MISTAKEN IDENTITIES

POETRY AND
NORTHERN IRELAND

PETER MCDONALD

CLARENDON PRESS · OXFORD
1997

Oxford University Press, Great Clarendon Street, Oxford OX2 6DP
Oxford New York
Athens Auckland Bangkok Bogota Bombay
Buenos Aires Calcutta Cape Town Dar es Salaam
Delhi Florence Hong Kong Istanbul Karachi
Kuala Lumpur Madras Madrid Melbourne
Mexico City Nairobi Paris Singapore
Taipei Tokyo Toronto
and associated companies in
Berlin Ibadan

Oxford is a trade mark of Oxford University Press

Published in the United States by
Oxford University Press Inc., New York

British Library Cataloguing in Publication Data
Data available

Library of Congress Cataloging in Publication Data
Data available

ISBN 0-19-818422-0

1 3 5 7 9 10 8 6 4 2

Typeset by Pure Tech India Ltd, Pondicherry
Printed in Great Britain
on acid-free paper by
Biddles Ltd,
Guildford and King's Lynn

FOR

John Lyon

Preface and Acknowledgements

This book collects and expands three essays which have appeared previously, and adds four new pieces. A shorter version of Chapter 2 appeared in *The Irish Review*, 12 (Spring/Summer 1992), and was reprinted in Eve Patten (ed.), *Returning To Ourselves: Second Volume of Papers from the John Hewitt International Summer School* (Belfast: Lagan Press, 1995); parts of Chapter 4 appeared as 'History and Poetry: Derek Mahon and Tom Paulin', in Elmer Andrews (ed.), *Contemporary Irish Poetry: A Collection of Critical Essays* (Basingstoke: Macmillan, 1992); and an earlier draft of Chapter 5 was published in Neil Corcoran (ed.), *The Chosen Ground: Essays on the Contemporary Poetry of Northern Ireland* (Bridgend: Seren Books, 1992).

I am greatly indebted to Professor Edna Longley who, as academic co-ordinator of the annual John Hewitt International Summer School in County Antrim, helped to create and foster an intellectual climate in which I and many others found one of the most fertile 'places where a thought might grow'. Chapters 2 and 4 began life as lectures delivered to the School, and Chapter 6 was helped considerably by seminar discussion there in 1995. While the emphases, errors, polemic, and 'politics' of this book are to be laid entirely to my own account, I have profited enormously from the arguments, observations, and disagreements of a number of participants at the Summer Schools, including Robert Crawford, Patrick Crotty, Cathal Dallatt, John Wilson Foster, Ben Hawes, Eamonn Hughes, John Hughes, Richard Kirkland, Eve Patten, and Norman Vance.

I have been fortunate throughout the writing of this book in the critical vigilance of Karen O'Brien, who has read and advised with generosity and perceptiveness. John Lyon has been helpful at every stage, and I owe much to his critical intelligence and sharp eye; I have gained greatly from his thinking about thinking in poetry. In a more general sense, I am indebted to my students and colleagues at the University of Bristol, from whom I have learned a great deal about the Englishness (and Irishness) of literature. I am much indebted to Tim Kendall, who provided valuable advice and criticism on Chapter 6. I am grateful for the practical help of Peter Foden, who found the OUP files on *The Character of Ireland*, and to Marjorie Dunderdale, who assisted invaluably with computers and printers at the appropriate times. It is a pleasure to acknowledge the guidance and assistance given to this book by Jason Freeman and Janet Moth.

I am grateful to the following for permission to quote copyright material: Faber & Faber, for poems by Seamus Heaney, Tom Paulin, and Louis MacNeice; Faber & Faber, Wake Forest University Press, and the author, for poems by Paul Muldoon; Secker & Warburg, and Jonathan Cape, for poems by Michael Longley; Gallery Press, for poems by Ciaran Carson and John Montague; Oxford University Press, Gallery Press, and Penguin Books, for poems by Derek Mahon.

The essays in *Mistaken Identities* have as their subject the relation between poetry and notions of 'identity' in Northern Ireland, and are especially concerned with poetry written in the years after 1969. I have referred throughout the book to the Troubles in Northern Ireland; I mean by this the civil unrest from c.1969, and my failure to provide inverted commas around the term reflects, not any lack of awareness of its inadequacy, but a reluctance to litter the text with marks whose warning function would soon become tedious and unnecessary. I have tried to keep such marks away from the term 'identity' as far as possible, and for similar reasons. It is difficult (and inadvisable) to relate periods of artistic achievement too closely to periods of historical development or crisis, and the poetry which is the subject of *Mistaken Identities* has been written by poets who will continue to develop beyond any point of resolution or change to the Troubles, just as many of them were developing well before the Troubles began. An effective cut-off date for the poetry I discuss comes in 1995 with Michael Longley's volume *The Ghost Orchid*; published during a ceasefire (which lends force to one of its most powerful poems), the collection may in due course seem to mark more than just a literary culmination. At any rate, I hope that my own analysis, in so far as it traces poetry's relation to violence from 1969 to the mid-1990s, will in time appear to coincide with a period of Northern Ireland's history which is recognizable and discussable (both within academic circles and beyond them) because it is at an end.

P.McD.

Bristol
May 1996

Contents

I

A Sixth Sense

In 1992 a project headed by Professor Torkel Opsahl listened in to what people living in Northern Ireland had to say about the conflict which had been in progress there for well over twenty years. The report of this independent commission (Initiative '92) was published in 1993, the result of a series of public hearings and written and oral submissions from over 3,000 contributors. One section of the report, 'Culture and Identity', opens with the following paragraph:

Few would question the idea that, central to our problems in Northern Ireland is a conflict, even a confusion, of identity. The 'troubles' and attendant political developments have shattered old certainties. Nationalism and unionism are no longer the monoliths they once were. The IRA's brand of republicanism has alienated many from the nationalist cause, and the Commission found little confirmation among ordinary nationalists— whatever about their political leaders—of the Protestant perception of nationalists as 'winning'. Nor was there much foundation for some nationalists' belief that unionists seek only to continue their ascendancy. Although we are still forced to use the language of stereotypes for analysis, the stereotypes no longer apply. This is the reason for the withdrawal into private life and apparent apathy of so many Northern Irish people—the fragmentation of the old identities, the abuses to which this has given rise, but the inability to arrive at anything new which carries the same clarity.[1]

Given its timing, a year before the conditionally permanent 'ceasefires' of the Provisional IRA and the loyalist paramilitaries in 1994, the Opsahl report might be read as a last—and the most detailed— attempt to record political opinion in Northern Ireland in one long and dreadful phase of the province's history. Certainly, it seems proper to hope that eventually it will be read as a document of primarily historical interest in the context of a political climate changed for the better. Nevertheless, the consensus that

---

[1] Andy Pollak (ed.), *A Citizens' Inquiry: The Opsahl Report on Northern Ireland* (Dublin: Lilliput Press for Initiative '92, 1993), 95.

'the stereotypes no longer apply' (together with its concession that 'we are still forced to use the language of stereotypes for analysis') is a conclusion which will continue to be of pressing relevance to all kinds of discussion of what is going on in Northern Ireland, or what has gone on there. 'The fragmentation of the old identities', along with the recognition that 'old certainties' have been 'shattered' is hardly news to the people of Northern Ireland; it remains, however, largely unwelcome information for many of the kinds of analysis that surround the Troubles. The idea of 'a conflict, even a confusion, of identity' as the cause of the Troubles has grown into a commonplace starting-point for analysis (even the Opsahl Commission's analysis); its validity is, as the report recognizes, bound up with the fact that 'identities', like the 'old certainties', continue to be lethal even when they have been outgrown. 'Identities' seem the cause of the problem; old notions of identity have been 'shattered'; and yet the problem continues to be discussed as one resolvable through identity. The report delivers what is arguably a fundamental insight (important both for its perceptiveness and its sense of paradox) in one sentence, which bears repeating: 'Although we are still forced to use the language of stereotypes for analysis, the stereotypes no longer apply.'

Political analysis (like actual politics) cannot take the possibilities of identity in Northern Ireland very far, since any conclusions are fated to come down to a 'new' offer of identity. As long as the problems of Northern Ireland are framed as problems of identity, solutions will always end up as identity-prescriptions of one kind or another; and these, by offering a fresh sense of identity, will not displace but tend further to entrench the identities already in place. When the Opsahl report senses change in the air, and hints that this change might undermine 'old certainties', it fails to understand the dangerous centrality of identity-thinking not just to the problem (which is clear enough), but to the whole spectrum of proposed solutions. Thus, a few pages after the important paragraph quoted above, Catholics are urged to 'help Protestants to feel more at ease by recognizing Protestant culture as part of an Irish identity', and the conclusion is reached that 'There should be a progressive depoliticizing of cultural beliefs, with attempts to find new Northern Irish symbols and emblems with which both traditions can identify.'[2]

---

[2] Pollak, A Citizen's Inquiry, 100.

This remains the language of stereotypes, and its retreat into the vagueness of cultural identity-talk is matched elsewhere by the explicitly political analogue which John Hume provides in the SDLP's submission:

> If our strategy for dealing with this problem were to be reduced to its most essential core, it would be the need to create new arrangements in this island to accommodate those two sets of legitimate rights: the right of nationalists to effective political, symbolic and administrative expression of their identity; the right of unionists to effective political, symbolic and administrative expression of their identity, their ethos and their way of life.
>
> No solution is available to us through victory for either of these identities. So long as the legitimate rights of both unionists and nationalists are not accommodated together in new arrangements acceptable to both, that situation will continue to give rise to conflict and instability.[3]

If *both* 'traditions' are indeed to have 'effective political ... expression[s] of their identity', it is certainly hard to see exactly how either identity can achieve a 'victory'. But Hume's solution is not the logical one, that both 'traditions' must, effectively, come to an end in terms of their perceived aspirations and demands; rather, he envisages 'new arrangements acceptable to both'—the abstract thing (like a new identity) which can be prescribed easily enough in abstract terms, but not so easily made real, when actual constitutional arrangements have to be made. The prescriptive element of all this is covert, but nevertheless important: Hume means that 'new arrangements' must be 'acceptable to both' traditions, but this denies the exercise of that 'effective political ... expression of their identity' to any 'tradition' which refuses to accept the 'new arrangements' in their concrete form. In a similar way, the notion that Protestants might be able 'to feel more at ease' for having their culture recognized as 'part of an Irish identity' is an almost purely theoretical proposition, and could be applied only in conditions where 'Protestant identity' and 'Irish identity' were perceived as compatible—and it is a politically awkward feature of 'Protestant identity' in Northern Ireland, as generally experienced and expressed, that this is not likely soon (or ever) to be the case. The inflexibility here is inherent in the conditions of the category of identity itself, for identities are made out of perceptions of hostile difference as well as passive distinctiveness, and they exist by virtue

[3] Ibid. 368.

of their interest in maintaining these differences. But 'identity', as a rhetorical term in cultural or political discourse, once liberated from the unwelcome tests of application in the sphere of actual political existence, can set its sights almost anywhere: one day, for instance, in some liberal and nationalist models, the Protestants of Northern Ireland will discover the truth of their Irish identity (and once this happens, in fact, the 'two traditions' will be able to find something with which they can both identify). Wishes like these are not without their own traces of identity-agendas, and what the Opsahl report calls 'a progressive depoliticizing of cultural beliefs' (with its assumption that culture necessarily finds expression in 'beliefs', as though its business were to provide these) betrays an assumption that identity-problems need identity-solutions. Thinking about real problems, however, can often mean thinking around those problems, and finding the language which, rather than plaintively declaring its inability to escape from stereotypes, challenges fundamentally the terms in which the problems have been expressed.

In this sense (though the parallel has to be maintained with some caution), thinking about literature can help in thinking about politics. But thinking about literature is a very difficult process; though easier than actually producing literature, it is still a rare (and necessarily a rarefied) activity. Where literature from Ireland is concerned, it is much easier not to think at all, and much literary criticism exists comfortably on the basis of taking on trust the assumptions of others. With the writing produced in, or out of, the Northern Irish Troubles, a crossover between not thinking about politics and not thinking about literature is especially easy. The following remarks, taken from a study by an American critic Robert F. Garratt, are in no way unusual, and the things they take for granted are indeed common currency in the study of Irish writing; Garratt speaks here from a consensus which he takes to be uncontentious:

Modern poetry in general is haunted by the divided mind, as we sense in Rilke, Eliot, and Stevens, poets who portray man cut off from his past, confused about meaning, and involved in an attempt to reconcile himself to his isolation. In the Irish literary tradition, that reconciliation is defined in cultural and national terms, that is, the struggle for reconciliation becomes embroiled in the question of identity.[4]

[4] *Modern Irish Poetry: Tradition and Continuity from Yeats to Heaney* (Berkeley: University of California Press, 1986), 101–2.

The fatuousness of the first sentence here is not irrelevant to the quality of the second sentence's analysis; Irish politics blends gracefully into the syllabus of modern literature, and its search for identity continues the project of those poets 'haunted by the divided mind'. It is an elementary (but necessary) objection to the literary analysis here that the three poets (in any case unlikely companions) were not, in any primary or accessible sense, attempting to reconcile themselves to isolation—or not, at any rate, in their writings: they wrote poems, and a lot of different poems. But Garratt is, one presumes, much more interested in 'modern man' and 'isolation' than he is in anything so unforthcoming as poetry; by the same token, his concern for 'the Irish literary tradition' leads to 'the question of identity' as that literature's inevitable and essential subject. When Garratt says that 'The difficulty, then, for Irish poets at mid-century came in the search for continuity, finding something that would suffice to provide cultural identity and also to admit the modern world',[5] he accepts an agenda far removed from what poets actually do (for better or worse, they write poems, which are themselves better or worse). Of course, poems are hard to write about, while cultural identity is very easy to discuss: so easy, in fact, that it tends often to write its own way through the kinds of critical discourse that accept it as their subject. In literary studies as in political analysis, it is always easier not to think than to think, and it is quite possible not to think in academically profitable ways: whole schools of not-thinking about literature have established solid institutional presences by finding new ways to ignore the difficulties and perplexities of literary analysis and evaluation. Inevitably, the crossover between contemporary literary criticism and contemporary political or cultural discussion of Northern Ireland is both easy and rewarding. Nevertheless, such a crossover has a price.

The recognition that identity has become a commonplace, or in some ways a cliché, in cultural and political discussion (even if it is, as the Opsahl report wearily and self-defeatingly claims, an unavoidable term) is seldom made in Irish literary criticism. Here, identity often remains the goal of Irish writing, and the foundation of real literary achievement; a certain amount of bad contemporary writing, especially in the Irish Republic, takes the critical agenda of

[5] Ibid. 168.

identity entirely seriously, and often comes down to no more than a series of roots proclaimed, allegiances declared, and set gestures rehearsed. It is hardly surprising that some of this writing finds its advocates among critics to whose preconceptions it is already in thrall. In Northern Ireland, fewer writers have been willing to make the (potentially lucrative) investment in identity which provides criticism with the correct answers to the pre-set questions. This may be owing to the degree to which the costs of identity-thinking have been all too visible in Northern Ireland, and the caution of writers in this respect (often, from the point of view of political discussion, a trivial or irresponsible caution) has paid longer-term dividends in terms of literary achievement. In arguing for this evaluation, one is arguing for the significance and value of poems as discrete achievements within larger bodies of work, as things which possess, so to speak, identities of their own. Such an argument is almost completely at odds with most of the assumptions of a good deal of contemporary critical theory, for which poetry is always and inescapably a mode of discourse, and therefore not to be separated from other elements of that discourse. These assumptions might be of literary and critical use if they arose from an awareness of the specific charges and liabilities which words in literature carry from other areas of discourse; but they tend more commonly to constitute a dogmatic rejection of the close scrutiny of words in their formal literary contexts, with a consequent rejection of the specific in the interests of larger propositions. Effectively, the answers of the critical discourse take priority over the questions posed by the details of its ostensible subjects; the agenda is set outside the poem, and the poem has to conform to what the agenda requires. It is only a poem, after all.

Such matters are finally, in the pejorative sense, academic ones, and have no direct bearing on the situation in Northern Ireland. This is not to say, however, that this situation can have no bearing on those academic questions, or that it cannot test their adequacy in fundamental ways. In any case, the matter of interpretation, and the grounds of interpretation, are by no means confined to the mandarin circles of professional academic discourse. It might well be argued that the situation of individuals in Northern Ireland is compromised in the political and cultural discourses which set out to take them into account. An act of violence, in this discourse, is more than just a violent act, since its meaning and conditioning are foregrounded in the political or historical interpretations that can deal with it; effectively, these patterns of interpretation take priority over the act itself, so that a man who murders (for example) can be defined and understood as a political offender—in this sense, he *is* his interpretation, and lives within a defining public identity. It is, if not a tragic, at least an appalling fact that many individuals in Northern Ireland over the past quarter of a century have killed, and died, in abject obedience to their interpretations. By the same token, patterns of interpretation have been imposed consciously at the cost of others' lives: the meaning of the victim and the meaning of the killer coexist within the same realm of discourse. One death cannot disrupt or divert the discourse by which it is interpreted. It is only one death, after all. In such a dreadful context, the innocent world of literature and its criticism assumes, perhaps, its proper proportions; nevertheless, the flirtation with identity-politics in which some of the literary intelligentsia (most commonly, academics and commentators from outside Northern Ireland itself) are able to indulge themselves is not entirely without its legitimating influence on those modes of discourse which have provided, especially in the USA, one kind of Irish identity with its lethal interpretative force. Again, it is always easier not to think than to think, and the reasons and excuses for not thinking are always abundant: fighting for a free Ireland, like fighting for God and Ulster, can put interpretation handily in the way of reality, and help the process of not thinking in which the facts of murder are soon and easily forgotten. There remains, however, a responsibility to resist the pervasiveness of such a discourse rather than accept its conclusions as inevitable.

There is a paradox in the contemporary use of 'identity' (a use going far beyond Ireland) which helps to explain why the term is especially problematic in relation to literature. A sense of identity might seem to point up the sheer individuality of experience, its unrepeatable particularity; in fact, the idea of identity is employed almost always to emphasize the *common* nature of experiences, and to provide these experiences with a significance and meaning already mapped out in cultural or historical terms. Thus John Hume's demand for both traditions to have 'effective ... expression of their identity' understands identity as something shared which transcends the individual. It is a short step from this to see the individual's responsibility as one of realizing his identity, and finding its expression; and, luckily for him, the identity is there already, waiting to be realized. The unease often felt by writers about interpretation is similar to the unease of an individual who is being told where his identity (his and many others') is waiting to be discovered, and Northern Irish writers have been especially reluctant to align themselves with critics' projections of their significance over the years. Any celebration of literature in terms of identity is finally prescriptive in nature, because it can only recognize things within strictly limited ranges, and cannot afford to put itself at the mercy of literature's actual unpredictability and variousness. In an excellent formulation (to which he has not always adhered in his own work), Seamus Deane has written of how 'Identity is here and now, not elsewhere and at another time';[6] similarly, poems are to be distinguished from their interpretations, and constitute the complex 'here and now' of literary attention, which remains more important and valuable than the assorted elsewheres of theoretical categories, just as literature is more important than the critical enterprise which may surround it. It is vital that this importance should continue to be measured outside the world of professional academe.

However, 'identity' is not a term which floats free in contemporary criticism, and the more recent academic engagements with the concept declare their attraction to it as part of a vocabulary of post-colonial interpretation. As far as the situation of Ireland is concerned, this particular interpretation (which is almost imperially ambitious in its geographical range) has been applied with rigour and determination. The English literary theorist, Terry Eagleton, has usefully digested the dogmas of post-colonial identity for the benefit of the Irish:

Nobody can live in perpetual deferment of their sense of selfhood, or free themselves from bondage without a strongly affirmative consciousness of who they are. Without such self-consciousness, one would not even know what one lacked; and a subject which thinks itself complete feels no need to revolt. In this sense, the 'negativity' of an oppressed people—its sense of itself as dislocated and depleted—already implies a more positive style of being. The true triumph of alienation would be not to know that one was alienated at all.[7]

[6] 'Remembering the Irish Future', *The Crane Bag*, 8/1 (1984), 91.
[7] *Nationalism: Irony and Commitment* (Londonderry: Field Day, 1988), 16.

For the Irish, it seems, a 'sense of selfhood' is inevitably a recognition of the 'bondage' they have suffered, and suffer; to deny the oppression is either to have failed to achieve an 'affirmative consciousness' of who one is, or to have been hoodwinked into believing that one has not been hoodwinked. There are no answers to arguments like these, since they are themselves already a series of answers which will brook no questions. However, as such arguments filter into actual critical dealings with Irish literature, and particularly Northern Irish literature, they set agendas for creative writing which good poetry has difficulty in following. In this sense, the theorist David Lloyd is entirely logical (if doomed to failure) in his dismissal of Seamus Heaney as 'a minor Irish poet' who has been elevated 'to a touchstone of contemporary taste within a discourse whose most canonical proponent [Matthew Arnold] argued for the study of Celtic literature as a means of the integration of Ireland with Anglo-Saxon industrial civilisation'.[8]

Lloyd's sophistication allows him to acknowledge the problems inherent in identity-discourses, but also to blame these on the English imperial discourses which they were fated to emulate: he writes of 'the specific relation of an "Irish identity" to the English literary—and political—establishment', and accuses that establishment of providing 'not only the language, but the very terms within which the question of identity is posed and resolved, the terms for which it is *the* question to be posed and resolved'.[9] It may be that Lloyd is correct to see in some of Heaney's work a 'chosen basis' in 'the concept of identity', and to be alert to the ways in which this can be a liability for some poems; but Lloyd, like other post-colonial theorists, is more concerned with what he calls 'The real basis of the present struggle in the economic and social conditions of a post-colonial state'[10] than with the different 'here and now' of poems. It is also important in such an argument that support for 'the present struggle' should legitimize the adverse criticism of a popular poet; the critique of identity-discourse offered by Lloyd and others must be at all costs (and at any cost) a radical one.

Radicalism like this has only to be declared loudly in order to be proven. In a report on a conference entitled Gender and

---

[8] *Anomalous States: Irish Writing and the Post-Colonial Moment* (Dublin: Lilliput Press, 1993), 37.

[9] Ibid. 23.

[10] Ibid. 19.

Colonialism, held in Galway in 1992, *Feminist Review* noted that 'There were 300 attenders, mainly from academic institutions in the British Isles, with some also from Canada and the US', and concluded rightly that this provides 'a strong indication of the growing popularity of colonial and postcolonial studies'. In keeping with this, it would seem that an insistent radicalism, or perhaps an indiscriminate radicalism, was also much in favour:

There were four plenary sessions. The opening lecture was given by Barbara Harlow (University of Texas, author of *Resistance Literature*, 1987). The 'occupied territories' of her title were Ireland, Palestine, Texas—she drew on prison and insurgent writings from the Sinn Fein Women's Department, the PLO and Chicano writers in the US. Her political support for these movements was refreshingly direct—no fashionable suspicion of 'grand narratives' here. For example, she attacked the recent wave of Irish 'revisionist' (or anti-nationalist) historians in a memorable phrase as 'the strip-searchers of academia'. This set the note for the majority of at least the Irish contributors to the conference—a clear pro-republican stance, opposed equally to the 'bourgeois nationalism' of the Irish state, and to the 'liberal revisionists'.[11]

One assumes that the Irish and British bourgeois states were not entirely unforthcoming in their subsidies for the not-very-oppressed academic contributors who made the journey to Galway, and enjoyed the 'remarkable hospitality of the conference organizers', along with 'the unexpected brilliance of the weather'. Perhaps the contributors, no doubt healthily refreshed by Harlow's directness, found further theoretical nuances for the expression of 'a clear pro-republican stance', and were confirmed in their belief that they were, indeed, up to something entirely novel and ground-breaking. But scepticism from beyond the academic fold seems in this case entirely reasonable; had the delegates ventured further north, they might have enquired profitably of people in Northern Ireland about the real differences between revisionist history and strip-searching. Other distinctions commonly made in the world of post-colonial theory are perhaps more difficult to grasp; for many of Northern Ireland's dead, the difference between being interpreted in the light of 'a clear pro-republican stance' or of a 'bourgeois nationalism' is indeed, in the narrowest sense, an academic one. Observations like

[11] Clara Connolly, 'Culture or Citizenship? Notes from the "Gender and Colonialism" Conference, Galway, Ireland, May 1992', *Feminist Review*, 44 (Summer 1993), 104–5.

this might well, on the other hand, spoil the fun; and the very act of making them within the context of academic discourse might seem to be in bad taste, if only because it breaks the conventions by which some of that discourse keeps itself safely and profitably at arm's length from the radicalism which it commends.

In contexts like these, disavowals of identity-discourse ring hollow: Lloyd's critique of Heaney, in the light of this, can be seen to amount to little more than a theoretically dense series of allegations that the poet, read in the totalizing discourse of cultural politics, fails to be republican enough. Arguably, it is greatly to Heaney's credit that someone of Lloyd's convictions so dislikes his poetry; but more commonly Heaney has found his work assimilated to vaguely nationalist cultural agendas, in which the privileging of identity allows recognition and praise of the poet's apparent validation of rootedness and origin. The extent of Heaney's critical and popular success has been significantly dependent on the acceptability of ideas of Irish identity in critical and journalistic currency, and the Northern Irish Troubles have added a *frisson* to this by seeming to present a drama of confused and tragically conflicting identities to which an art like Heaney's might minister. Yet (perhaps as a result of this) critical discussion of Heaney has been, with a few notable exceptions, largely passive and undistinguished.[12] Some poets spawn weak imitators, who publish poems in which they try to sound like their master; in Heaney's case, the imitators would seem to include many of his critics, and their prose restagings of his poetic habits and procedures are as weak and derivative as the outpourings of any poetaster. Maurice Harmon, for example, has written of Heaney's poems as 'chords [*sic*] of attachment binding him to the landscape' and 'mating calls by which the land rises to delight the poet', adding that 'what is verifiably real is drawn into metaphor, intimately mated in the act of poetic speech'.[13] Critical arousals like these are not rare, and they are capable of being adapted to suit even theoretical agendas, as when Henry Hart

---

[12] Notable exceptions include Neil Corcoran, *Seamus Heaney* (London: Faber & Faber, 1986); Bernard O'Donoghue, *Seamus Heaney and the Language of Poetry* (Hemel Hempstead: Harvester Wheatsheaf, 1994); and Tony Curtis (ed.), *The Art of Seamus Heaney* (Bridgend: Seren Books, 3rd edn. 1994).

[13] '"We pine for ceremony": Ritual and Reality in the Poetry of Seamus Heaney, 1965–75', in Elmer Andrews (ed.), *Seamus Heaney: A Collection of Critical Essays* (Basingstoke: Macmillan, 1992), 73, 74.

remarks on how 'For a postcolonial poet who feels that the religious, political, and linguistic hierarchies imposed on his country by a foreign empire still watermark his psyche, deconstruction is as much a gut response as a well-thought-out strategy of exposure and demolition.'[14] Heaney's poetic identity, which is often to be a repository and purveyor of Irish identity, is laid down in a great deal of the criticism which sings his praises. That he is in fact a much more complex figure than this, whose work relates to notions of identity in various and variously questioning ways, is something less likely to be noticed, and much less likely to be welcomed, by many of his warmest admirers.

The Heaney of the 1980s and after does not inhabit the discourses of identity in any very comfortable way, and a good deal of his writing is possessed by the consequent discomfort involved in finding ways around the positions which those discourses prescribe. While a case might be made for the literary unsatisfactoriness of some of the poetry in which Heaney most strenuously attempts such relocations, the artistic necessity of the effort need not be in question. In the long (and only intermittently successful) 'Station Island' (1984), Heaney begins tentatively to assess the risks involved in abandoning a poetry of solidity, roots, and firm location for one bereft of the certainties of cultural identity, in which the figure of the poet might be exposed and at large. In section IX Heaney confronts his own image:

> 'I hate how quick I was to know my place.
> I hate where I was born, hate everything
> That made me biddable and unforthcoming,'
> I mouthed at my half-composed face
> In the shaving mirror, like somebody
> Drunk in the bathroom during a party,
> Lulled and repelled by his own reflection.[15]

This instant of confrontation seems at first entirely futile, like a moment of bad temper that will pass. But the rejection of the self's ready acceptance of typecasting, or the foreordained tracks of a secure identity, even as it seems to acknowledge its own futility, starts to build up a counter-momentum:

---

[14] *Seamus Heaney: Poet of Contrary Progressions* (Syracuse, NY: Syracuse University Press, 1992), 7.
[15] *Station Island* (London: Faber & Faber, 1984), 86.

> As if the cairnstone could defy the cairn.
> As if the eddy could reform the pool.
> As if a stone swirled under a cascade,
> Eroded and eroding in its bed,
> Could grind itself down to a different core.

The insistence of 'As if...' is starting to get somewhere in these lines, and Heaney begins effectively to push towards the 'different core' of unpredicted strangeness on the other side of a given sense of identity. Although the passage is marred by the whimsy of the final two lines which follow ('Then I thought of the tribe whose dances never fail / For they keep dancing till they sight the deer'), Heaney's determination can be felt to work its purpose here. The familiar metaphorical life of the idea of identity often involves cores, essences, and centres; for Heaney, whose work in the 1970s had so frequently explored the metaphorical possibilities of unearthing and delving, the 'core' laid bare by imagination in Northern Ireland had taken a mythic, historical, or archaeological form—the sense of identity being dug up, explored, by a volume like *North*, is increasingly impersonal and perhaps forbidding in its fossilized remoteness. The frustrations of 'Station Island', on the other hand, are those of an authorial self impatient with the given possibilities of its identity, and the poem goes around in circles (or, more exactly, in circuits) in its protracted consideration of the likelihood of finding 'a different core'.

It may be, however, that even metaphorical cores have their limitations. In an interesting poem from *The Haw Lantern* (1987), Heaney speaks for 'The Stone Grinder', a figure who prepares lithographic plates by repeatedly erasing what has been engraved there ('Me, I ground the same stones for fifty years / and what I undid was never the thing I had done'[16]). The core of this enterprise is (literally) erasure, and the stone grinder's profession centres him on absence:

> For them it was a new start and a clean slate
> every time. For me, it was coming full circle
> like the ripple perfected in stillness.

Heaney's growing interest in things having vanished, in absences and gaps, allows him to speak for the stone grinder (who is himself,

[16] *The Haw Lantern* (London: Faber & Faber, 1987), 8.

of course, a vanished figure) in terms that risk incompleteness
rather than the completeness of a knowable identity:

> So. To commemorate me. Imagine the faces
> stripped off the face of a quarry. Practise
> *coitus interruptus* on a pile of old lithographs.

The voice's commands to posterity do not allow for the satisfac-
tions of secure identification, for they emphasize the persistence of
the unfinished (and the unstarted) in a future of absences as well as
presences. The stone of this poem is all surface, and no core; it may
be, indeed, that the core turns out to be all surface. In a perceptive
aside on this poem, the critic Michael Allen has asked, 'I wonder if
what [Heaney] is representing here is the tension between popular
and aesthetic commitment in the writer, writing poetry for "the
ear" or for "the people" in the terms of "Exposure"'.[17] Certainly
Heaney's popularity does not always sit easily alongside the terms
in which he sometimes expresses his 'aesthetic commitment', and
his increasingly complex (or increasingly mystical) sense of identity
as a core which is known by its absence, 'a space / Utterly empty,
utterly a source' in the terms given in 'Clearances',[18] seems to have
led the poet away from the earthed certainties in which his own
popular appeal was founded. The metaphorical tendency of Heaney's
writing has shifted from the earthy to the ethereal, and his volume
Seeing Things (1991) represents the poet's most sustained attempt
to achieve imaginative lift-off into a kind of poetry less constrained
by identities (Irish or otherwise) and more openly metaphysical in
its concerns. Undoubtedly, the enterprise is a risky one, and Paul
Muldoon's gentle satire in *The Prince of the Quotidian* is not
without its point:

> the great physician of the earth
> is waxing metaphysical, has taken to 'walking on air';
> as Goethe termed it, *Surf und Turf.*[19]

Heaney's 'walking on air', whatever the artistic merit of *Seeing
Things*, is not without a point of its own, since the poet has found
himself occupying the unmistakably solid ground of popularity and

---

[17] '"Holding Course": *The Haw Lantern* and its Place in Heaney's Development',
in Andrews (ed.), *Seamus Heaney: A Collection of Critical Essays*, 197.
[18] 'Clearances', 8, *The Haw Lantern*, 32.
[19] *The Prince of the Quotidian* (Oldcastle: Gallery Press, 1994), 14.

critical authority to an increasing extent, and his artistic reflexes have directed him away from this, towards something altogether more difficult to express, or to stand firmly upon. Bernard O'Donoghue's explanation that 'The secular mysticism of the book is a celebration of the ordinary, sometimes in its transcendent form, and ordinary language can be drawn on in representing it'[20] is perhaps too confident of Heaney's abilities, but it accurately describes the volume's ambitions. Despite possible liabilities of style, however, Heaney's poetry seems determined to concentrate on the things inherent in absence, leaving behind the stony determinisms of the core for something less constrained and more open:

> Strange how things in the offing, once they're sensed,
> Convert to things foreknown;
> And how what's come upon is manifest
>
> Only in light of what has been gone through.
> Seventh heaven may be
> The whole truth of a sixth sense come to pass.[21]

Heaney's 'sixth sense' has assumed a major place in his poetic imagination, and it is more at odds with the assumptions of his early writing (and perhaps with the foundations of his popular success) than his admirers will admit.

In terms of the identity-discourses and the cultural politics with which Heaney's reputation (especially in Northern Ireland) has been entwined, 'what has been gone through', along with 'things in the offing', may assume a particular prominence. The effort made in the poet's final lecture as Professor of Poetry at Oxford to exercise a 'sixth sense' in relation to Ireland results in a complex presentation of a cultural and historical map of the island, drawn according to the intuitions and revelations of the literary imagination. What Heaney calls (after Sir Thomas Browne) his 'quincunx' is a figure connecting 'five towers', the first (and central) one being 'the tower of prior Irelandness, the round tower of original insular dwelling', but the others belonging to Edmund Spenser, W. B. Yeats, James Joyce, and Louis MacNeice.[22] The figure is ingenious as well as elegant, and might be seen as providing a satisfying instance of literature imperiously exercising its own imaginative capacities on

[20] *Seamus Heaney and the Language of Poetry*, 128.
[21] 'Squarings', xlviii, *Seeing Things* (London: Faber & Faber, 1991), 108.
[22] *The Redress of Poetry: Oxford Lectures* (London: Faber & Faber, 1995), 199.

a map to which the narrowest of politics had previously laid claim. Yet Heaney's imaginative instincts are perhaps reduced in scope as soon as he translates them into the language of politics and culture, where the available vocabulary sends the writer back to precisely those terms and definitions from which poetry repeatedly manages to escape. The language in which good intentions find expression tends to be compromised despite the best of those intentions:

> Those who want to share [an Irish] name and identity in Britain's Ireland should not be penalized or resented or suspected of a sinister motive because they draw cultural and psychic sustenance from an elsewhere supplementary to the one across the water. Unresented, they could more easily stop resenting. For they, in turn, must not penalize or resist the at-homeness of their neighbours who cherish the primacy of the British link. The Unionists' refusal to be 'outcast on the world', in Hewitt's poetic formulation, expresses itself politically as a refusal to be included in an integral Ireland. And that refusal has to be imaginatively comprehended as well as constitutionally respected.[23]

Heaney's use of 'identity' drags down the imaginative buoyancy of his argument, and he is forced (like John Hume) to hope that incompatible identities can be reconciled through finding untrammelled expression. The constitutional respect urged by Heaney for a unionist 'refusal to be included in an integral Ireland' begs precise political questions, and allows a degree of vagueness to enter an issue where prosaic clarity is essential. It does not take Heaney long to urge the unionists to 'start to conceive of themselves within—rather than beyond—the Irish element', and 'make their imagination press back against the pressure of reality and re-enter the whole country of Ireland imaginatively, if not constitutionally, through the northern point of the quincunx'.[24] By now, Heaney's prose is fanciful rather than imaginative, deaf to the contradictions of its terminology, and (at least) mistaken in its estimate of literature's hold over the business of living (and living with the business of dying) in Northern Ireland. Heaney finds himself betrayed into the arrogance which is the flip-side of his sense of literature's authority; the betrayal comes, as usual, from the fixed agendas inherent in the discourse of identity, which write themselves into the prose just as surely here as in a speech by a politician or an academic analysis by a cultural theorist. Perhaps, after all, the

---

[23] Heaney, The Redress of Poetry, 201–2.   [24] Ibid. 202.

imaginative confinement of Louis MacNeice in Carrickfergus
Castle signals an underlying weakness in Heaney's 'quincunx'.

Heaney's integrity is not unique in its capacity to be compromised even at its most honourable; to varying extents, all writers
from Northern Ireland have come into contact with the problematic dynamics of language and political interpretation during the
Troubles. From the point of a view of a literary critic, this may be
precisely the thing that makes the achievements of Northern Irish
poetry most engaging and revealing; poetry's integrity here makes
apparent its difference from other kinds of integrity in political or
cultural discourses, not by rejecting them (it may well, at some
levels, accept them), but by maintaining and insisting upon the
privileges and proprieties of its own existence. It is worth repeating
the truism that good intentions cannot of themselves write a good
poem; a critical culture distrustful of evaluation (though it may be
silently efficient in enforcing its own evaluations and canonical
judgements) is able to ignore such a truism, but poets themselves
have found it less easy to forget. An active and alert kind of literary
criticism is engaged unavoidably in the business of evaluation,
however tentative it may be in making its conclusions, and it
cannot afford to make judgements on the basis of ideas or allegiances that are to be validated outside a poem. Thus, to praise a
poem, or the works of a poet, in terms of a perceived fidelity to
some notion of shared identity is really to recruit the writing itself
to a project in which the identity in question is propagated and
strengthened. In Northern Ireland, such an activity is no contribution to 'progress' (to employ a term already sullied by various
vested interests), but part of the deeper, obstinately rooted problem.

The ambitions of the present book are, in one way, limited: it
brings together a series of essays which, although interrelated, are
intended also to stand independently as studies of particular poets
and poems, and the contextual situations in which they are
involved. In another sense, it is more ambitiously angled, attempting as it does to discard as far as possible the agendas of identity-
discourse; since the book addresses only Northern Irish poetry, this
attempt is likely to be read by those discourses as politically conditioned or even politically engaged. To some extent, any attempt
at argument on this matter is bound to be in vain: at any rate, the
book accepts Northern Ireland as (over the last quarter-century at
least) a place very different *de facto* from the Irish Republic, and its

literature as sufficiently distinct from that of the South to require in this case separate treatment. A second 'political' dimension can be readily acknowledged: that is, the author of *Mistaken Identities* is no more free than any other writer from the pressures of identity discourses, and his own origins (as a Belfast-born Presbyterian) are visible plainly enough in the book's style and in certain emphases of its polemic. Yet the assumptions central to the essays in this book, and the implications of the space which it tries to open for literary criticism in Northern Irish poetry, are not necessarily friendly to any specifically 'political' application. Certainly, the criticism of identity-discourses here is willing to accommodate the caveat issued about such suspicion by the historian Gearòid O Tuathaigh:

Those who are suspicious of or hostile to the Irish-Ireland idea, who continue to warn against monochrome definitions of cultural identity, must themselves guard against intolerant dismissal of what they do not know but yet fear. There is a form of intolerance also in seeking to deny that there is any point or purpose (indeed, in hinting that it may be dangerous and socially divisive) in calling on Irish people to cherish and cultivate those particular marks of Irishness which have a long historical continuity in Ireland and which other peoples acknowledge as being distinctively Irish.[25]

Intolerance is, indeed, the reflex which both 'traditions' in Northern Ireland need to unlearn, however painful such a process will prove. But the language of essence and distinctiveness is not unconnected to that intolerance, and it is one of the things which will have to be forgotten also if the darker side of Ireland's 'historical continuity' is to be defeated.

Yet such admissions are in a sense incidental, for the primary business of this book is with poetry and not with political identity, and its arguments and interpretations are to be judged against the evidence of the Northern Irish poetry which it discusses. It is important, however, that the subject-matter of the essays is not understood as narrowly contemporary: the book does not see recent poetry in historical isolation or as some freak cultural growth, and, besides material on John Hewitt and W. R. Rodgers, the significance of Louis MacNeice is a recurring theme. In the final

[25] 'The Irish-Ireland Idea: Rationale and Relevance', in Edna Longley (ed.), *Culture in Ireland—Division or Diversity*, proceedings of the Cultures of Ireland Group conference, 27–8 September 1991 (Belfast: Institute of Irish Studies, 1991), 68.

chapter, the degree to which Northern Irish poetry is lodged in contemporary English literary concerns enlarges on another theme present throughout the essays. As regards contemporary Northern Irish writing itself, the selection of poets and poems is not made with an intention of providing an adequate survey or guide, still less any definitive series of canonical rankings, and readers will doubtless be well aware of the excellence and distinctiveness of a number of poets who are not discussed in the present book—amongst whom Medbh McGuckian, Frank Ormsby, Robert Johnstone, James Simmons, and Gerald Dawe are likely to be numbered. Even a modestly adequate critical survey of Northern Irish poetry since the 1960s would make a hefty volume, and this in itself raises a number of important issues.

The quality of much writing from Northern Ireland offers critics an especially complex challenge, since it brings to the surface problems and areas of awkwardness more often forgotten or ignored. One such area is, clearly, that of the relation between political contention and the literary imagination; but there are other (arguably more fundamental) matters at stake as well: what, for example, is poetry's distinctiveness as a mode of discourse? And how might a critical language be found to account for this distinctiveness which is not itself compromised by the insistent crises and demands of its cultural and political context? Is criticism able to imagine a liberation from 'identity' which will move into the spaces opened up by different kinds of poetic achievement? Perhaps a kind of criticism responsive to questions like these might make the transformation of culture into 'cultural beliefs' less easy, and have applications beyond Northern Ireland. In any case, the essays in this book make an effort to take poetry seriously as (to use Heaney's term) Northern Ireland's 'sixth sense'; this is something less, or more, than a 'cultural belief', and something in which the present author is content to put his trust.

2

The Fate of Identity: John Hewitt, W. R. Rodgers, and Louis MacNeice

The brief foreword to John Hewitt's *Collected Poems 1932–1967* (1968) covers more ground than is usual for such preliminaries: along with the customary obligations of acknowledgement, its four short paragraphs map out in miniature a journey that the book itself will go on to describe. Central to this piece is the modest adequacy of Hewitt's description of himself—'by birth an Irishman of Planter stock, by profession an art gallery man, politically a man of the Left'[1]—which properly owns up to and helps to account for the first-person voice so prominent in the poems. But the identity given this shorthand delineation is not one to be limited to a single place: some of the poems, Hewitt informs his readers, 'originated in frequent sojourns in the Glens of north-east Antrim'; and finally the poet's journeying goes beyond 'sojourns' to residence in 'the English Midlands' where he 'settled' in 'the spring of 1957'. The trajectory thus plotted from one settlement to another is mirrored by Hewitt's account of the migratory movements of the poems themselves: 'a number figure in about two dozen anthologies, British and American', 'some have found place in textbooks', 'Half a dozen...have travelled farthest and have been used most often'. What might appear at first to be no more than meticulous bookkeeping seems eventually to record a long journey away from points of origin.

Hewitt's 1968 foreword, with its careful initial indications of ground travelled, prepares the way for the journey implied in the poems' arrangement, from 'Ireland' (the first piece in the book) towards the final poem, 'To Piraeus'. Between these points, there is the poetry of sojourn, of exploration, of ideological engagement,

[1] *Collected Poems 1932–1967* (London: MacGibbon & Kee, 1968), 5.

and that of departure, of exile, of disengagement and disillusion. The poetic voice, buttressed by the statements of instinct and belief that seem to confer its identity, does indeed remain remarkably consistent as it tests its changing surroundings against measured and steady convictions or habits of response. 'Ireland' (dated by the author 1932) begins by speaking as 'We Irish', but the voice soon discovers that 'We are not native here or anywhere', and the poem closes with intimations of departure:

> So we are bitter, and are dying out
> in terrible harshness in this lonely place,
> and what we think is love for usual rock,
> or old affection for our customary ledge,
> is but forgotten longing for the sea
> that cries far out and calls us to partake
> in his great tidal movements round the earth.[2]

Given this as a beginning, it is appropriate that the *Collected Poems* should end at sea—another sea, the Aegean—this time with the lonely voice in the company of 'a strong small barrel-built man' who takes out 'his tasselled string of beads' to pray after lunch. Hewitt ends 'To Piraeus', and 'To Piraeus' ends the book, by escaping for the moment from solitude, and in readiness to move on further still: 'I would feel safe / Travelling to the moon with him'.[3]

The parabola described by Hewitt's 1968 collection is not entirely in keeping with the poet's formulations of 'regionalism': if the book's travels are those of 'a *rooted* man',[4] then he has his roots in something other than place alone. The fact that John Hewitt went on to embark on a second (and prolific) phase of his literary career after the publication of *Collected Poems 1932–1967* might encourage readers of the poet to forget that the 1968 volume was arranged so as to put on display a process of engagement and disengagement, placing and displacement which, in its way, entombs the regionalist enterprise with which Hewitt's name was (and remains) associated. It is clear that Hewitt's subsequent poetry

---

[2] Ibid. 11–12; repr. in *The Collected Poems of John Hewitt*, ed. Frank Ormsby (Belfast: Blackstaff Press, 1991), 58.

[3] *Collected Poems 1932–1967*, 144; *Collected Poems*, ed. Ormsby, 108.

[4] John Hewitt, 'The Bitter Gourd: Some Problems of the Ulster Writer' (1945), in *Ancestral Voices: The Selected Prose of John Hewitt*, ed. Tom Clyde (Belfast: Blackstaff Press, 1987), 115.

often revisits regionalism's grave, but only to pay its respects, and not to witness some authentic resurrection. The failure of Ulster cultural regionalism in the 1940s and 1950s is a part of Hewitt's career, inextricable from the achievements for which it is a context; it may be, also, that Hewitt's posthumous success is itself largely dependent on more recent attempts at a regionalist resurgence in Northern Ireland. It should be added, however, that the 'failure' of regionalism does not vitiate such success as Hewitt's poetry achieves; rather, it forms a necessary component of that success, and is even perhaps its inescapable condition.

It is true that the connotations of failure in political discourse are harsh; but in literary activity the 'failure' of an idea, project, or group of beliefs can lay bare unexpected and imaginatively fertile areas. The present chapter will address some aspects of the writings of three poets—Hewitt himself, and his contemporaries W. R. Rodgers and Louis MacNeice—with an eye to the possibilities of 'failure'. It is necessary to take account of the formation, in the post-war years, of a literary idea of regional identity in Northern Ireland, of the different kinds of testing this idea undergoes in the work of the three poets, and of the implications of certain artistic unsuccesses that result from such points of contact. The journey represented in (and by) Hewitt's 1968 *Collected Poems* shows how poetry can negotiate a way around the mixed fortunes of ideas; the ideas are, in any case, not destinations but staging-posts in the kinds of journey good poetry has to make. Rodgers and MacNeice also, in their different ways, engaged with and disengaged from notions of allegiance, place, and identity. Moreover, all three poets were of a generation for whom ideas of identification, common interest, and solidarity (often expressed in explicitly political terms) were significant pressures. If MacNeice encountered such pressures relatively early, in the various imperatives of the British intellectual left of the 1930s, the experiences of Hewitt (himself 'a man of the Left') in the post-war promotion of Ulster regionalism form a suggestive parallel. It may be possible to ask how far, or how effectively, the poetry of Hewitt, Rodgers, and MacNeice contrives to outlive certain ideas in the midst of which it sometimes places itself, and to consider how usefully this process of survival can inform an understanding of Northern Irish writing of later decades and from younger generations.

Writing under the double cover of anonymity and the dialogue form, W. R. Rodgers contributed 'Conversation Piece' to the Irish literary periodical *The Bell* in 1942: the subject for discussion here was what might now be called the cultural identity of the Northern Irish Protestant. When one of the dialogue's voices makes use of the term 'racial difference', he is pulled up and forced to explain what he means:

It is a convenient term by which I refer to that backward pull of custom and forward pluck of morality, that common fund and accumulation of interest which makes the character of a group of people distinctive. The racial difference is, I think, fundamental to an understanding of Ulster.[5]

Remarks like these may seem (at least) infelicitous, given their date. Indeed, W. J. McCormack has cited this piece as one of the 'disturbing invocations of "race" and "rootedness" even among writers who were otherwise notably and courageously liberal'[6] to be found in Irish Protestant literature. Yet what Rodgers says (or, more properly, what Rodgers lets be said) is part of a poetic agenda before it has contact with a political one, and is, in all likelihood, imperfectly aware of its own ideological overtones. The existence of a validating source of a regional (or—problematically—'racial') identity is precisely in the nature of a 'common fund' for the poet W. R. Rodgers, enabling him to subsidize his own creative bargaining between 'pull' and 'pluck'—romantic reassurance and individual unease, or melodic comfort and staccato urgency. For Rodgers, a common 'character' has to exist in order to give meaning to the poet's departures from, or heightenings of, its available orthodoxies and distinguishing traits. Even so, this division between the 'pull' and 'pluck' in Rodgers's poetry is a severe one, often expressed violently, and is an internal rift which he cannot finally close. When the proposition is made, later in 'Conversation Piece', that 'We are really a "split" people, we Protestant Ulstermen', Rodgers's rather simple division of allegiances ('Our eyes and thoughts are turned towards England, but our hearts and feet are in Ulster'[7]) relies upon an opposition which his own poetry embodies and to which it gives (sometimes strident) expression. An identity,

---

[5] Anon. [W. R. Rodgers], 'Conversation Piece', *The Bell*, 4/5 (Aug. 1942), 307.

[6] 'The Protestant Strain', in Gerald Dawe and Edna Longley (eds.), *Across a Roaring Hill: The Protestant Imagination in Modern Ireland* (Belfast: Blackstaff Press, 1985), 62.

[7] 'Conversation Piece', 310.

or 'character', for Ulster is therefore poetically necessary for Rodgers; in its implications it is also, we might remember, necessarily poetical.

'Oh this division of allegiance!'[8] Louis MacNeice's more than half-ironic exclamation, roughly contemporaneous with Rodgers's 'Conversation Piece', still seems to sum up a perceived problem which the ideas of Ulster regionalism also tried to address. In his article of 1947, 'Regionalism: The Last Chance', John Hewitt made a point of the subsidy on offer to the individual artist from this common fund of a regional identity, a solution which, 'although it begins with the individual, must immediately pass beyond the individual and react upon the community'.[9] Again, there is some ambiguity involved in the argument: does regionalism give birth to the individual artist, or does the artist create for his community the viable concept of regionalism? Hewitt's own definition of 'the region' does not greatly help in this respect: 'an area which possesses geographical and economic coherence, which has had some sort of traditional and historic identity and which still, in some measure, demonstrates cultural and linguistic individuality.'[10] As a practical, or broadly speaking a political, definition, this is obviously enough flawed: Hewitt is smoothing over some very rough patches of analysis with his 'some sort of' and 'some measure'.[11] As was to become more apparent, the gap between artist and community, so quickly bridged in Hewitt's definitions, was more difficult to close than this post-war enthusiasm would admit. Like Rodgers, Hewitt can be seen engaging himself in the creation of a 'common fund' to back up his own poetic enterprises, a source of deep solidarity that will give coherence and significance to the departures and innovations of the artist. As in his poetry, so in his arguments for regionalism, Hewitt returns time and again to the tropes of stability, rootedness, and community; but again, as in his poetry, his arguments for these things, and his habitual attraction towards them serve also to indicate how far they remain from any successful realization. In a way perhaps analogous to the forced

    [8] *The Strings are False: An Unfinished Autobiography* (London: Faber & Faber, 1965), 78.
    [9] *Ancestral Voices*, 122.
    [10] Ibid.
    [11] On 'geographical coherence', see Barra O Seaghda, 'Ulster Regionalism: The Unpleasant Facts', *The Irish Review*, 8 (Spring 1990), 54–61.

smoothness of his favoured iambic pentameters, Hewitt's regionalist argument often reaches its conclusions by loading certain points
with more stress than they will easily bear.

It is true, however, that Hewitt's poetry cultivates from the start a
certain feeling for distances. Sometimes the poet chooses to present
these as gaps between urban and rural identities, as in 'O Country
People':

> I recognize the limits I can stretch;
> even a lifetime among you should leave me strange,
> for I could not change enough, and you will not change;
> there'd still be levels neither'd ever reach.[12]

This recognition of limits, an intuition of levels of community out
of reach of the individual speaking voice, comes later to condition
Hewitt's judgement of the regionalist project as a whole. In a way,
the poetry's feeling for 'limits' operated substantially in advance of
Hewitt's prose arguments that tried to 'stretch' over too great a gap
between self and 'region', the individual and a 'common fund' of
identity. Interviews late in the poet's life offer final perspectives on
such questions, treating them (with the benefit of hindsight) as in
some respects historically conditioned. In 1985, for example:

I became a regionalist in my thinking during the war years. That was
important because the North of Ireland was cut off from England...So
we were different and I thought this emphasised our difference and identity
...but I was wrong. Ulster is not one region, it's several regions...My
concept of regionalism was trying to bring together incompatible pieces.[13]

Or again, from the same year: 'I thought that if we could establish a
regional consciousness for the north of Ireland it would give us
something to cling to, a kind of key to our identity. . . . I did a lot of
agitation with no result whatsoever.'[14] If this sounds like a meditation on failure, we must bear in mind that the artistically fruitful
meditations had taken place much earlier, in the fabric and design
of Hewitt's poetry—and notably in the very shape made by the
1968 *Collected Poems*, with its brooding on the significance of
place counterpointed by the announced mobility and constant
displacement of the poetic voice. Late in that volume, in one of

---

[12] *Collected Poems 1932–1967*, 70; *Collected Poems*, ed. Ormsby, 73.
[13] Interview with Ketzel Levine, *Fortnight*, 213 (4–17 Feb. 1985), 17.
[14] Interview with Damian Smyth, *North*, 4 (Winter 1985), 14.

his poems set in Greece, Hewitt finds himself waiting in the ancient
theatre at Epidaurus:

> But only near the dark green grove
> with the pine-scent and light airs
> among the fronded fans,
> was I somehow strangely at home,
> receiving, open, myself.[15]

Here 'the limits I can stretch' have become unexpectedly wide; the
poet can be 'strangely at home' while being simply 'myself', un-(or
up-)rooted, without any region or community. Stretched open like
this, Hewitt's poetic identity can travel away from its geographical
starting-points for a fresh 'sojourn'. But this freedom, with which
the poet brings his *Collected Poems* to a close, is something quite
distinct from 'some sort of traditional and historic identity which
still, in some measure, demonstrates cultural and linguistic individuality'; here, it has no agenda, and it demonstrates nothing, but
what it imagines is a kind of autonomy, a freeing of the self in
writing to become 'receiving, open', rather than constant and
confined.

This is not to imply that Hewitt's poetry should make us treat
lightly his later expressions of disappointment and disillusion: the
failures of regionalism are real, and they matter—especially so at a
time when some of the regionalist terminology, notably in the
rhetoric of 'identity', remains in circulation. Hewitt's struggle
with 'incompatible pieces', carried out 'with no result whatsoever'
continues to exercise a fascination in contemporary Northern
Ireland. Indeed, the stubborn materials to which the poet applied
himself are still present, still problematic, and still susceptible to
regionalist analysis. The literary critic John Wilson Foster's propo-
sals for 'radical regionalism', almost half a century after the beginnings of Hewitt's ideas, pay explicit acknowledgement to their
precursor;[16] yet cultural agendas like these still hope for much
more in the way of a definable 'identity' than Hewitt, for one,
was ever able to smoothe out from that rough, uneven, and recalcitrant matter. For the purposes of neo-regionalist arguments, the
poet John Hewitt is asked to perform a symbolic function: in John

---

[15] *Collected Poems 1932–1967*, 136; *Collected Poems*, ed. Ormsby, 55–6.
[16] See John Wilson Foster, 'Radical Regionalism', *The Irish Review*, 7 (Autumn 1989), 1–15.

Wilson Foster's reading, for example, 'it is precisely because his Irishness is problematical that Hewitt's worrying of the matter for decades has enabled him to forge the conscience of the Scots–Irish in Ireland, and that may be his chief significance'.[17] Similarly, for the historian Roy Foster it is Hewitt 'who articulated that quintessential combination of Protestant scepticism and commitment, linked with a sense of place that was absolutely Irish'.[18] The language of formulations like these—'the conscience of the Scots–Irish', 'that quintessential combination', 'absolutely Irish'—is underwritten by an acceptance of the possibility, and the desirability, of concepts of identity. (Two *OED* definitions may answer to this sense: 'Absolute or essential sameness; oneness'; 'The sameness of a person or thing at all times or in all circumstances'.) However, such judgements approach poetry with too little caution; as literary criticism, they offer too easy an assessment, importing categories of broad description into a body of work which finds such categories workable only at its weaker moments. The question is not whether neo-regionalist appropriations of Hewitt are parts of an otherwise unjustifiable cultural agenda, but whether their discourse of 'identity' can survive its being set in context by the procedures of literary history and criticism.

Perhaps it is useful to compare this situation with another context that runs parallel to regionalism, that of the British poets of the 1930s generation. Hewitt and Rodgers, no less than MacNeice, could well be placed here: it was W. H. Auden's poetry, for example, which inspired the apprentice Hewitt in the early 1930s and which influenced heavily much of Rodgers's earlier work, as well as setting the terms and challenges for a good deal of MacNeice's writing of the period. The apparent flirtation of a number of poets at the time with left-wing politics has always tempted their critics into political rather than literary judgements, regardless of any resistance to such analysis put up by much of the writing under discussion. Here again one finds the importation of fundamentally inappropriate categories: notwithstanding the several excellent works of literary history which have begun to clear away the rubble of dogma and myth from the poetry of Auden

[17] John Wilson Foster, '"The Dissidence of Dissent": John Hewitt and W. R. Rodgers', in Dawe and Longley (eds.), *Across a Roaring Hill*, 144.
[18] 'Varieties of Irishness', in Maura Crozier (ed.), *Cultural Traditions in Northern Ireland* (Belfast: Institute of Irish Studies, 1989), 22.

and his contemporaries, it was possible as late as 1991 for a literary critic to remark regretfully that 'In the politics and aesthetics of the poets...nowhere have we encountered any sustained attempt to develop a Marxist poetic or a Marxist poetry.'[19] This critic goes on to find what he is looking for in some obscure corners which have been neglected (of course) through the liberal ideological bias of other critics. Yet the writer's own bias prevents him from considering the possibility that developing 'a Marxist poetry' might be rather like cultivating Marxist flower-arranging or golf—a purely speculative theoretical perversity, with no real bearing on the activity in question. That such expressions of critical or political dogma should seem such an easy target, and should be so evidently anachronistic in their assumptions, is a sign (perhaps) of critical progress or (more likely) of the simple passing of time. However, there is a similar inadequacy in the attempts at a critical neo-regionalism, which involve a very familiar importing of unsuitable categories and criteria. The fact that abstract constructions like 'the conscience of the Scots–Irish' or the 'quintessential combination of Protestant scepticism and commitment' are commonly given a hearing and even granted plausibility, whereas the earnest search for a lost Marxist poetry is more likely to be seen now as slightly embarrassing, could quite easily obscure what is a deep affinity. If we are to reject the confusion between ideology and value in critical attempts to interpret the British 1930s, we need to be just as wary of blurring the distinction between marks of 'identity' and signs of value in approaching the work and significance of Hewitt and his contemporaries in Northern Ireland's 'thirties generation'.

Despite all this, it remains difficult to avoid mentioning 'identity' in dealing with Hewitt's poetry, or indeed with that of Rodgers or of MacNeice: very often, it is the poets themselves who draw attention to this concept in their work. Any critical argument which is suspicious of 'identity' in contemporary Northern Irish critical discourse has to admit that the concept is not new, and that its literary credentials are powerful ones. It is possible, however, to trace the fortunes of 'identity' in even Hewitt's poetry without treating the idea as a self-evident good in itself, or as the writing's self-validating goal. Furthermore, the Hewitt generation might not be uniformly rich in 'identity', even though later, neo-regionalist

[19] Adrian Caesar, *Dividing Lines: Poetry, Class and Ideology in the* 1930s (Manchester: Manchester University Press, 1991), 203.

arguments confer such treasures indiscriminately upon them; later generations may flatten out and simplify the inconsistencies of their predecessors. It is worth remembering, for instance, that Louis MacNeice was often found wanting in identity by the regionalists themselves: the article of regionalist faith which stated (in John Boyd's formulation of 1943) that 'no writer, however talented, should uproot himself in spirit from his native place'[20] made Mac-Neice something of a sapless hybrid in the Hewitt circle: 'There is little in either his work or his outlook to identify him as an Ulster-man', wrote J. N. Browne in 1951, 'and the influences which have moulded him have not been the regional ones.'[21] The same critic suffered no such difficulties when he went on to contemplate appetizingly in Hewitt's verse 'the wholesome, nourishing grain that makes us think, somehow, of wheaten bread'.[22] By the same token, the fluffy patisserie of much of Rodgers's poetry was insufficiently substantial for many regionalist appetites. If, then, both MacNeice and Rodgers can be seen to engage with notions of 'identity' in their writing, it does not follow that this 'identity' is the same concern as that so important to Ulster regionalist think-ing (of course one might also make this point, though with more caution, of some of the poetry of Hewitt himself). Another consideration should be that, although all three poets find uses for 'identity', their poetry also tests the concept, turning it in sometimes unexpected directions and on occasion fracturing it altogether: it is neither an unquestioned good, nor an end in itself in this writing.

In falling back on the cliché of 'a "split" people' to describe 'Protestant Ulstermen', W. R. Rodgers had in mind an 'identity' clearly distinct from the *OED*'s 'sameness...at all times or in all circumstances'. When he negotiates his own 'identity' in poems, Rodgers encounters other splits and divisions, as for example in the opening lines of 'Ireland', which embody their own 'backward pull and forward pluck':

> O these lakes and all gills that live in them,
> These acres and all legs that walk on them,

[20] John Boyd, *Lagan*, 1 (n.d. [1943]), p.5. On regionalism and MacNeice, see Peter McDonald, 'Ireland's MacNeice: A *Caveat*', *The Irish Review*, 2 (1987), 64–9.
[21] 'Poetry in Ulster', in Sam Hanna Bell, Nesca A. Robb, and John Hewitt (eds.), *The Arts in Ulster: A Symposium* (London: Harrap, 1951), 142.
[22] Ibid. 145.

> The tall winds and the wings that cling to them,
> Are part and parcel of me, bit and bundle,
> Thumb and thimble. Them I am . . .[23]

There is something outlandish about this putting-on of a composed identity, or at least a degree of licence which the poetry, with (as so often in Rodgers) its finally irritating verbal play, simply has not earned. Rodgers's feeling that his poetry came from 'a clash between two opposites' is of course relevant, but one notices that here, as all too often, words, imagery, and ideas do not really manage to 'clash'; rather, they stage a mild disagreement, easily reconciled both by the poet's musical arrangements and by his explicit first-person authority—'Them I am'. This overly controlled conflict in habits of perception (and composition) never seriously calls into question Rodgers's authorial identity; his attitudes towards, or memories of, Ulster tend on the whole to serve a similar purpose, one that corroborates rather than unsettles:

Maybe it is the liking for strong black and white contrast that makes me partial to the Belfast I knew, with its long files of women and girls in black shawls, streaming out of the linen mills; or the dark city at dusk with the rain stippling the puddles and silvering the pavements, and the 'Islandmen' thronging the red tramcars and filling the red-blinded pubs.[24]

This is just as vivid, and in its way just as detached, as MacNeice's reminiscences of the North of his childhood; but whereas Mac-Neice, in works like *The Strings are False*, allows such memories their resonances of the inconclusive and the ambiguous, Rodgers makes them serve to underwrite his own authority as a poet. Essentially, Rodgers encounters in memory the 'strong black and white contrast' of his own poetic imagination, so that in remembering Belfast he constitutes for himself a literary identity.

The habit of linking a sense of identity with authority is evident in Rodgers's short poem 'Words', where the speaking poet and the island of Ireland merge into each other:

> Always the arriving winds of words
> Pour like Atlantic gales over these ears,

---

[23] *Collected Poems* (Oxford: Oxford University Press, 1971), 42; repr. in *Poems*, ed. Michael Longley (Oldcastle: Gallery Press, 1993), 40.

[24] W. R. Rodgers, script for *The Return Room*, as quoted in Darcy O'Brien, *W. R. Rodgers (1909–1969)* (Lewisburg, Pa.: Bucknell University Press, 1970), 23–4. An edition of Rodgers's *The Return Room* by Douglas Carson is forthcoming.

These reefs, these foils and fenders, these shrinking
And sea-scalded edges of the brain-land.[25]

The conceit is no more convincing when Rodgers ends the poem by
anticipating how words, 'Arrowed and narrowed into my tongue's
tip', will finally 'speak for me—their most astonished host'. Here
again, the assertion of identity between the underwritten poetic
voice and the words it employs is either a disingenuous statement
of a fallacy or an indication that the poem is not fully engaged with
its own language, and has forgotten that words are more than
vessels of images or sounds. As with the perception of 'a "split"
people', there is an insufficient regard here for language's need to be
answerable to something other than the private agendas and
requirements of the self.

Although he has remarked acutely on Rodgers's belief that 'he
could fashion oneness merely out of his love for Ireland and in the
finitude of his poems', John Wilson Foster follows the poet's logic
too faithfully when he explains the constant duality lodged in the
poetry by noting that 'life in Ulster has always been at one crucial
level twofold, Protestant and Catholic'.[26] To posit this as the cause
of Rodgers's stylistic habits seems perverse; to suggest it as in some
way analogous to them, though a more plausible proposition, is to
miss the deficiencies and problems involved in the 'finitudes' of this
poetry. Perhaps this is a critical difficulty similar to that presented
by much of Hewitt's work: where Hewitt has an often unwarranted
smoothness of texture and ideas, Rodgers offers a consistent division and splitting-up of both perception and verse. Both evenness
and fracture can have the reflex quality of habit. The techniques of
both poets claim to answer to something in the 'identity' of Ulster,
but neither operates with the subtlety or circumspection proper to
such an undertaking. I have suggested already that some of Hewitt's
poetry takes account of the problems inherent in this kind of
enterprise, and relocates its senses of 'identity' as a result. In the
case of Rodgers also, the best poems outgrow the complacencies of
his slacker work by opening ideas of 'identity' to the challenges of
artistic exposure and doubt.

In 'Summer Holidays', a long and in some respects derivative
poem heavily influenced by such 1930s panoramas of urban life

---

[25] *Collected Poems*, 2; *Poems*, ed. Longley, 27.
[26] '"The Dissidence of Dissent": John Hewitt and W. R. Rodgers', 153.

as MacNeice's 'Birmingham', Rodgers ends with an evocation of
the human condition that goes beyond the bolt-hole of 'split'
identity to lay bare a sense of friction which is at the core of his
own work:

> The spin of flesh on the spindle of bone
> Concentring all, with its brute ambitions,
> Its acute and terrible attritions.[27]

The very familiar verbal tricks are operating here as usual, but to
greater than usual effect: the idea of an individual identity as something *concentred*, put together from the delicate and the durable,
the blunt and the sharp, finds its best expression in the poem's final
phrase. Already, in this relatively early piece, Rodgers has found the
proper description for his imaginative process of self-identification
—not conflict, or the clear, decisive 'clash of opposites', but
the 'acute and terrible attritions' of, amongst other things, sound
against sound. At the centre, the point where the poet's memories,
skills, beliefs, and imagination consort, there is not an 'identity', a
coherence and sameness continually sustained through mastering
division, but a changing self, alive to and worn down by the
processes of attrition. One sense of 'attrition' (though Rodgers's
use of the plural is unusual) is the *OED*'s 'action or process of
rubbing one thing against another; mutual friction'. Perhaps the
word also carries here overtones of its specifically theological
meaning, 'An imperfect sorrow for sin, as if a bruising which
does not amount to an utter crushing.' The 'spin of flesh', and its
development into the more solid 'spindle', hovers close to that
'spine' which Rodgers imagines his 'Ulster Protestant' as possessing
in 'Conversation Piece'. In this situation, words are altogether more
substantial things than 'arriving gales': 'He would *like* to have
eloquence. But he suspects and hates eloquence that has no bone
of logic in it. It seems to him glib, spineless, and insincere. It freezes
him into silence.'[28] It is as though Rodgers is imagining a negative
pressure that could be brought to bear on his own writing, with its
relentless gift of the gab: as against his poetic preference for verbal
harmony, he presents the Protestant voice as 'sharp, expulsive,
jerky', the noise perhaps of a resistance that rubs away at the
more luxuriant mouth-music of Rodgers's own lines of verse.

---

[27] *Collected Poems*, 26.   [28] 'Conversation Piece', 309.

Although Rodgers learns how to turn this process of 'attrition' to poetic advantage in his best work, it is still possible to see, in a fragmentary poem written late in his career, the workings of an instinct to shore up the poetic voice through the projection of an 'identity' for Ulster. In this case, the poem is Rodgers's unfinished 'Epilogue' to the never-completed project *The Character of Ireland*, a book of essays which was to be coedited with Louis MacNeice. Here, the poet returns to the 'sharp, expulsive, jerky' Ulster accent and, as in his earlier poem 'Words', serves self-consciously as 'host' to its antagonistic sounds:

> I am Ulster, my people an abrupt people
> Who like the spiky consonants in speech
> And think the soft ones cissy; who dig
> The *k* and *t* in orchestra, detect sin
> In sinfonia, get a kick out of
> Tin cans, fricatives, fornication, staccato talk,
> Anything that gives or takes attack,
> Like Micks, Tagues, tinkers' gets, Vatican.[29]

This *tour de force* of mimicry crosses the line into caricature: its entertainment value aside, the dramatic identity assumed by Rodgers's voice is a limiting one in the end, heightened and distorted into poetic melodrama. The hailstorm of fricatives develops from comic effect into a line of sectarian abuse, of angry and offensive noise. Of course, this aspires to an effective ironic detachment; at the same time, though, the verbal excess betrays a certain complacency, a willingness to schematize, generalize, and divide:

> An angular people, brusque and Protestant,
> For whom the word is still a fighting word,
> Who bristle into reticence at the sound
> Of the round gift of the gab in Southern mouths.

The angular and the round, like Rodgers's other paired opposites, are answering to forces at work inside his poetry more fully and satisfactorily than to his ostensible subject-matter. The division between a distrust of language and a linguistic rapture is Rodgers's distinctive concern, and is a fundamental instability which makes the daring of the balance achieved in poems like 'The Swan' and 'The Net' so remarkable. But the Rodgers who can announce that 'I

---

[29] *Collected Poems*, 144; *Poems*, ed. Longley, 106.

am Ulster' has lost his balance, and has fallen into mere 'identity' from that riskier, more precarious openness in which words are the agents of freedom rather than fixity. Unfinished as it is, this 'Epilogue' is a significant failure—or belittling—of Rodgers's powers, which exposes a shortcoming in his hold upon the Ulster he takes as his subject. Terence Brown has noted how the poem tries to approach 'the cultural neuroses and psychoses in the collective mind of Ireland', an abstract construction assembled from 'the sum of her inhabitants' warring myths and identity problems', but he has also remarked on how Rodgers falls short of any 'simple therapeutic solution' to the problem he confronts.[30] Perhaps this line of investigation can be pursued further: is Rodgers's failure here the result of a deficiency in imaginative and intellectual resources, or might it be the outcome of applying those resources to what is a phantom subject—to what the poet calls, in a letter accompanying his 'Epilogue', 'my favourite theme, the characteristics of Irishmen'?

Rodgers is hardly the first writer to set out after this particular chimera, and certainly both Hewitt and MacNeice are on occasion hot on its trail. Writing for an overseas audience during the Second World War, MacNeice approaches the subject of 'Northern Ireland and her People', paying special attention to stereotypes. He examines, for instance, the 'one word that at once jumps to the Englishman's lips: the word "dour"'.[31] The poet meets this half-way, admitting that it 'is certainly appropriate to the typical Belfastman', and picturing 'tough figures in cloth caps whose first glance at you seems to imply antipathy and whose mouths are shut tight like a money-box'. After more of such description, he admits that 'in general the Northern character...can be described as dour'. However, MacNeice will not leave the matter there, showing how the outsider's perspective turns out to be doubly misleading. On the one hand, the 'dourness' is, 'in nine cases out of ten', 'very deceptive', concealing what MacNeice calls 'hospitality' and a willingness to 'go out of their way to help you and refuse to take any reward for it'. But on the other hand, there is something behind 'dourness' which does not accord quite so well with the tourist-brochure tones:

[30] *Northern Voices: Poets from Ulster* (Dublin: Gill & Macmillan, 1975), 88.
[31] 'Northern Ireland and Her People' [?c.1941–4], in *Selected Prose of Louis MacNeice*, ed. Alan Heuser (Oxford: Clarendon Press, 1990), 144–5.

What, however, disturbs the Englishman more than the Ulsterman's dourness is what is often called his bigotry. Party feeling takes a more savage
form here than in any other part of the British Isles.... Some of this
political vehemence can be taken with a grain of salt; it is a standing joke
that the Irish, whether South or North, love an argument—or a fight—for
its own sake. The root of the matter, however, lies in history—and a very
tangled history it is.[32]

The manifest deficiencies of this, and of the potted history of Ulster
which follows, are too great to be excused on the grounds that
MacNeice is addressing here an international (and possibly a largely ignorant) audience. The poet is too ready to dismiss politics
and history as elements to be taken with a pinch of salt, and his
provision of an Irish stereotype to help explain this hardly helps
matters. Is this, then, MacNeice playing exactly the role which
many of his contemporaries in Ireland (and many Irish critics since)
have assigned to him: the outsider, the tourist in his own country,
forever alienated by his English education and manners? And yet
the blind spots here—most notably the blanket description of the
Ulster character, the lack of attention to the realities of sectarian
division or the machinery of Protestant power (we are told that the
Orange Order's 'bark is worse than its bite'[33])—along with the
focus on local colour and provincial oddities, are in fact not typical
of MacNeice's writing. Indeed, in his own poetry on Irish topics
from the 1930s and after these are the very blind spots that are
illuminated as focal points. However, they seem very close to the
deficiencies of Rodgers on the Ulster 'character', or to certain of
Hewitt's recurring themes. Trying to serve up an easily comprehensible 'identity' for Northern Ireland, MacNeice has recourse to the
techniques of regionalist analysis, the combination of simplification
with generalization, and ignores as far as possible those areas
which prove recalcitrant to such an approach.
    It would be wrong, of course, to dismiss either MacNeice's
wartime article on Ulster, or the arguments of regionalism to which
it seems to be indebted, on the grounds that they do not accommodate problems of political violence in post-1969 experience. Yet
there is a reticence, perhaps something of a principled shyness, in
the approach to issues of allegiance and nationality amongst
those writers who were raised, after all, in a decidedly 'political'

[32] Ibid.   [33] Ibid. 149.

generation in the 1930s. It seems that the very process of addressing Ulster, and Ireland, leads the writers to exclude or postpone the problem which is central to any consideration of 'identity'—that of a national definition of the subject. The discourse of 'identity' was employed in such a way as to put problems of definition, and division, on the back burner (as, arguably, it continues to do in neo-regionalist practices). Hewitt's well-known sliding definition, which elides the Ulsterman of Planter stock with Irish, British, and European identities, might be seen as passing off personal self-definition as something more widely significant or exemplary. The same elision of awkward problems of group definition could be found in John Boyd's 1951 announcement that 'Ulster is part of Ireland, which is part of the British Isles, which is part of Europe', so that 'Our literature should belong to our own country, to the British Isles, to Europe.'[34] But 'our own country' remains undefined here, as in many other archipelagic formulas. With the inevitable arrogance of hindsight, it is all too easy to see that with so much on the back burner, these particular pots were bound eventually to boil over.

However, one ought not to make use of later understanding of the weaknesses or inadequacies of ideas behind some regionalist writing in order to deliver snap judgements on its literary worth: a critic inclined to a relatively low estimate of, say, Hewitt's poetry, is under the same obligation of historical perspective as its admirers. The harsh term 'failure' (used by Hewitt himself) is sometimes necessary in coming to terms with regionalism, but this has to be balanced by a feeling for the kinds of success which might also be involved. As far as Rodgers and MacNeice are concerned, there is one 'failure' in particular which is suggestive in its relation to the question of creative writing and the agendas of 'identity': *The Character of Ireland*. Rodgers's unfinished 'Epilogue', discussed above, is just one crumbling component of the unstable, and in the end unviable, project—a coedited collection of essays, with MacNeice and Rodgers in charge, which stumbled on for at least fifteen years before its complete abandonment. Although the book's scope was obviously more wide-ranging than a discussion of Ulster regionalism alone, its beginnings are closely associated with the period of greatest effort by Hewitt and others. The idea for a

[34] 'Ulster's Prose', in Bell, Robb, and Hewitt (eds.), *The Arts in Ulster*, 99.

volume of this nature seems to have occurred to Rodgers in the late 1940s, and by 1952 he and MacNeice were in a position to put together a list of contributors, both possible and already signed-up. At this stage, this included Elizabeth Bowen on 'The Big House', Frank O'Connor on 'English Literature', Sam Hanna Bell on 'The Six Counties', and John Hewitt on 'The Visual Arts'; also involved were Sean O'Faolain, Geoffrey Taylor, Estyn Evans, J. C. Beckett, Theodore Moody, and Conor Cruise O'Brien. As the project began to take shape under the aegis of the Clarendon Press in 1952 it seemed promising, a gathering of materials on Ireland North and South by a literary and academic generation who had for the most part come to maturity in the post-Partition, or post-Independence years. Rodgers, whose field-researches on Irish 'character' of all kinds had been successful in his 'radio portraits' of Irish writers, was a natural choice as editor; MacNeice, with his stricter and apparently more aloof interests in Ireland seemed an excellent complement. And yet, as the project's long-suffering (and long-subsidizing) publisher Dan Davin recalls in his memoirs of the two poets, *The Character of Ireland* floundered for many exasperating years before finally coming to grief with the deaths of its two editors.[35] Conceived at a high point of enthusiasm for the possibilities of putting on paper some broad and many-faceted approach to or definition of 'the Irish character', the project dragged on through the 1950s and half of the 1960s: contributors defaulted or withdrew; completed articles went out of date; ideas of 'balanced' coverage proved hard to sustain. Above all, as Davin's memoirs make clear, the editors themselves could hardly finish their own contributions: MacNeice's verse 'Prologue' did finally arrive in 1959, seven years after it was first promised, but Rodgers never brought his 'Epilogue' close to completion. It is difficult to tell, so great is the catalogue of setbacks, mistakes, and delays, whether *The Character of Ireland* was a failure in collaboration or a collaboration in failure.

The whole story of delay and vacillation is related effectively by Davin, who sees the near-tragic significance of the failing project for Rodgers during his last, exhausted years (indeed, Davin's memoir was first printed as an introduction to Rodgers's posthumous *Collected Poems* in 1971). The role played by *The Character of*

---

[35] See Dan Davin, *Closing Times* (Oxford: Oxford University Press, 1975).

Ireland in MacNeice's later career is less sombre, crossing as it does
into his final period of imaginative renewal and poetic strength
rather than, as in Rodgers's case, coinciding with the progressive
failing of imaginative powers. It would appear, in fact, that Mac-
Neice's interest in the project was at its strongest in the early
1950s—for him poetically a strained and difficult time—but tailed
off as he found his own poetic resources renewing themselves in the
late 1950s and early 1960s. In the cases of both poets, the need to
invest in 'character' and 'identity' may be linked to the necessity of
drawing on a 'common fund' that might help to float their own
work. By the time he completed his 'Prologue' to the volume,
MacNeice was already past this need, and the poem indicates this
in its lengthy meditation on Ireland in terms of the imagery habitual
to many of his other poems—the prismatic colours of light on
landscape, and above all the fluidity and clarity of water. What
MacNeice specifically excludes from his 'Prologue' is any settled
notion of 'identity', going so far as to question the founding
assumptions of the project itself:

> 'The Character of Ireland'? Character?
> A stage convention? A historical trap?
> A geographical freak? Let us dump the rubbish
> Of race and talk to the point: what is a nation?[36]

The recognition of 'identity' for a country, or indeed for a self-
identifying 'race' within that country, as 'a historical trap', makes
good the kind of poetic intuition which MacNeice's 'Prologue'
explores. Ireland's status as 'nation' soon dissolves to become
'this land of words and water', something unfixed and unfixable.
Along with the images of flowing water (which always carry overtones of Heraclitean flux for MacNeice), the figure of the prism
helps make solid the many paradoxes which the poet observes in
Ireland:

> The water
> Flows, the words bubble, the eyes flash,
> The prism retains identity, that squalor,
> Those bickerings, disappointments, self-deceptions,
> Still dare not prove that what was love was not...

---

[36] 'Prologue', in Terence Brown and Alec Reid (eds.), *Time Was Away: The World
of Louis MacNeice* (Dublin: Dolmen Press, 1974), 1–4; repr. in Jon Stallworthy,
Louis MacNeice (London: Faber & Faber, 1995), 488–91.

The Irish become here the 'Inheritors of paradox and prism', putting themselves in possession of an 'identity' far removed from the constructions of writers like Rodgers or Hewitt—removed, indeed, from the ideas behind a project like *The Character of Ireland*. MacNeice's wartime 'Northern Ireland and Her People' had remarked how 'sunlight in Ireland has the effect of a prism; nowhere else in the British Isles can you find this liquid rainbow quality which at once diffuses and clarifies'.[37] The poet had used the same image in his book on W. B. Yeats in 1941, noting the 'pantomimic transformation scenes' of the Irish landscape: 'one moment it will be desolate, dead, unrelieved monotone, the next it will be an indescribably shifting pattern of prismatic light.'[38] The prism that 'retains identity' is associated with the dual processes of clarification and diffusion, bringing about both concentration and separation. It is in this sense that MacNeice uses the prism to figure identity: if one aspect of this is the brilliant colour and light celebrated as flux in the 'Prologue', another is the 'dead, unrelieved monotone' of completely united, fully identified colours. This is the aspect of Ireland which had entered MacNeice's much earlier poem, 'Valediction', as 'inbred soul and climatic maleficence', where the Irish must 'pay for the trick beauty of a prism / In drug-dull fatalism'.[39]

Fatalism may be one corollary of a sense of 'identity', an unforeseen one perhaps, as in the case of regionalism, but something sensed in poetry by MacNeice and others. To discover and define an 'identity' for the self, and beyond that for a broader community, is also to flirt with ultimately determinist conceptions of character. One question which has to be asked about 'identity' is how far the term encodes a purpose, forcing discussion and thought in a predetermined direction. When, for example, a Northern Irish Protestant 'identity'—however that might be defined—is accepted as a usable concept in political or cultural discussion, the term itself favours certain lines of development in reasoning, thus aligning the perspective in vital ways with certain determinist assumptions fundamental to nationalism. Solidarity, community, place: all of these values, which strengthened and helped to mark out a

[37] *Selected Prose*, 151.
[38] *The Poetry of W. B. Yeats* (London: Oxford University Press, 1941; 2nd edn. London: Faber & Faber, 1967), 50.
[39] *Collected Poems*, ed. E. R. Dodds (London: Faber & Faber 1966), 53.

generation on both sides of the Irish Sea, proved in the end less flexible and liberating than some of the creative writing they helped bring to birth. As a part of the same complex of ideas, 'identity', whatever plurality it might claim, cannot accommodate the fluidity into which 'character' in all good writing necessarily dissolves.

Perhaps *The Character of Ireland* fell into 'a historical trap' of its own construction: certainly, the passing of time turned the project's initial bright ideas into ever darker and more involved problems. In particular, the required coverage of Northern Ireland proved difficult: despite John Hewitt's efficiency on 'The Visual Arts' ('one of the earliest and most promptly delivered articles' according to Rodgers in 1955, and dutifully revised in 1957[40]), important dimensions were missing. Again, the reticence of regionalism with regard to 'politics' seems to play a part: where southern contributors were on the whole willing to give outspoken views, the Northern Irish authors were more guarded. Writing to Dan Davin in 1957, Rodgers touches on the area of difficulty:

You'll recall that initially we asked Sam Hanna Bell to contribute a piece on the Six Counties: he refused, partly, I think, because he thought it would involve dealing with political issues. I still think, and Louis agrees, that a general article on Ulster by Bell would balance the book better. Otherwise we won't get the feeling or flavour of that determined place.[41]

Here the natural frustration of the editor rubs against the poet's instinct for the *mot juste*: 'that determined place' combines exasperation and felicitousness in its registering of the double pressures exerted by 'identity'. 'Determined' stretches both to 'self-willed' or 'independent', and to 'foreordained' or 'fated'. In witnessing the slow failure of *The Character of Ireland*, as well as participating in and contributing to it, Rodgers re-encounters the desperate gaps his own poetry continually sets out to bridge, between 'pull' and 'pluck', 'spin' and 'spindle'. Like that of Hewitt and MacNeice, Rodgers's best poetry understands that ambitions for 'identity' in a place like Northern Ireland are inevitably worn down by what they hope to transcend, the 'acute and terrible attritions' of 'that determined place'.

[40] W. R. Rodgers, letter to Dan Davin, 21 Mar. 1955, OUP archives.
[41] W. R. Rodgers, letter to Dan Davin, 7 Mar. 1957, OUP archives.

3
Poetry, Narrative, and Violence

I Violence and 'Violence'

It is one of the current vices of critical style to hedge vocabulary with the visible protection of quotation-marks, a tricksiness which, in proclaiming so clearly the awareness of danger, succeeds often in conveying no more than the author's anxiety to be seen as intelligently self-conscious. Sometimes, of course, the quotation-marks can function as a species of commentary upon the vocabulary: these words, they may imply, are clichés, and both author and reader are able to understand them as such. Alternatively, the quotation-marks may signal contention, and point out terms whose meanings are bound up in the very disagreements over what these meanings might be. Thus, the poetry and violence in the title of this chapter ought rather to be, it might be argued, poetry and 'violence'. In Ireland at present, the argument might run, the word 'violence' is subject to both interpretation and dispute: the chapter acknowledges the fact of that dispute in contemporary literature and criticism, and the quotation-marks would register an awareness of disagreements of a fundamental kind. That there has been violence in Northern Ireland, and that poetry has been written there, are both pieces of uncontentious information; but the status, function, and implications of both poetry and violence are altogether different matters, and they involve interpretations of various, and variously contentious, kinds.

It is customary to repeat in the context of such discussions (and, sometimes, in almost any critical discussion) that no literary discourse is transparent or innocently self-sufficient. Certainly, an awareness of this has contributed to a number of the most forceful critical responses to Irish writing in recent years. Such responses have been provoked as much by the discussion of history as by the interpretation of literature: events, in this way, have made matters of understanding and narrating the contem-

porary Irish situation complicated, so that the distinction between objective and strategic knowledge has become hard to
maintain. For example, the question of the significance of 'revisionist' Irish history has become commonplace, and extends now
well beyond anything one might describe as narrowly defined
professional circles, with the result that most Irish cultural commentators are expected to have some position on 'revisionism'
in contemporary historiography. One influential interpretation
of contemporary historical writing, at any rate amongst literary
critics, is to insist upon its mistaken assumptions about language and meaning, and the mistaken nature of its claims (or
supposed claims) to shed light on events through information
about them. Seamus Deane's attack on Roy Foster's *Modern
Ireland*, for example, makes the point that, for historians, the
'bottom line' is that 'Events took place', then takes this naïve faith
to task:

But historical facts or events are artefacts. Once an event is characterized as
'historical', it has entered into the world of historical discourse. Even
discourse itself is an event, but it is often the case—in recent historical
writing in Ireland at any rate—that the written word, when treated as
historical evidence, has a very peculiar relation to action, especially action
of the revolutionary kind.[1]

Historians like Foster, in this reading, forget that history is textually
situated, is not so much history as 'history', so to speak, and are (at
best) imperfectly aware of their own linguistic or textual medium.
The literary critic, on the other hand, is able to interrogate 'events'
in a less innocent way, and to read the ideologies behind 'facts'. For
Deane and others, it is one distinguishing feature of the postmodern
intellectual that she or he knows which concepts to enclose in
quotation-marks.

The suspicion of 'revisionism', or, rather, the attempt to expose
contemporary historical writings as (to varying degrees) ideologi-
cally conditioned acts of political intervention, emerges from a
literary or academic culture open to the industry of 'theory'.
Clearly, this is part of a trend in literary and cultural studies which
goes far beyond Ireland; but in Ireland such a trend finds itself in
more immediate contact than elsewhere with the realm of the

[1] 'Wherever Green is Read', in Máirín Ní Dhonnchadha and Theo Dorgan (eds.),
Revising the Rising (Londonderry: Field Day, 1991), 103.

political. In the case of Seamus Deane, a rejection of 'revisionism' in history is part and parcel of a larger series of rejections, or refusals, which embrace literature along with history:

There is no such thing as an objective factual history which has somehow been distorted by a series of mythologies invented by various bigoted groups. There is no such thing as objective history, and there is no innocent history. All history and literature, as far as I understand them, are forms of mythology. This is not to take away other functions from literature and not to deny it its specific features, but to make the point that all literature is linked to various forms of historical mythology.[2]

The specifics of both literary and historical discourse seem to be granted a place within Deane's larger dismissal of the 'objective', but in fact they are being put very firmly in their place by the assertion of the overarching 'mythology', something which the critic is especially able to interpret. Where 'revisionist' historians mistake the fruits of their researches for facts with a bearing on received narratives of national history, the literary interpreter can see this as part of a process of constant adjustment of 'specific features'. The analogy between this and the process whereby literary theory places within its discourse the specifics of literary texts is fairly clear: the 'specific features', while not usually being denied their place, must always be put within the primary frame of theoretical interpretation. To overrate such particular features is to fall for an ideological trick:

To believe that there is such a thing as fine writing, and that it is somehow autonomously separate from a speech by Ian Paisley, John Hume or Margaret Thatcher, is to show that you truly have been brainwashed. It shows that you actually do believe that there is a stable place called 'culture', to which you can retreat from the shouts and cries of the street, from the murder and mayhem that takes place there, and that you can go into that realm of humanist subjectivity in which literature or great art prevails. When you do that you are actually responding to an invention of 19th-century bourgeois culture, the idea of autonomous individual character.[3]

The 'cries of the street' mean that theoretical interpretation is necessary, and that any talk of specifics without reference to such

[2] 'Canon Fodder: Literary Mythologies in Ireland', in Jean Lundy and Aodan Mac Poilin (eds.), *Styles of Belonging: The Cultural Identities of Ulster* (Belfast: Lagan Press, 1992), 26.
[3] Ibid. 26–7.

interpretation amounts to an act of 'retreat'. Where, then, does this leave the issue of Northern Irish poetry and its relation to violence?

In posing the question at all, of course, one is already admitting to some measure of 'mythology', in so far as the central terms are not announced as problematic ones. Is 'poetry' an abstract category, or a specific body of work? Beyond this, is 'violence' as neutrally descriptive a term as it initially seems? Both terms try to make into broad categories what are in fact selective areas of concentration: which poems in particular, for example, does 'poetry' account for? Whose violence exactly does 'violence' cover, and whose does it ignore? Is there a sense, a critic influenced by Deane might ask, in which the critical conjunction of 'poetry' and 'violence' is predisposed in favour of 'poetry' as a humanistic escape from the barbarity of 'violence', thus setting up a comparison in which the various 'mythological' values implicit in the literary are bound to be vindicated from whatever demands the 'cries of the street' may make upon them?

'Violence' is, like 'poetry', a term open to critical interpretation, and by no means a word of uncontested, descriptive function in contemporary Irish forms of discourse. If one separates, provisionally, political from literary discourse, then this point is of some importance; it amounts, perhaps, to little more than an alertness to the facts of rhetoric and the need for suspicion of the vocabulary of such rhetoric in the political sphere. But this kind of provisional separation is precisely the thing that critics like Deane reject, insisting that any such division is ultimately false, since it encourages the idea of the work of art as somehow self-sufficient and at a remove from the expediencies or polemical purposes of the more immediately 'political'. Just as 'revisionist' history is to be read as either covert or self-deluding polemic in favour of (usually unwelcome) political agendas, so criticism of literature which seems to hold the text at a distance from political analysis and argument is indulging in a humanistic fantasy of art's 'innocence'. To quote Deane again, 'you never read a clean text', and this fall into the state of experience means that the critical reader in Ireland inevitably brings to bear on the text the knowledge of both politics and violence.

There is no such thing as an innocent text, even if it was only published yesterday. Reading is never innocent, interpretation is never innocent. Writing is never innocent: it belongs to culturally specific situations and moments. Therefore northern writing, if we want to categorise it so, belongs to a culturally specific moment which is the atrocious moment of the last 20 years.⁴

In a sense, this is no more than a reiteration of an orthodoxy of Marxist criticism, and is hardly a novelty, in terms of its theoretical assumptions, in literary studies. But its force derives from more local circumstances, and especially from the atrocities which go into the formation of Deane's 'atrocious moment' in Ireland. Violent things, Deane would seem to insist, are inescapably present in the text, like 'categories of discrimination, categories of determination and, indeed, incarceration'; moreover, like the 'cries in the street', there is, for the critic dealing with Irish writing, 'no avoiding them'.

In the face of such urgency, it is clearly important to decide what is meant by the 'atrocious moment' of contemporary Irish violence. Is it a series of particular atrocities, or rather a phrase encoding a narrative, or 'mythology', which the critic must interpret? According to David Lloyd, a scholar of nineteenth-century Irish literature whose theoretical concerns with nationalism, post-colonialism, and politics have put him in the same area of cultural and literary debate as Deane and others, 'violence' in Ireland is always tied up with one narrative pattern or another: this pattern may be perceived by the critical reader of history, whether that history is 'nationalist' or 'imperialist and, perhaps much the same thing, revisionist'.⁵ Where one school, according to Lloyd, sees the violence as 'the unrelenting struggle of an Irish people forming itself in sporadic but connected risings against British domination', for the imperialist/revisionist school, 'Violence is understood as an atavistic and disruptive principle counter to the rationality of legal constitution as barbarity is to an emerging civility.' For Lloyd, 'both tendencies concur', in that 'the end of violence is the legitimate state formation', thus enabling the literary theorist to read deeply into the narratives of both parties:

From such a perspective, violence is radically counter-historical, even against narrative, always represented as an outburst, an 'outrage', spasmodic and without a legitimating teleology. Violence is always without the law. For, within nationalist history, what was violence becomes, in Walter

---

⁴ Lendy and Mac Poilin, *Styles of Belonging*, 25.
⁵ *Anomalous States: Irish Writing and the Post-Colonial Moment* (Dublin: Lilliput Press, 1993), 125.

Benjamin's terms, 'sanctioned' and thereby ceases to be violence insofar as bloodshed is subordinated to the founding of the state. Nationalism itself requires the absorption or transformation of justifiable but nonetheless irrational acts of resistance into the self-legitimating form of a political struggle for the state.[6]

If the narratives even of opposed readings of history make violence into meaning, then it is the theoretical 'perspective' which is able to redeem violence from the narratives in terms of which it is habitually understood. Interestingly, this does not lead to an insistence on the plurality and particularity of acts of violence in themselves, but to a mimicry, on Lloyd's part, of the narratives his theory affects to transcend: 'justifiable but nonetheless irrational' concedes little to particularity but, like Deane's 'atrocious moment' into which the atrocities of twenty years are compressed, it manifests its own tendency towards totalizing narrative.

Nevertheless, the desire to read violence as narrative is a significant part of what might be called the theoretical perspective on Irish literature; in the practice of literary history, for example, such a narrative can be exposed and considered from the position of a contemporary understanding of the story in question—in Lloyd's case, the story that issues in 'a political struggle'. The phrase, as used by Lloyd, does not find itself inside quotation-marks, nor does it earn these in contexts such as 'the continuing anti-colonial struggle in Northern Ireland'[7] elsewhere in Lloyd's prose. Yet the language is not uniquely Lloyd's, for 'struggle' to describe terrorist violence for republican political ends in Northern Ireland is a rhetorical commonplace. The limits of such rhetoric are suggested by Gerry Adams's writing:

From defensive origins the IRA campaign developed into an offensive against the state, and there is no denying the fact that innocent bystanders were killed and injured as a consequence of IRA actions. Death by violence is always a sickening tragedy and no talk of 'the inevitable casualties of guerrilla warfare' can do anything to alter the fact. I deeply regret all deaths and injuries which occur in the course of this struggle...[8]

Adams's rhetorical technique allows him to pretend to sense the inadequacy of language to experience, as he seals off 'inevitable

---

[6] Lloyd, *Anomalous States* 126.

[7] Ibid. 3. Cf. the quotation at n. 6 above.

[8] *The Politics of Irish Freedom* (1986), repr. in Seamus Deane (gen. ed.), *The Field Day Anthology of Irish Writing*, 3 vols. (Londonderry: Field Day, 1991), iii. 797.

casualties' within quotation-marks, but the hollowness of this gesture is exposed in his clichés—'sickening tragedy', 'deeply regret'—
and in his ultimate recourse to 'struggle' in order to contain such
problems within a larger narrative of justification. Despite all this
'regret', the narrative remains intact: 'By its very nature British rule
cannot be just or peaceful and, while this is so, revolutionary
struggle will continue to strive to overthrow it in pursuit of true
justice, peace and happiness.'[9] 'Struggle' here is no more ironic or
shadowed by doubt than is the confidence in the IRA's 'true justice'.
Common experience suggests otherwise, however, and urges some
caution in the use of such terms. Language's adequacy to experience is at issue here, as well as the extent of its inadequacy, both
issues which Adams's rhetoric has to bypass. For Adams's purposes
there is always, as it were, violence and 'violence'.

If a faith in validating narrative is understandable in the writings
of a man like Gerry Adams, it would be more surprising in the work
of contemporary theorists. It is curious, perhaps, that critics like
Deane and Lloyd are able, on the one hand, to air a radical scepticism about the 'objectivity' of historical discourse and its attitude
towards 'specific features', while, on the other hand, taking for
granted an agreement on the frameworks for a historical understanding of Ireland—those of colonial and post-colonial 'struggle'
—which function in their work as, so to speak, unsuspected narratives, or narratives above suspicion.[10] The forensic tone of much
theoretical discourse often helps to give the impression that, for the
cultural critic, narratives can be detected and dissected in a precise,
almost 'objective', manner. Thus Clair Wills, writing on 'Language
Politics, Narrative, Violence', expresses the wish to 'examine the
theory of narrative suggested by acts of political violence', and asks
whether 'terrorism, in all its various forms, [can] be said to harbour
a theory of narrative and temporality'.[11] The suspicion that a phrase
like 'political violence' might be said to harbour its own narrative is

[9] Ibid. 803.
[10] Deane's ironic formulation that 'The North can read the South; the South
cannot read the North' ('Wherever Green is Read', 94) misfires when considered in
the context of the actual level of political and cultural understanding of Northern
Ireland in the Irish Republic; what Deane intends as sarcasm has an air of mundane
truth. The discomfort at the idea of being 'read' by the wrong readers perhaps
indicates how central a concern narrative remains to post-colonial analysis.
[11] *Improprieties: Politics and Sexuality in Northern Irish Poetry* (Oxford:
Clarendon Press, 1993), 107.

either ignored or suppressed in such formulations, and in this respect Wills follows Deane and Lloyd closely, allowing the language of literary and cultural theory to assume an uncontested position in which it can appear, if not 'objective', at least settled and transparent. Wills's treatment (in a footnote) of 'revisionist' readings of history shows the style at its most rigorous and, apparently, scientific: 'one could argue', she writes, 'against revisionist and post-nationalist claims that militant nationalism sets itself against pluralism, diversity, and heterogeneity, that the very indeterminacy of violence runs counter to the notion that it sets up a notion of unity.'[12] If this is less brisk than Lloyd's 'imperialist and, perhaps much the same thing, revisionist' label for the historians' covert narrative, it manages to reclaim 'violence' for 'pluralism', and set its 'indeterminacy' against the all-too-determined narratives of the 'revisionist and post-nationalist' interpretations.

The situation, then, is in some ways a paradoxical one: cultural theory enables the critic to gain a perspective beyond the circumstantial pressures of 'specific features', from which the narrative of violence will become clear; at the same time that theory, which rejects narrative as a goal, accepts as valid the narrative of Irish history as anti-colonial 'struggle'. When this is applied to the field of literary criticism, the particular texts under examination tend to be searched for their latent narratives, or their contributions to other such narratives, rather than being considered as 'specific features' of the literary terrain—that is, features with specificity, differing from one another and capable of being apprehended and appraised in and for themselves. Deane's rejection of the 'realm of humanist subjectivity' is a rejection of interpretation without an enabling narrative, and disowns 'specific features' in both historical and literary studies that do not find their proper place within such a narrative. This position (which is, in truth, something of a commonplace) is reiterated by Terry Eagleton's contribution to the Irish theoretical debate, his Field Day pamphlet *Nationalism: Irony and Commitment*, and his overview there of the 'specific features' issue:

This is not to say, on the other hand, that the aesthetic as 'disinterested' mythic solution to real contradictions is not in evidence in Ireland at all. There are Irish critics and commentators who deploy the term today as a privileged mark of that decency, civility and cultivation of which an

[12] Wills, *Improprieties*, 106.

uncouth nationalism is fatally bereft. In the stalest of Arnoldian clichés, the poetic is still being counterposed to the political—which is only to say that the 'poetic' as we have it today was, among other things, historically constructed to carry out just that business of suppressing political conflict. Imagination and enlightened liberal reason are still being offered to us in Ireland today as the antithesis of sectarianism: and like all such idealised values they forget their own roots in a social class and history not unnoted for its own virulent sectarianism, then and now.[13]

Here Eagleton provides a good example of the utility of narrative: in dismissing the 'realm of humanist subjectivity' in Irish criticism as something either deceitful or self-deceived, he recasts this insistence on 'specific features' in terms of a narrative which has its conclusion in the present—'virulent sectarianism, *then and now*'. Both '"disinterested"' and '"poetic"' are put within quotation-marks that may indicate an Arnoldian line of descent, but also announce the interpreter's grasp of the larger narrative within which they seem to function. Eagleton's analysis is, then, overtly hostile to the 'poetic' and to 'imagination'; but how would this kind of approach receive poetry, or rather the various 'specific features' of a period's literature which are individual poems?[14] If this is a question which is applicable to a good deal of European and American literary theory, its obviousness should not preclude its being asked in the context of contemporary Irish criticism.

Any critical narrative which rejects 'objectivity' in history and the 'aesthetic' in literature as varieties of politically compromised illusion is, plainly, faced with certain problems in its interpretation of literature and violence in contemporary Ireland. In his general introduction to *The Field Day Anthology of Irish Writing*, Seamus Deane raises this central question, but again is anxious to argue against any aestheticizing opposition of literature and violence:

If there is an association between violence and writing, how can it be understood? . . . The aesthetic ideology, which claims autonomy for the work of art, is a political force which pretends not to be so. But within that assertion, this ideology has produced a very powerful form of

---

[13] *Nationalism: Irony and Commitment* (Londonderry: Field Day, 1988), 12–13.
[14] Some indication of Eagleton's critical principles in practice may be found in 'From the Irish', *Poetry Review*, 75/2 (Aug. 1985), 64–5, where James Simmons's line, 'laughing in spite of Stalin and the IRA' is condemned (perhaps a little smugly) as a 'glib *Daily Telegraph* analogy between genocidal tyranny and—whatever you feel about them—a national liberation force'. Eagleton goes on to refer to Simmons as 'a bit of a smug bastard'.

auto-critique, sometimes known as literary criticism and sometimes not.... The idea that that which is chaotic, disorganized and 'rude' can be converted to order and civilization was shared by English colonial writers and English literary critics, at least until very recent times. It is also shared by those who see a connection between northern Irish violence and the northern Irish literary 'revival'. The literature—autonomous, ordered—stands over against the political system in its savage disorder.[15]

Deane's way with quotation-marks is again clinically distancing, so that the phrase 'disorganized and "rude"' (compare Eagleton's 'uncouth nationalism') is put under the same suspicion as the 'northern Irish literary "revival"': to fall for one of these phrases as something 'objective' entails—whether one knows it or not—falling for the implications of the other as well. It becomes apparent that the very idea of literature and violence being in some kind of relation belongs to a narrative other than Deane's which, in detecting the hidden narratives of others, quietly enforces its own denials of any 'order' which is to be finally distinguished from the 'order' of the coercive colonial state.

However, there is a sense in which, no matter how often the relation between literature and violence in Northern Ireland is dismissed by Deane and others as part of 'the aesthetic ideology', the question of that relationship refuses to go away. The contingencies of its critical reception aside, Northern Irish poetry's subject-matter over the last quarter of a century has inevitably been, in part at least, marked and shaped by the actual violence of its contexts. For poets, the current language is both the inescapable medium of writing and something perpetually open to infection from the ungovernable conditions of its own currency: cliché, cant, inexactitude, and complacency are always ready to seize the initiative, even in the language of poems. The degree of attention paid to the meaning, and the particularity, of 'violence' is also a measure of Northern Irish poets' capacity to inoculate their language against infection from forces complicit with the violence itself. Compared to poems, critical analyses and discourses are often prone to forget what J. L. Austin, as quoted by Geoffrey Hill, calls 'the demands of the world upon language',[16] even while their inverted commas

---

[15] *Field Day Anthology of Irish Writing*, vol. i, pp. xxv–xxvi.

[16] J. L. Austin, *Sense and Sensibilia, reconstructed from the manuscript notes by G. J. Warnock* (Oxford: Clarendon Press, 1962), 62, quoted in Geoffrey Hill, *The Lords of Limit: Essays on Literature and Ideas* (London: André Deutsch, 1984), 142.

try to display familiarity with such demands. Indeed, the confidence of such marks of forensic treatment may itself be a sign of infection.

II 'Specific Features'

Poems setting out to deal with the Irish Troubles always, in one way or another, run risks from the language of violence and the kinds of rhetoric it contains. In establishing the difference between successful and unsuccessful ways of taking risks, it is necessary to look very closely at work where the poetic language gives way to rhetorical pressures, relying on stock responses to give coherence to the things presented. A poem by John Montague, 'Foreign Field', tries to compass the shooting of a British soldier in a narrative centred on a house which belongs to 'Paddy':

> Paddy's whole place was a clearing house:
> A public phone in the hallway,
> Folk huddled around a tiled fireplace.
>
> But we were given tea in the front parlour,
> Chill as the grave, a good place to talk,
> Among brass trinkets, Long Kesh harps.[17]

The setting has parable-like overtones, and the act of violence which occurs just outside the house attracts first the curiosity and then the (measured) sympathy of those within ('"When a man's got, he's a non-combatant,"/ Paddy apologises, shepherding us inside.') The poem, with an ironic allusion to Rupert Brooke in its title, indulges in pity for the misled and abused, so that the first-person voice can rise above the mere hatred and callousness of some local inhabitants: 'Out playing / Again, the children chant: "Die, you bastard!"' Yet Montague's pity, and what appears to be his careful attention to the particulars of a violent incident, find expression in language with a callousness of its own:

> But Paddy led us to where he lay,
> A chubby lad, only about eighteen,
>
> That hangdog look, hair close-cropped,
> Surplus of a crowding England, now
> Dying in a puddle of wet and blood.

[17] *Mount Eagle* (Oldcastle: Gallery Press, 1988), 19–20.

Montague takes his eye off the subject in 'Surplus of a crowding England', looking away from the broken human body towards an explanation for or contextualization of the violence that has just taken place: does Montague see 'A chubby lad' or a 'surplus' here? A phrase like 'Surplus of a crowding England' contains a great deal in the way of political or quasi-historical analysis, but this is something accepted by Montague rather than discovered or felt by him in the poem: it is a solution to the problem posed by the horror of the subject-matter. If Paddy's distinction between combatants (fair game) and non-combatants (permitted sympathy) is morally specious, and the children's 'Die you bastard!' is saddeningly callous, Montague's own moment of imported analysis is an infected rhetoric at odds with the specific suffering it tries to explain and forget.

The poet of 'Foreign Field' puts himself in the position of a passive witness of violence, and the figure of poet as wise spectator is a particularly alluring one for some Northern Irish poets. Seamus Heaney's bog-poems in *North* are a complicated and ambiguous instance of the phenomenon, troubled as they are by the complicity with violence which is present in any apparently privileged perspective upon it, but the voice of the overview is always latent as a possibility (or danger) in poetry relating directly to violence. Where this possibility comes through into poems as a technique, it brings with it the need for a narrative to provide the necessary coherence. Such narratives can be public, like history or tradition, or private and peculiar to the poet, but their function in dealing with the subject-matter of violence often puts them under particular strain.

Seamus Heaney's poem 'The Toome Road', in which the speaker recalls an encounter with British forces in rural Ulster, contemplates the visible consequences of violence in what seems to be an alien presence on the known landscape:

> One morning early I met armoured cars
> In convoy, warbling along on powerful tyres,
> All camouflaged with broken alder branches,
> And headphoned soldiers standing up in turrets.[18]

The poem's opening words suggest the movement and incident of a ballad, but the actual speed and pace of what follows provides

---

[18] *Field Work* (London: Faber & Faber, 1979), 15.

something quite different, a dwelling on the details of intrusion, so that the alien soldiers not only stand up, but stand out in the landscape which they attempt to appropriate. Against this, there is the straightforward question, 'How long were they approaching down my roads / As if they owned them?' Of course, this is not in fact quite so straightforward as it is simple, for an answer to 'How long...?' would possibly entail a sweep of history far beyond the reported scene: this sense of depth is, as it were, taken for granted by the poem, in which the movement of the soldiers' approach is set against a more profound stability or fixity located in the observing voice. It may be that the very density of the description is that of a voice in no hurry to establish itself (the third line, for example, slows down the presentation by taking the time to notice that the camouflage is provided by 'alder branches' rather than any more generally described greenery, and does so in a descriptive phrase that holds a full, end-stopped line). As the poem progresses, the poetic voice continues to take a stand against whatever narrative the presented incursion might try to represent. This is done by an enumeration of the solid possessions of local knowledge:

> I had rights-of-way, fields, cattle in my keeping,
> Tractors hitched to buckrakes in open sheds,
> Silos, chill gates, wet slates, the greens and reds
> Of outhouse roofs.

The listing here slows the verse down almost to a halt. This stasis of the intimately known is set in contrast to the military approach and the 'warbling' of its technology, so that the poem presents a juxtaposition of movement and steadiness which parallels that of invasion and possession. Indeed, the voice displaces action of any kind into an unanswered question, 'Whom should I run to tell...?', and aligns its own apparent passivity with a community's slow patience as 'Sowers of seed, erectors of headstones...', a line in whose aposiopesis even the motive power of syntax is disengaged. Narrative, it seems, belongs in a realm other than that of the rooted poetic voice; yet narrative of another order may be present in that apparent (or comparative) stasis.

Heaney's three-line apostrophe to the soldiers allows the force of the static to reach expression, in a way that combines the rhetoric of the traditional ballad with a register of vocabulary altogether more idiosyncratic:

> O charioteers, above your dormant guns,
> It stands here still, stands vibrant as you pass,
> The invisible, untoppled omphalos.

'Stands . . . stands' makes a point of its repetition within the rhythmic pattern of the lines; it is, perhaps, coarsely rhetorical in the crudeness of its rhythmic propulsion of the word 'vibrant' to contrast with the 'dormant' guns. Yet this reversion to the techniques of a poem which might begin 'One morning early I met . . .' is made problematic by the strangeness of the thing which emerges in the last line, 'The invisible, untoppled omphalos'. In a poem much exercised by the tension between the native and the alien, the final and climactic appearance of an 'omphalos', a word scarcely naturalized from the Greek in English usage,[19] is a poetic turn of some significance. In the intransigence of these three lines, the poem stages an assertion of possession and permanence, in which the specificity and individuality of the 'omphalos' is the ultimate mark of resistance to a narrative of usurpation.

It is important for 'The Toome Road' that 'omphalos' can be glossed by reference to something other than a dictionary, and Heaney's prose-piece 'Mossbawn' provides the necessary information:

I would begin with the Greek word, *omphalos*, meaning the navel, and hence the stone that marked the centre of the world, and repeat it, *omphalos, omphalos, omphalos*, until its blunt and falling music becomes the music of somebody pumping water at the pump outside our back door.[20]

As Heaney's reminiscence of childhood develops, the *omphalos-pump* begins to stand against the processes of 'history' that surround it, offering its own, different, narrative of stability:

It is Co. Derry in the early 1940s. The American bombers groan towards the aerodrome at Toomebridge, the American troops manœuvre in the fields along the road, but all of that great historical action does not disturb the rhythms of the yard. There the pump stands, a slender, iron idol, snouted, helmeted, dressed down with a sweeping handle, painted a dark green and set on a concrete plinth, marking the centre of another world.

This is, perhaps, an anti-narrative, for the pump becomes a magnet for adjectival description (again, as in 'The Toome Road', Heaney's

---

[19] The *OED* records Heaney's sense of the word (*sb* 1b) only once, in 1850.
[20] *Preoccupations: Selected Prose 1968–1978* (London: Faber & Faber, 1980), 17.

description serves to slow down any narrative development). Finally, the pump becomes its sound, and the sound is identified with that of the Greek word: 'The horses came home to it in those first lengthening evenings of spring, and in a single draught emptied one bucket and then another as the man pumped and pumped, the plunger slugging up and down, *omphalos, omphalos, omphalos.*' Sound is above and beyond narrative, or is another, deeper narrative of its own here, and this sense of depth is what 'omphalos' in 'The Toome Road' tries to invoke. Stability puts itself in the path of new narrative designs, and thus it ultimately guarantees possession, just as the poetic voice of Heaney himself possesses the word 'omphalos'. To return to the question which 'The Toome Road' asks of the armoured cars—'How long were they approaching down my roads / As if they owned them?'—any answer which attempts precision ('For the last five minutes', for example) is rendered ludicrous by the meta- or hyper-narrative of the 'omphalos': in this perspective, the soldiers have always been approaching, just as the 'invisible, untoppled' navel-stone has always stood in their way.

Critical readings of 'The Toome Road' tend to fall in with Heaney's resistance to narrative, and gloss the 'omphalos' more or less according to the poet's prompting. If there is a certain cracker-barrel innocence about Henry Hart's identification of the 'omphalos' as a point 'where political and religious turmoil was eclipsed by pastoral calm and where beliefs were more certain, more stable',[21] readers more closely attuned to the political resonances of Heaney's writing have come up with less comforting interpretations of the 'untoppled' stone. Neil Corcoran, noting Heaney's 'oracular' tone in the final lines of the poem, understands the 'omphalos' as 'the navel of nationalist Irish feeling, maintaining on the road to Toome (with its 1798 associations) its persistent, defiant opposition to the colonial power.'[22] Michael Parker elaborates on this with some gusto, in an attempted paraphrase which follows the observation that the last three lines (the lines which take the poem over the fourteen-line mark of a sonnet) are added 'as if determined to snatch victory from the colonial power':

[21] *Seamus Heaney: Poet of Contrary Progressions* (Syracuse, NY: Syracuse University Press, 1992), 136.
[22] *Seamus Heaney* (London: Faber & Faber, 1986), 134–5.

Although the power and glory belong to the 'charioteers', the professionals concerned with extending or defending Empires, ultimately it is the 'Sowers of seed', like his forebears, who will inherit the Kingdom. Their champion is the *omphalos*, a transcendent, ever-present, unseen being which 'stands' and will remain standing long after all these warriors, with their anachronistic chariots and 'dormant guns' will have passed away.[23]

It is interesting to observe the critical language here attempting to mimic the tone of Heaney's poem; it is more perplexing, perhaps, to determine how far the confusions and vulgarities of the critical response are indeed true to something in the poetry. After all, 'it stands here still, stands vibrant as you pass' is not, on first reading, too distant from ' "stands", and will remain standing'; the rhetoric is, in both cases, an explicit matter, and its implicit denial of one kind of narrative is in the interests of something beyond the mere particulars of any specific situation. In Parker's reading, the time-less vitality of a 'Kingdom' resists the historical encroachment of empires in the naming of the 'omphalos'. Heaney's poem is not, of course, so flat-footed as this paraphrase, but neither is it entirely distinct from the deep narratives such a paraphrase celebrates. Corcoran's identification of the 'omphalos' with 'nationalist Irish feeling' returns Heaney's navel-gazing to some kind of specificity, but seems to hint at possibilities of irony in the poem which the rhetorical drive of the last three lines simply rules out.

Disruption and calm are both present in 'The Toome Road': disruption is figured by the approaching soldiers, calm by the voice's assured possession of its territory. In rejecting disruption, the poetic voice rejects the imposition of event, of a new narrative, in the name of a more deeply grounded continuity. This is, in effect, the stony stability of 'identity', as the word is commonly under-stood in Irish politics and cultural discussion, and the rejection of the 'armoured cars' is not a rejection of narrative *per se*, but of this version of imposing narrative in particular. While the vehicles 'warble', the 'omphalos' remains in place, 'invisible' perhaps, but assuredly there. It is worth thinking about this poem in terms of the larger questions which the problem of poetry and violence in Northern Ireland brings to the surface: specifically, does poetic language uncover the encoded narratives of current discourse, or

---

[23] *Seamus Heaney: The Making of the Poet* (Basingstoke: Macmillan, 1993), 159.

does it collude with or reinforce them? In one sense, 'The Toome Road' makes the language its own, by the insistence on 'omphalos' as an irreducible linguistic element, one which carries personal and cultural meaning; in another sense, though, the poem's reliance on one deep narrative—of possession and identity—over the rejected narrative of incursion entails an acceptance of the already formed historical and political narratives which the critical comments on 'omphalos' quoted above make explicit. The defiance voiced in Heaney's 'stands... stands' speaks from a narrative in which meanings are always finally clear: even a word like 'omphalos', apparently alien, is ultimately guaranteed a meaning within the narrative of identity, as a touchstone of authenticity. But the resultant combination of lexical idiosyncracy and ballad rhetoric is forced, putting strain on the poem as a whole: in the end, 'The Toome Road' relies on the reader's acceptance of its deep narrative as a way of making such pressures bearable. The poem achieves, or offers to achieve, a final coherence, but there is nevertheless a price to be paid for such a completion.

At this point, the issue of the degree of relation between the poetry itself and a contextual field of violence is unavoidable, though to evade this in favour of a more closely circumscribed understanding of the poet's personal aesthetic procedures is undoubtedly more comfortable for the reader. Asking hard questions about 'The Toome Road' risks much, and James Simmons's comment that 'I am amazed at Heaney's hatred of the soldiers... his identification with paramilitary nationalism'[24] seems to be in danger of a hard-faced philistinism. Yet the poem's strategies do tend to protect its narrative from such doubts: to return to Heaney's question about the armoured cars—'How long were they approaching down my roads / As if they owned them?'—there are answers which might be given, but these are rendered inappropriate by the poem's underlying narrative coherence. If 'five minutes' is an absurd response to the question, because over-literal in spirit, other responses might stem from the kinds of narrative which the poem rejects: the armoured cars may, for example, be approaching down these particular roads because of other incursions elsewhere; rather than violating the home ground of the

[24] 'The Trouble with Seamus', in Elmer Andrews (ed.), *Seamus Heaney: A Collection of Critical Essays* (Basingstoke: Macmillan, 1992), 63.

speaker, these vehicles may be serving to protect against violations that take place on other home grounds. If 'The Toome Road' reconfigures violence as territorial violation, it also sacrifices the specificity of its perceptions in order to simplify its mythic/political perspective. To push the matter further, the coherence which the 'omphalos' supplies must obscure the kinds of actual violence which have given rise to the military presence; for the reader to understand and appreciate the poem's conclusion is to forget all that the 'omphalos' insists has to be forgotten.

Such a reading may perhaps be unreasonable, in the sense that Heaney's work as a whole allows itself a much wider range of remembering and particularity when it comes to the issue of Irish violence, and it is certainly arguable that the simplicities of 'The Toome Road' are made more difficult by some of the poems which surround it in *Field Work*. However, the poem in itself suggests certain things about poetic language, narrative, and violence which are of some importance in approaching Northern Irish poetry, and which a good deal of contemporary criticism and critical theory ignores. 'Omphalos' contains a whole narrative within itself, and this narrative does things to the representation of violence; so, in the work of other Northern Irish poets beside Heaney, the language of poetry invests itself in a narrative which makes sense, in some way, of violence. But this relation is artistically a weak one; if 'The Toome Road', for example, fails in important respects, so a good deal of poetry fails by accepting the all-too-inviting chain of connection that leads from language to narrative to violence. Better poems show that sense is not made all that easily, and that the poet's control of language in these matters can be something of an illusion. As the critic Jahan Ramazani has written (on Heaney's bog-poems in *North*), 'To make sense of these atrocities, he risks making them seem sensible'.[25]

Ciaran Carson's poetry is much occupied by the difficulties and liabilities of narrative, but retains a compelling narrative subtlety and design. Much more than Heaney, Carson dwells on violence and its locations: both *The Irish For No* and *Belfast Confetti* are collections in which the context of the Northern Irish Troubles impinges constantly on the various narrative voices. There are

[25] *The Poetry of Mourning: The Modern Elegy from Hardy to Heaney* (Chicago, Ill.: University of Chicago Press, 1994), 337.

ways in which Carson's writing always complicates its subjects at the same time as its narrative lines tangle and intertwine, with the result that the narrative momentum of anecdote constructs strange and unexpected kinds of coherence out of the material on hand in various series of events. In *First Language* Carson takes this complication of voice and narrative further, by exploring linguistic and formal registers of great complexity and peculiarity. One poem in this collection opens up a line of intertextual relation with Heaney's 'The Toome Road', unsettling the earlier poem in ways which suggest a destabilization of the kinds of narrative upon which it relied. In 'All Souls' Carson, like Heaney, observes the British army and its 'headphoned soldiers', but his poem begins with language quite distinct from Heaney's:

The un*Walkman* headphones stick out awkwardly, because they are
   receiving
Not the packaged record of a song, but real-time input, a form of blah
Alive with intimations of mortality, the loud and unclear garbled static.[26]

Carson's language, rather than distancing the poem from its subject and creating a detached, observing voice, incorporates the confusion of 'real-time input', in which 'intimations of mortality' are present, alongside that which they are not—the 'packaged record of a song' received on the headphones of a personal stereo. Even in these first three lines, the poem deploys oxymoron and cliché—'Alive with intimations of mortality', 'loud and unclear'—and the poem goes on to develop this combination of the familiar with the strange. Where in 'The Toome Road' the familiar (and the familial) is invaded by the alien, in 'All Souls' it is much more difficult to take bearings in the 'garbled static'.

   As Carson promises to bring things into focus, the soldiers come into view along with 'The Toome Road' itself:

Like putting on spectacles, when what it was was blurred, then swims
Into your focus. You can see they come from the Planet X, with their
   walkie-
Talkies, the heavy warbling of their heavy Heaney tyres and automatic,
Gyroscope-type-tank-surveillance technique, their faces blacked like
Boots. Their antennae quivered on that Hallowe'en encountered just
   beyond Sans
Souci.

   [26] *First Language* (Oldcastle: Gallery Press, 1993), 40–1.

A metaphorically alien presence is here comically literalized, so that the paraphernalia of military technology are identified with creatures 'from the Planet X', and the complex compounds of technological language include also the 'heavy Heaney tyres', 'warbling' as they had done in 'The Toome Road'. Carson's narrative here is not to be distinguished from the poem's language and its intertextual detours (Keats's 'watcher of the skies' is also present, ushering in, perhaps, the little green men); the particularity of the language, both in describing the hardware and in placing the incident, is also important, specifying a point 'just beyond Sans / Souci'. The distance between Sans Souci Park, in south Belfast, and Heaney's Toome is a considerable one, in more than just geographical terms—Heaney might well have been indulging in a degree of intertextual dialogue with himself, recalling his poem 'Toome', as well as touching on the historical connections of that town;[27] Carson seems to defamiliarize the landscape by specifying the French name of the Irish road, then splitting that name across two lines, the slight catch in the breath of 'Sans / Souci' for a moment giving the lie to its promise of being without regret. It is the poem's language, in its unexpected juxtapositions and turns, which takes a major part in the narrative of 'All Souls', 'Sans / Souci' leading to the fire station nearby, and the firemen providing in turn further 'intimations' of what is heard through the 'static' of confused communication. 'All Souls' is a poem haunted by codes which cannot—quite—be deciphered, but which are nevertheless heavy with menace:

> Demonic intimations went on daily; routine, undercover orchestrations
> Of the nominated discipline of alphabetic, proscribed areas
> That ended, as they always do, in tragic, tired recriminations; rhetoric.

The language here is aware of the designs which the world might have upon it, and its deadpan, flat tone is also a register of the pressures which drain language of meaning. 'Rhetoric' is not something which can simply be disowned, and Carson's use of 'tragic' already puts on display its own inadequacy, emptied of meaning by the 'rhetoric' which this narrative cannot compete with by offering some alternative pattern of meaning and coher-

---

[27] See Seamus Heaney, 'Toome', *Wintering Out* (London: Faber & Faber, 1972), 26: 'a hundred centuries' / loam, flints, musket-balls, / fragmented ware, / torcs and fish-bones.'

ence. Instead, Carson concludes 'All Souls' with further narrative complication:

It then occurred the Firemen had a Ball, it was at Hallowe'en. Ecstatically,
  they
Didn't have false faces on. They were plastic, not explosively, but faces.
  Then
They tore their faces off. Un*Walkman*like. Laconic. Workmanlike.

What is happening here? The narrative focus appears to be on the firemen, though the soldiers of the beginning of the poem are recalled in the return of the personal stereo to Carson's lexicon. The firemen at their Hallowe'en ball are not wearing false faces, but plastic ones—this strange, apparently nonsensical distinction is made with Carson's characteristic concern for precision, so that the plastic of the faces is distinguished from that of plastic explosive, thus bringing that substance to the reader's attention. 'Plastic' can of course be used to mean 'Susceptible of being moulded or shaped' (*OED* 5a), 'pliant, supple, flexible' (*OED* 6a), so the faces' plasticity remains as a disturbing note behind 'Then / They tore their faces off'. The overtones of 'Ecstatically', similarly, may add to the sinister atmosphere, hinting at a literal standing outside of the self, and making the question of who is tearing off whose face all the more pressing. But at the point where the narrative would usually resolve itself, clarifying and making coherent what has been happening, Carson ends the poem in word-play: 'Un*Walkman*like. Laconic. Workmanlike.' This is in itself grimly laconic, linking the negative comparison of the beginning of the poem to a final, flat word, one which suggests perhaps that someone somewhere is only doing his job. What has actually happened here, in terms of narrative, is lost in the 'static' of language, 'loud and unclear'.

'All Souls' rewrites 'The Toome Road' in more than just its particulars, for it replaces the assertion of narrative with the subversion of narrative by language; in Carson's hands, poetic language absorbs violence by destabilizing narrative, making it harder to 'make sense' of the shower of particulars—no transcendent 'omphalos' provides a centre of gravity for this writing. At the same time, 'All Souls', like much of Carson's poetry, has nothing to say about violence; the poetic voice has to do with narrative rather than commentary, even if that narrative is often bizarre and confusing. The resistance to 'rhetoric' is understood by Carson to be a matter of linguistic performance rather than statement, and the poetry of *The Irish For No* and *Belfast Confetti* pulls away from the force of commentary which, in presenting acts of violence, can reduce even the best intentions to an essentially rhetorical function. In the short poem 'Campaign', for example, poetic language has no special or compensatory status:

They had questioned him for hours. Who exactly was he? And when
He told them, they questioned him again. When they accepted who he was, as
Someone not involved, they pulled out his fingernails. Then
They took him to a waste-ground somewhere near the Horseshoe Bend, and told him
What he was. They shot him nine times.[28]

The solution to 'Who exactly was he?' is not found in these lines, or at least proves not to be relevant once the unspecified 'they' have 'told him / What he was'; a formulation such as 'Someone not involved' takes on a sinister blandness here, since it merely allows the question of 'Who?' to be superseded by the fact (not open to questions at all) of 'What he was'. Carson's reticence is crucial to the disturbing effect of these lines, and the rest of the poem offers its own version of 'Who exactly was he?'

A dark umbilicus of smoke was rising from a heap of burning tyres.
The bad smell he smelt was the smell of himself. Broken glass and knotted Durex.
The knuckles of a face in a nylon stocking. I used to see him in the Gladstone Bar,
Drawing pints for strangers, his almost-perfect fingers flecked with scum.

The poem's last detail may be anecdotal, but it is not casual, for it sets up a relation between the 'almost perfect fingers' of the working barman and the pulled-out fingernails of the eventual victim. This relation is expressed within a context of other details, less easily rendered into a narrative coherence, of violence and waste in which, finally, every particular is indeed 'involved'. 'Campaign' is a poem whose title, like much of its language, is already infected by rhetoric, by unscrupulous usage and determination, and which makes that infection visible in its insistence upon flat presentation

---

[28] *The Irish For No* (Dublin: Gallery Press, 1987), 36.

of detail. Again, narrative coherence belongs to the questioners who translate 'Who?' into 'What', rather than to the poetic voice, which clings to particulars of memory and experience, however unpalatable or disconcerting these may be.

A poem like 'Campaign', which tempers its narrative with a final, first-person recollection, touches upon a common trope in Troubles poetry, where presentation of events is turned in an elegiac direction by the intervention of the individual poetic voice. Yet 'Campaign' is not an elegy, and much of Carson's writing maintains a distance from that genre which is made all the more manifest by the voice's capacity to provide first-person corroboration. (If anything is the subject for elegy in Carson, it is the city of Belfast itself, the losses in whose fabric are detailed with something like grief.) When Heaney writes elegies for the victims of violence, the first-person poetic voice ministers, so to speak, to the particular narrative; the most obvious ministration comes in 'The Strand at Lough Beg', where Heaney performs intimate, formal rites for his murdered cousin:

> I turn because the sweeping of your feet
> Has stopped behind me, to find you on your knees
> With blood and roadside muck in your hair and eyes,
> Then kneel in front of you in brimming grass
> And gather up cold handfuls of the dew
> To wash you, cousin.[29]

Allowing for the conventions of elegy within which the poem operates, it is worth considering what the poetic voice does here to the narrative. Memory leads to involvement, so that the first part of the narrative (Colum McCartney's murder) is completed by a second phase, in which the poet's voice performs the acts of commemoration and completion. One anti-elegiac interpretation of this procedure is to see the poet as making the atrocity somehow bearable (it is this, essentially, of which Heaney allows himself to be accused by his cousin's ghost in section VIII of 'Station Island'). Another interpretation, however, would read the elegist's voice as a drive to correct the narrative, and to set right the terrible details by establishing a counter-narrative of completion and consolation. The lack of this in Ciaran Carson's poetry, for example, means that his writing is both more difficult to interpret than Heaney's

---

[29] *Field Work*, 18.

and more disturbing; just as its narratives are more tangled, so its refusal of resolution and coherence takes away from it the possibility of elegiac consolation.

The distrust of narrative need not be a distrust of the particulars that narrative contains; it may be rather, as Carson's poetry demonstrates, a distrust of the tendencies towards coherence which narrative generates. In this, Carson is not alone amongst Northern Irish poets: the poetry of Paul Muldoon and of Michael Longley shows similar wariness, and it is in relation to violence that this becomes particularly apparent. Longley's 'Wounds' receives its narratives from different sources: the first half of the poem presents 'two pictures from my father's head',[30] while the second gives details of two separate incidents, the murders of 'three teenage soldiers' and of a bus-conductor. It is the poetic voice, then, which links these various pieces of information, and whose narrative effort might put them into a meaningful relation. Yet 'Wounds' provides little in the way of coherent relation between the incidents remembered and described: such connections as are made in the poem serve to increase the sense of incomprehension which links the father's memories of the First World War with contemporary Irish murders. Recollection of 'the Ulster Division at the Somme / Going over the top with "Fuck the Pope!"' prompts 'my father's words / Of admiration and bewilderment'; while in the murder of the bus-conductor, at the end of the poem, the killer speaks 'to a bewildered wife'. There are two bewilderments here, but their placing does not produce a symmetry that can be translated into a mutual illumination. The voice which carries these pieces of narrative is explicitly the poet's, but it refrains from providing the interpretations that will bring these specifics into an achieved coherence. The poem's ending is unsettling, precisely because it refuses to be a conclusion:

> Also a bus-conductor's uniform—
> He collapsed beside his carpet-slippers
> Without a murmur, shot through the head
> By a shivering boy who wandered in
> Before they could turn the television down
> Or tidy away the supper dishes.
> To the children, to a bewildered wife,
> I think 'Sorry Missus' was what he said.

[30] Michael Longley, *Poems 1963–1983* (Edinburgh: Salamander Press, 1985), 86.

The bewilderment spreads here from the wife to the murderer, whose 'Sorry Missus' is so incongruously caught between brutality and good manners. In this, the poem itself is open to the force of bewilderment, its abrupt ending catching appropriately another kind of unexpected termination: the persistence of detail, in the slippers, the television, and the supper dishes, is determinedly irrelevant to any larger designs for meaning which might be applied to the narrative itself.

Like Carson, Longley both appropriates narrative elements and resists narrative resolution. The formal gestures of a poem like 'Wounds', in which the contemporary violence is made part of a burial-rite for the poet's father, are counterpointed by the eerie casualness of the details and of anecdote ('I think "Sorry Missus" was what he said'). Specifics outweigh design, even in this formally symmetrical poem, and the 'bewilderment' which unites the poem's two sides is tenacious of these specific things. In Carson's work, and especially in his longer poems, there is a similar resistance to conclusion, and an embracing of 'bewilderment' almost as the condition of knowledge. In important ways, this procedure is at odds with elegy, and the formal tones of a poet like Longley should not be mistaken for those of achieved consolation. In a memoir, Longley has written of how 'I find offensive the notion that what we inadequately call "the Troubles" might provide inspiration for artists; and that in some weird *quid pro quo* the arts might provide a solace for grief and anguish':[31] the wariness of rhetoric here is in line with the poet's distrust of any 'solace' which neglects the particular.

In poetry there is no obligation to accommodate specifics within completed structures of interpretation; what most readers and poets recognize as 'poetry' is, indeed, a matter *entirely* of specific effects that establish their own, original patterns of coherence. In the case of Northern Irish poetry and violence, interpretative accommodation is fraught with danger, and is always open to rhetorical infection. At the same time, 'bewilderment' may seem a risky poetic strategy in itself, since nothing could be easier, in one sense, than to reject the idea of 'making sense' of events, or rather making other people's sense of them. But this is to forget that poetry makes sense of things in distinctive ways, which defeat the

[31] *Tuppenny Stung: Autobiographical Chapters* (Belfast: Lagan Press, 1994), 73.

patterns offered by rhetorical and political coherences. If Heaney's 'The Toome Road' fails to make this distinctive kind of sense out of its perceptions, later poems show the poet more open to 'bewilderment' in the face of violence, and less liable to have recourse to patterns of interpretation and reassurance outside the poem in order to put narrative into a framework of public meaning. The 'Squarings' sequence from *Seeing Things* returns, in section xxvi, to a scene reminiscent of 'The Toome Road' or 'From the Frontier of Writing' in *The Haw Lantern*, but now sees the encountered soldiers with 'their gaze abroad / In dreams out of the body-heated metal', and holds in parallel the strange and the mundane in the situation:

> Silent, time-proofed, keeping an even distance
>
> Beyond the windscreen glass, carried ahead
> On the phantasmal flow-back of the road,
> They still mean business in the here and now.[32]

Heaney's 'here and now' is greatly expanded by refusing the rhetorical bolt-hole of poems like 'The Toome Road', and the soldiers witnessed in 'Squarings' move from the context of violence into a Dantean perspective, 'like a speeded-up / Meltdown of souls from the straw-flecked ice of hell'. The significance of all this is complex, contingent, and original, bound up as it is with Heaney's insistence on an autonomous, transcendent imaginative drive; such narratives as are on offer here are both unpredictable and individual, developing away from the facts of experience rather than accommodating such facts to the narratives of others.

The intricacies and liabilities involved in telling a story about contemporary violence in Northern Ireland, which Ciaran Carson's poetry makes especially visible, are significant elements in the narrative structures of Paul Muldoon, and it is arguable that it is Muldoon, more than any other writer, who works most powerfully, persuasively, and entertainingly against grand narratives in relation to violence. The narrative complications of 'Madoc: A Mystery' or '7, Middagh Street' are foreshadowed in 'The More a Man Has the More a Man Wants', the long poem which concludes *Quoof*, where terrorist violence mixes with the shape-changing of the native American Trickster figure, and sequences of events become tangled

---

[32] *Seeing Things* (London: Faber & Faber, 1991), 84.

and indeterminate. Although the poem makes the reader's provisional construction of a narrative difficult, and any definitive establishing of the narrative content impossible, discrete elements within the story are given an often disarming clarity. One critic has noted that 'if the characters of "The More a Man Has . . . " are somewhat hard to follow, then their actions take place against a surprisingly clear background', and goes on to observe how 'specification of time and place seems only to reinforce the obscurity of the third and fourth elements that contribute towards Muldoon's drama: character and action.'[33] The specifics of Muldoon's narrative are lavish and precise, but its sequence and organization are far from clear.

If 'The More a Man Has . . .' (or indeed *Quoof* as a whole) may be transposed from performance into 'meaning', then the intent of Muldoon's convoluted and involuted narrative lies in the specifics it contains. The dynamics of such specific features belong to Muldoon's language and his poetic forms, but they belong also to the felt relations between these things and the events to which they seem to stand at an angle. One of the incidents in the poem features an explosive end for a local politician:

> Once the local councillor straps
> himself into the safety belt
> of his Citroën
> and skids up the ramp
> from the municipal car park
> he upsets the delicate balance
> of a mercury-tilt
> boobytrap.
> Once they collect his smithereens
> he doesn't quite add up.
> They're shy of a foot, and a calf
> which stems
> from his left shoe like a severely
> pruned-back shrub.[34]

Part of the shock of this writing lies in its playing off verbal and formal *brio* against the brutality of the incident described; rather than a pre-formulated language of description, or of analysis

[33] Tim Hancock, 'Identity Problems in Paul Muldoon's "The More a Man Has the More a Man Wants"', *The Honest Ulsterman*, 97 (Spring 1994), 57–8.
[34] *Quoof* (London: Faber & Faber, 1983), 53.

(condemnatory or otherwise), Muldoon deals in a deadpan precision which uses the quasi-sonnet form of the stanza to enact its own 'delicate balance' between cliché and surprise. The specificity of the description (presenting an incident whose place in the larger narrative scheme of 'The More a Man Has...' is far from clear) is a source both of shock and of mundane plausibility. The councillor's car is a Citroën—a detail whose significance is partly that the stanza's way with rhymes will mutate 'Citroën' into 'smithereens', a transformation parallel to that of the councillor from someone who 'straps / himself' into the car to a 'shrub', through the oblique rhyming of 'straps', 'ramp', 'trap', and 'up'. The pivotal point in the stanza—and for the councillor—is the 'boobytrap' of the eighth line. The last detail, the 'foot, and a calf', with its final vivid simile of the 'pruned-back shrub', lingers over something which in fact cannot be found on the scene. Detail here, as elsewhere in Muldoon, is both powerfully specific and at the same time subject to the mutations of form and the problematic consequences of such changes and accommodations: like the 'foot, and a calf', detail niggles away at attempts to make things 'add up'.

   In the often hallucinatory world of *Quoof*, and in much of Muldoon's poetry, distinctions between narrative foreground and background are difficult to establish. In 'A Trifle', a poem in which a great deal of detail is on offer, the apparent mundanity of the anecdote makes the foreground everyday and conversationally flat:

> I had been meaning to work through lunch
> the day before yesterday.
> Our office block is the tallest in Belfast;
> when the Tannoy sounds
>
> another bomb alert
> we take four or five minutes to run down
> the thirty-odd flights of steps
> to street level.[35]

The accumulation of detail here is apparently casual ('four or five', 'thirty-odd'), but its context of 'another bomb-alert' makes the time taken in relaying such information time under a certain pressure: the difference between four and five minutes in such situations might be a far from casual matter. Yet Muldoon's poem remains

35 Muldoon, *Quoof*, 30.

true to the false normality of the procedure it describes (this is *'another* bomb-alert', after all), and the sestet concluding the sonnet dwells again on a single detail on the downward journey to 'street level':

> I had been trying to get past
> a woman who held, at arm's length, a tray,
> and on the tray the remains of her dessert—
>
> a plate of blue-pink trifle
> or jelly sponge,
> with a dollop of whipped cream on top.

By concluding in this way, 'A Trifle' turns away from the expected development from perceived detail towards comprehended coherence. The encounter with the woman who brings her dessert along with her on the evacuation of the office is indeed an interruption of such narrative designs: her dogged attachment to lunch is its own ironic comment on emergency and normality, and their coexistence. At the same time, the trifle itself is presented with a queasy precision, and again its mundane nature seems to threaten a hallucinatory transformation—though one from which the poem finally holds back—into other 'remains' and jellies of blue and pink. Like the victim in Carson's 'Campaign', the potential victim leaving her office is 'not involved', and by that token, ironically, she is liable to be caught up in the totalizing narrative of violence which can render a word like 'involved' lethally opaque. Although violence seems to be outside Muldoon's poem, it is implicit in every detail; it is also ignorable, if to ignore the implicit carnage can be analogous to the simultaneous emergency and normality which the poem records.

'A Trifle' may perhaps set itself up as a trifling poem, but its trifling is part of an unsettling process in which perceptions are both sharpened and made complex. In an interview, Muldoon has described a procedure in which detail is the end as well as the means of his poetry:

I'm interested in new ways of looking at things. I don't mean in a nasty way necessarily... but I want my own vision to be disturbed, I want never to be able to look at a hedgehog again or a... briefcase again—or at least the poem wants me never to be able to look at a hedgehog or a briefcase again—without seeing them in a different way.[36]

---

[36] Interview with Kevin Smith, *Rhinoceros*, 4 (n.d. [1990]), 90.

Muldoon's habit, which manifests itself in a number of interviews, of setting his designs on the poem aside in favour of the poem's designs on him, disclaiming a proprietorial authority over interpretation, reflects a basic reluctance to fix boundaries for language or for language's relation to the world. There is no room for an 'omphalos' to guarantee identity, or rootedness, in Muldoon's idea of 'what the poem wants'. Asked by his interviewer whether seeing things in a different way is not in fact a 'function of art', Muldoon's response is emphatic:

For me it is. Absolutely. I've never understood some of these notions about art—'the end of art is peace': Coventry Patmore...the idea that, for example, poetry embodies 'what oft was thought, but ne'er so well expressed'—none of these ideas mean anything to me. I'm interested in some new, arresting vision.

The Coventry Patmore tag has its currency through Seamus Heaney, who uses it both in an epigraph to *Preoccupations* and in the poem 'The Harvest Bow'; Muldoon's allusion here seems to gesture towards Heaney, and touches on an issue which does divide the poets. Muldoon's poetry (leaving aside, for the moment, Muldoon himself) is indeed untroubled by 'the end of art', whereas Heaney's writing is more inclined to relish this as a theme in itself. It is this which puts Muldoon in a perpetually 'trifling' relation to narratives—mythic, personal, and political—which drive towards given ends. With regard to language, also, the distinction between the two poets is important: where Heaney discovers that language can reveal and give expression to identity, Muldoon's poetry relishes the dissolution of identity in language, allowing rhyme, pun, and cliché to undo the coherences which all 'identity'—personal or otherwise—has for its foundation.

'New, arresting vision' is as difficult in Ireland as elsewhere, and the context of contemporary violence makes it no easier to achieve. In the best Northern Irish poetry relating to the Troubles, there is an insistence on individuality of perception which is also, necessarily, an insistence upon artistic risk. This does have a corollary for the whole critical question of the relation between poetry and violence, in that to insist upon the particular is also to refuse the consolation (political or otherwise) offered by any reduction of the specific to the general in the matter of violent events. It is this, perhaps, which accounts for the kinds of hostility expressed by some critics of Northern Irish poetry, who search the writing either for political positions or for a blameworthy lack of commitment to such things. Poetry does not offer the kind of solidarity with political interpretations of the 'situation' which some critics desire, but it does present the reader with a different kind of solidarity, or rather solidity, in which the writing relinquishes nothing of the specific, or of the individuality of the poet's perception.

Michael Longley's 'The Ice-Cream Man' is a poem in which the weight of the specific is finely judged, and precariously balanced against the felt need for consolation and coherence in the wake of a sectarian murder. Interestingly, the poem allows the narrative of violence to diminish to just over one line, and puts in front of this another kind of narrative, where gestures of grief are associated with the workings of memory along very individual lines:

> Rum and raisin, vanilla, butter-scotch, walnut, peach:
> You would rhyme off the flavours. That was before
> They murdered the ice-cream man on the Lisburn Road
> And you bought carnations to lay outside his shop.[37]

In this ten-line poem, these opening four lines contain and frame the murder itself; what follows puts the poetic voice in the position where it can offer its own narrative in compensation for the loss which the killing represents. Such compensation is not for the victim, but for 'you', the addressee whose memory has now been darkened by the violence, and the poetic 'I' provides another list to balance the ice-cream flavours. The list of wild flowers, prolonged over five lines, makes 'The Ice-Cream Man' a very long poem indeed:

> I named for you all the wild flowers of the Burren
> I had seen in one day: thyme, valerian, loosestrife,
> Meadowsweet, tway blade, crowfoot, ling, angelica,
> Herb robert, marjoram, cow parsley, sundew, vetch,
> Mountain avens, wood sage, ragged robin, stitchwort,
> Yarrow, lady's bedstraw, bindweed, bog pimpernel.

In one sense, the density of the particular here says nothing about the violence against which it is set; in another sense, its accuracy,

---

[37] *Gorse Fires* (London: Secker & Warburg, 1991), 49.

delicacy, and fullness speak decisively against forgetting, and provide another kind of narrative, a verbless one, in which the poetic voice can displace the narrative of murder with an absorption in the specific. Again, the performance of this act of listing ('I named for you') cannot mend anything; the poet's voice is involved in an act of memory which ministers intimately to one addressee, but does not try to construct some kind of public coherence in order to explain its procedure. The echoes of *The Winter's Tale*, Act IV, scene iv (where Perdita enumerates the flowers she distributes) and of 'Lycidas', 142–51 (the list of 'every flower that sad embroidery wears') add to the complexity of Longley's effects, while also suggesting another context within which the formal 'naming' carried out by the poetic voice might be understood. Such consolation as 'The Ice-Cream Man' offers is fragile, and will dissolve altogether when taken out of the intimacy of its immediate surroundings; any elegiac impulse is undercut by the pressure of actuality, so that Milton's closing reflection on the list of flowers in 'Lycidas' has relevance also to Longley's poem: 'For so, to interpose a little ease, / Let our frail thoughts dally with false surmise'(152–3). Poetic narrative may give 'ease', but this kind of interposition does not defeat the actualities it must come between.

If 'The Ice-Cream Man' gives something of an extreme example of the difference between the narrative of action in which violence figures, and the narrative of resistance to action which the poetic voice can set up, it does serve nevertheless to suggest the way in which Longley's poetry makes use of obliqueness, particularity, and form in confronting violent subjects. In this, Longley has a good deal in common with other Northern Irish poets, and his successes are, like those of Carson, Muldoon, and others, hard to accommodate within critical models for what might constitute a 'position' on the problems posed for poetry by violence. In cases where critical theory is applied to these problems, it is the resistance to 'bewilderment' which most hampers an understanding of the kinds of poetry involved; even the most apparently sophisticated searches for theoretical coherence in these matters can be alarmingly single-minded. If poetry sabotages such enterprises, the nature of its successes is significant both for Northern Irish literature and for the climate of contemporary writing and criticism beyond that country.

III   Distaste and Repudiation

It may be that the subtlety and pervasiveness of the connections between violence and critical discourse are illustrated by the metaphor of sabotage used to suggest a relation between poetry and critical or historical narratives in Ireland. Certainly, no critical analysis is likely, in present conditions, to be immune from the vocabulary of violence, and all that such a vocabulary brings in its wake. While this is a problem in the criticism of contemporary Northern Irish literature, in ways just as pressing as in the creation of poetry itself, it is one which is seldom acknowledged: critical and (meta-)historical narratives do not tend to carry health warnings about the adequacy, or inadequacy, of their language to events—or even, perhaps, the complicity between their language and those violent events. Bearing this in mind, it may be as well at this stage to set out some points which could be made in objection to the treatment of poetry above, and the argument made there for poetry as a subversive force in relation to other kinds of narrative.

First, it may be thought that to put poetry in a position where it unravels the narratives which somehow 'make sense' of pressing and difficult series of events is to reduce it to an agent of mere debunking, relieving it at the same time of any obligation to provide a better narrative. Secondly, and more seriously perhaps, the use of poetry in the kind of critical discussion of Section II above could be accused of a strategic aestheticism which conceals its own political agenda: the term 'poetry', it might be argued, is being employed in a way that recalls Matthew Arnold in its attempt to separate literature from ideology. And that, the argument might run, *is* the ideology hidden behind liberal criticism, which announces its distaste for 'theory' and preference for 'specifics' only to maintain the *status quo* by which, ultimately, it has itself been produced. It follows that an attempt to question current theoretical assumptions about violence and literature in Northern Ireland should be read as ideology in disguise—even when wearing that long-seen-through false face of 'practical criticism'.

There are no straightforward responses to such objections, partly for the reason that the critical language in which those responses have to be made is contested ground. That is, a rejection of 'debunking' as a description of what the language and procedures of good poems do to the grand narratives of Irish history and politics is not going to convince someone who feels that something valuable and coherent is under threat from a debunker; by the same token, an insistence that the disciplines and resultant values of 'practical criticism', when applied to individual poems, are not 'ideological' in the same way as, say, critical toying with the 'narrative of violence', cannot do anything other than exacerbate the disagreements involved. Such disagreements seem to reveal antagonists who are, at a fundamental level, speaking different languages.

Yet the language of criticism, like any public discourse, is in the end accountable to a consensus of understanding, and its attempts to establish special areas of privilege are doomed to fail, whatever short-term advantages they may enjoy. To claim poetry as a privileged zone would be a mistake; but the accountability of poetry means that it cannot take for granted any consensus of narrative-hungry interpretation, and must rely instead on the larger, and more daunting, consensus which is that of—and in—the language itself. More dauntingly still, as any lexicographer knows, consensus and contention are not always distinguishable: such difficulties almost amount to a precondition of literary activity. If on the one hand poetry has to avoid complete identification with a documentary 'truth', which will always require the support of some larger narrative, it needs to avoid, on the other hand, becoming the merely 'poetical' (*OED* 1b): 'Such as is found only in poetry or imaginative writing: fictitious, feigned, imaginary, ideal.' Accountable language exists between these two poles, and often acknowledges, or bears the signs of, the pull of both.

It is here that a critical theory which tries to convert attention to specific features of poems into a veiled ideological manœuvre begins to look unsatisfactory, especially in relation to the issue of violence. Whereas the language of poems has to be constantly on guard against the rhetoric of other narratives, always (as it were) listening to itself, too much literary theory listens only to the language of others, and knows in advance what it will find there. In the field of Irish literature and the application of theory, it is Seamus Deane's work which has been the most significant and influential contribution to a theoretical school of interpretation; there is good reason, then, to look again at Deane on 'violence'. First, Deane insists on the *relative* nature of a word like 'violence':

Since 1968, in Northern Ireland, the demonising of the 'men of violence' has been only partially effective because of the unpunished violence of the police and army...It is true that there is in Ireland a species of double-think about violence; but it has been learned from harsh experience of the link between political power and the manipulation of the legal system for the sake of retaining power in the name of justice.[38]

Even while he diagnoses 'a species of double-think', Deane engages in untroubled contradiction: the identification of 'men of violence' as a rhetorical phrase makes *this* 'violence' problematic, but the other 'unpunished violence' is straightforward, and by implication non-rhetorical, something clear for all (except those who can fall for phrases like 'men of violence') to see and interpret. 'Unpunished violence' is in fact a phrase so difficult in this context as to be almost opaque (if the assumption is that all violence ought to be punished, does this mean that the 'men of violence' should also be punished, or is punishment merited only by those who are not provided with the protection of quotation-marks?)—but Deane's critical language does not listen to itself quite so closely as this.

More detail is on offer in a 1985 essay on Burke, in which Deane examines different kinds of 'violence' as reflected in the narratives by which states, and those trying to subvert states, explain their operations:

Liberalism, as Burke had indicated, is not incompatible with violence. The use of violence must, however, be based on the consent of those on whose behalf it is (ostensibly) exercised. Radical violence is not, from this same point of view, justifiable since it is exercised by a faction or party, which claims the right to use it even against the wishes of the majority of the people on whose behalf it nevertheless is ready to exercise it. More often, and especially in Ireland, that kind of violence has been used by those who claim the right to use it on ideological grounds which do not include the consent of the aberrant majority. So we have the violence of the state as against the violence of the party which has not yet become co-identical with the state.[39]

The violence here is being examined from a very great distance, a distance which is, essentially, that of historical narrative. The

[38] Introduction to 'Political Writings and Speeches 1900–1988', in Deane (gen. ed.), *The Field Day Anthology of Irish Writing*, iii. 683.
[39] 'Edmund Burke and the Ideology of Irish Liberalism', in Richard Kearney (ed.), *The Irish Mind: Exploring Intellectual Traditions* (Dublin: Wolfhound Press, 1985), 155.

narrative altitude is sufficient to permit generalizations like 'the aberrant majority' which, whatever their specific function in Deane's argument here (this may even stretch to a degree of irony) are bound to have resonance in the context of contemporary Irish violence. Indeed, the historical distance dissolves in the next paragraph, when Deane aligns Burke's liberalism with that of Conor Cruise O'Brien, and his 'distaste for republican violence in Northern Ireland'. Here the rhetoric of Deane's argument comes into view very clearly: after all, to have a distaste for something is not an unambiguous condition. Distaste does not usually apply to things of much real significance (as one might express a distaste for a certain kind of shellfish or a particular colour of curtain), while distaste might also betray an attitude towards what is being rejected, allowing, or even encouraging, the inference that one is somehow above such things (as for example an announced distaste for bingo or soap-operas might do in certain contexts). After the historical distancing and relativizing of 'violence', Deane's reference to O'Brien's 'distaste for republican violence' implies O'Brien's inability to understand 'violence' within the historical narrative in question, and at the same time reduces 'violence' to something subject to 'distaste' rather than, say, horror or loathing. Deane soon develops the implication that O'Brien is in no position to express distaste, by returning to the theoretical point that 'violence' is present within the state itself, speaking of 'his willingness to condone and support state violence in Northern Ireland and even, by omission, loyalist violence which is directed to the preservation of the state'. Thus a distaste for violence becomes support for violence, 'by omission'. The logic here seems to be that O'Brien's not being involved makes him 'involved'. In the process, 'violence' has become little more than a verbal counter, a label for something no longer specified (though a reliance on 'specific features', of course, is itself under ideological suspicion).

It is important to recognize the significance of a narrative foundation in making such rhetorical manœuvres possible. Although the narratives of opponents are always liable to be exposed by Deane and his followers, their own narratives are much more important to their critical enterprise than, say, the ideology of liberalism could ever be to the close reading of a poem. Where language itself is put in the foreground of discussion, its inadequacy or partisan nature is established in relation to governing narratives.

Thus, 'violence' is said to be involved in the establishment and maintenance of the state as much as it is in radical opposition to the state, but the question of how such radical opposition is to be identified is not raised—and it need not be, as long as the critical discourse relies on a narrative setting in which republicanism is granted legitimate oppositional status, and the 'state' is identified as the British government. Yet the particular contours of violence in Northern Ireland since 1969 make this narrative, at best, just one among many available models, and in historical terms no more satisfactory a framework than that in which an aberrant minority could be said to have used and justified violence to gain an otherwise unattainable political advantage. Narrative sense distorts specifics; specifics distort narrative sense; and between these, language is available for use and abuse.

An attachment to narrative design, though seldom announced as such in Deane's writing, is persistently present, and is close to the surface in his various denunciations of the ruptures in the national historical fabric supposedly made by 'revisionist' historians. Interestingly, this narrative design can be called 'ideology':

It is now fashionable to discuss as too simple-minded any 'colonial' analysis of the existing crisis in Ireland. This derives, in part, from an assumption of what is still sometimes called 'revisionist' history—that is to say that a recognition of the unique complexities of a specific situation precludes the possibility of interpreting it satisfactorily in the light of an 'ideology'. Ideology is something abstract, schematic, biased and an illness to which revisionist historians are themselves immune...[40]

Deane's irony covers his own identification of nationalist historical narrative with ideology (as opposed to 'ideology', perhaps, just as state violence can be balanced against 'violence'). More significantly in the present context, Deane's other name for the enabling narrative, which (amongst other things) allows the critic to tell the difference between violence and 'violence', is poetry. In a sensitive and revealing essay on Seamus Heaney, Deane considers the bog-poems of *North* in the light of 'modern political killings' and the poet's 'apparent sanctification of the unspeakable'. The discussion is arguably a little too sensitive to the resultant artistic and moral dilemmas:

[40] Introduction to 'Political Writings and Speeches', 685.

It is a grievous tension for him since his instinctive understanding of the roots of violence is incompatible with any profound repudiation of it (especially difficult when 'the men of violence' had become a propaganda phrase) and equally incompatible with the shallow denunciations of it from quarters not reluctant to use it themselves. The atavisms of Heaney's own community are at this stage in conflict with any rational or enlightened humanism which would attempt to deny their force. Heaney's dilemma is registered in the perception that the roots of poetry and of violence grow in the same soil; humanism, of the sort mentioned here, has no roots at all.[41]

This takes Heaney more in the direction of 'The Toome Road''s 'omphalos' than towards the lyric airiness and freedom of 'Squarings', but its insistence on 'roots' lays bare the essence of Deane's enabling narrative. In fact, Deane's attempt to give roots to poetry is a way of planting poetry in the same ground as violence; identity is opposed here to a despised 'humanism'—something feared as well as hated, perhaps, since it can indeed serve to dig up roots, to destabilize identity, and to ask hard questions of grand historical narratives. To contend that this would be a good thing, and that Heaney's poetry, like poetry by other Northern Irish poets, has in fact gone in this direction, is doubtless to admit an 'ideology', but it is also a more accurate account of the best Northern Irish poetry than Deane's rooted narrative is able to supply.

Along with a reliance upon the primacy of narrative, Deane brings to his criticism the common theoretical dogma that language, or rather discourse, accounts for everything. The inadequacies of language, then, are inadequacies not to experience or verifiable (extra-linguistic) realities, but signs of control by hegemonic forces seeking to direct discourse. Thus, a 'profound repudiation' of violence is 'especially difficult when "the men of violence" had become a propaganda phrase'. And yet, without those academically alert quotation-marks (which serve to align the discourse of critical sophisticates with the bread-and-butter rhetoric of Sinn Fein and other political groups) a profound repudiation of violence in Northern Ireland *does* remain possible, and must remain so. Deane's argument here is deeply flawed, though it is in line with the logic of discourse as a totalizing element. If 'the men of violence' was, in the 1970s and 1980s, a phrase much used on television and in newspapers, as well as by politicians, it was not

---

[41] *Celtic Revivals: Essays in Modern Irish Literature 1880–1980* (London: Faber & Faber, 1985), 180–1.

by that token simply 'a propaganda phrase'. For Deane's sentence
to mean anything, more information is needed: propaganda by
whom, and to what end? When 'men of violence' is uttered or
written, is it always 'propaganda'? When a bereaved relative uses
the phrase, is she participating in the same 'propaganda' exercise as
that involved when the same words are used by, say, a spokesman
from the Northern Ireland Office? Is not Deane's 'a propaganda
phrase' itself already something of a propaganda phrase? A phrase
like 'the men of violence' is indeed weakened by over-use; its
weakness is perceived, however, in differing ways, and the effects
of such perceptions include an awareness of the gap between language and adequacy to experience. This kind of perception is
perhaps inherent in the way all clichés are used, and certainly in
the way they are identified as clichés: in this respect, the language of
literature both steers clear of such weaknesses, and also, on occasion, approaches them in order to make the distance between
words and reality palpable. At all events, to reduce cliché to 'propaganda' is to rely very heavily indeed on the privileges accorded by
a narrative of historical overview; it is also, more seriously, to
neglect the complexity of language, and to obliterate specificity in
the interests of an already determined interpretation. For Deane, in
the end, 'the men of violence' is a simple phrase, simply dismissed
and lightly consigned to its ideological box. Its status as cliché (read
as straightforward, and not complex, fraught with circumstance or
pathos) means that it cannot conceal anything so unfortunately
clear as a truth.

Critical intelligence needs to be able to do more than simply
recognize clichés, in any case, and Deane's identification of a cliché
with 'propaganda' is itself a terminally clichéd identification. Alert
writing deals with clichés actively, and riskily, rather than seeing in
them proof of some simple failure. Christopher Ricks's formulation
is a useful one:

The deliberate and responsible use of cliché can foster critical self-
consciousness; not a paralyzed self-consciousness of the narcissistic kind
that disappears into itself, but the kind that properly grounds its imaginative flights in the cliché's unservile acknowledgement that it is a cliché.[42]

Northern Irish poetry bears this out, though the work of poets like
Muldoon and Carson gives Ricks's remarks a much darker tinge:

[42] *The Force of Poetry* (Oxford: Oxford University Press, 1987), 364.

'When they accepted who he was, as / Someone not involved, they pulled out his fingernails.' The intelligence and precision of judgement behind the use of cliché here is utterly distinct from the kinds of intellectual and imaginative failure which can dismiss (other people's) clichés as 'propaganda'.

Good poems live with language's inadequacies in ways that a great deal of contemporary critical discourse cannot afford to do. There is no general observation which will account satisfactorily for the relation between violence and Northern Irish poetry, but certain features of the poetry become clearer for being contrasted with the critical, theoretical, and ultimately political agendas by which it is surrounded. Even when employing narrative modes, contemporary Northern Irish poetry distorts, hybridizes and problematizes narrative, resisting any sense of coherence which might provide a larger placing or direction within other available narratives. Poetry facing events in the Troubles tends to avoid the elegiac, and is more closely attuned to bewilderment than consolation, insisting on the integrity of specifics at the same time as the individuality of the poetic voice. Successful poetry 'about' violence is always aware that it is apart from that violence, just as all good poetry understands its own linguistic medium as something which, while in a comprehensible (and thus finally accountable) relation to reality, is not the same thing as the reality it addresses. If terms like 'successful' or 'good' are problematic in critical theory, their usefulness is nevertheless clear when poetry and violence come into such close conjunction as they do in contemporary Northern Irish writing, when so many judgements of value—for both readers and poets—become pressing issues, and when the difference between 'good' and 'bad' means something. It is a necessary truism to say that, as a proportion of the total number published and written, there are relatively few good poems in Northern Ireland, as elsewhere. In the painful and exacting context of Northern Ireland's violence, there is no such thing as an innocent poem, or one which is 'not involved': good poems know this, and act accordingly. Bad poems, like bad criticism and bad politics, too easily convinced by their own prior versions of events, are likely to remain in the aberrant majority.

4

Derek Mahon, Tom Paulin, and the Lost Tribe

There is an inexact rule of symmetry in certain kinds of critical overview, by which identities, as they find their cultural expressions, tend to match and answer each other. Thus, if Seamus Heaney is found to represent especially one model of identity in Northern Ireland, which could be called either Irish or Catholic, the full meaning of this representation comes with cultural understanding of the other identity, which might be called either Ulster Scots or Protestant. This much is the common currency of identity-discourse as it affects Northern Ireland, but finding a poet who can serve to articulate the essence of the Protestant tradition is not perhaps all that simple a process. John Hewitt is a relatively straightforward candidate for the post, and Louis MacNeice might also seem suitable (if trickier), but contemporary literature has been singularly slow to yield up its essentially Northern Protestant poet. The reasons for this are complex: in some readings, for example, the essence of Northern Protestantism is something much too primitive and reactionary in character to find expression in anything so subtle as a literary medium; in other interpretations, poets with roots in the Northern Protestant tradition make this identity available through their critique of, or distance from, it in their writings. To some extent, it is this latter kind of reading (not always unconnected to the assumptions of the former one) which has conditioned the reception of both Derek Mahon and Tom Paulin. Yet the inadequacy of this interpretation, in which the poets are allowed to supply information to the identity-discourse, is easy enough to detect; the achievements of both poets are distorted by the conditions of the contextualization which a 'Protestant' label enforces.

However, damage to poets' reputations is hardly the most serious thing that inadequate habits of interpretation can do, and the kinds of stereotype variously tested in Mahon's and Paulin's work have a vigorous life quite independent of those writers. As far as attitudes in the Republic of Ireland are concerned, the identity of Northern Irish Protestants is as settled as it is inconvenient and (largely) incomprehensible. This has certain clear political implications, but it feeds through also to matters of literary discussion. The arguments resulting from the publication of *The Field Day Anthology of Irish Writing* (1991) had been in the process of formation for (at least) a decade before the work appeared, and the stereotyping of Northern Protestant writing in the *Anthology*'s coverage of poetry sums up a tradition of passive reliance on identity as a way of bringing together political and literary perspectives. Gerald Dawe's angry reaction is instructive:

Over recent years, intellectual and cultural attitudes have hardened towards northern Protestants and, particularly, to those who consider the union with Britain a personal and emotional lifeline separate from the perceived introversions and hypocrisies of the Catholic country to the south and west. . . . The significance of this unease plays across the cultural and political life of Ireland. It moderates from good-humoured banter and wit, perplexity and arrogance to bewilderment and contempt with an average mean in sorrow, bemusement and superiority complexes all round.
    'Protestants' are considered 'unionists' (or, more fashionably, 'neo-unionists') unless they publicly declare to the contrary and seek asylum in 'Irish Literature'. Failure to do so unsettles the kind of cultural agendas that the media, publishing and academic worlds rely upon, both in this country [Ireland] and abroad.[1]

Dawe's sense of the basic laziness, or habit of neglect, to which the available categories of identity pander allows him to see in the *Anthology*'s dealings with contemporary poetry a failure which parallels other failures in the book's direction and purpose. The result of this is, in Dawe's formulation, 'The sense of not having the freedom to be one's self';[2] as usual, the discourse of identity means that individual identities are circumscribed rather than allowed to develop. To put the matter crudely, for the identity-discourse of Field Day, an Ulster Protestant ought to know who he is; and to discover who he is, he needs to consult the solutions contained in the *Anthology* itself. The project's intent is nothing if not colonial in its relation to the Protestant 'tradition', and as such it reflects the tendency noted in more general terms by John Wilson Foster:

[1] *False Faces: Poetry, Politics and Place* (Belfast: Lagan Press, 1994), 60.
[2] Ibid. 61.

The Ulster Protestant, feeling the perpetual threat of being taken over, already experiences in some sense, and exhibits the symptoms of, the condition of being colonized. His legendary intransigence is the anticipation of a calamity. It is true that this colonization is a mere project called reunification of the motherland, and that the Ulster Protestants have been called Irish by the projectors. Outside this context they are regarded as interlopers, alien, the spawn of colonizers. They too have been stereotyped and essentialized, invested with the aura of a negative mystique.[3]

As if in obedience to the imperatives of identity-discourse from the Irish Republic, there has been no shortage of Northern Irish attempts from within the Protestant community to develop and express a distinctive Protestant identity in terms of historical and mythic interpretations of the past, a cultural shorthand occasionally put in the service of (sometimes sinister) politics. Interestingly, the specifically literary is generally missing from such projects.

The urge to identify and essentialize Protestants from Northern Ireland is not, of course, one confined in any way to the island of Ireland. As a sampling of a number of given prejudices and associations, the following assessment by an English journalist is efficient and instructive:

Where once discrimination and gerrymandering assured them [Protestants] of jobs, now they face unemployment like everyone else in Northern Ireland. The Harland and Wolff shipyard, for example, which once employed 20,000 Protestants employs only 2,000 today. Once they had their own 'Parliament' and security forces; now they are ruled from Westminster. They used to be kings in their own dung-hill; now they find themselves the butt of the world's derision for their ludicrous marching, Masonic regalia and implacable resistance to change. One was reminded of those lines from Auden: 'History to the defeated / May say alas but cannot help or [sic] pardon'.[4]

The accuracy (or otherwise) of the historical grasp here is entirely secondary to the rhetorical drive; the prejudicial energies of this are themselves bigoted ('They used to be kings in their own dung-hill') as well as ignorant, and the appeal to a consensus of contempt finds its common ground in W. H. Auden's (apparent) common sense. That Auden later cancelled the lines in question, with the comment that 'This is a lie', is irrelevant to the intent and effect of a passage

---

[3] *Colonial Consequences* (Dublin: Lilliput Press, 1991), 271.

[4] John Naughton, 'Tribalism, Bigotry and Omelettes', *Observer*, 10 July 1994, review section, p. 25.

like this, which deals in complacency and the lazy stocktaking of things 'one' already knows. This cheap knowledge comes from somewhere, and its reliance upon the simplest of identity-discourses is, in so far as it might affect actual political events in Britain, potentially dangerous.

How far is literature involved in the stereotypes of Protestant identity? Amongst literary critics, certainly, a hearty acceptance of such stereotypes seems almost compulsory, as when Declan Kiberd rejoices to concur with his common reader on 'that curious blend of resolution and hysteria, of barbarous vulgarity and boot-faced sobriety, which lies beneath the emotions of Ulster Protestantism'.[5] There are instances of literature's obedience to the kinds of stereotype which fuel news reports and journalistic prejudice, but these come largely from outside the Protestant community itself, like John Montague's 'A New Siege', in which history explains the present point by point (Londonderry is 'still flaunting / the bloody flag / of "No Surrender"') and second-hand images stand in for straightforward contempt:

> the white elephant
>   of Stormont, Carson's
> raised right claw
>   a Protestant parliament
> a Protestant people
>   major this and
> captain that and
>   general nothing
> the bland, pleasant
>   face of mediocrity
> confronting in horror
>   its mirror image
> bull-voiced bigotry[6]

The chain of associations here, which runs from Edward Carson (and more particularly the statue of Carson outside Stormont) to Unionist mediocrity in power, then to the 'bull-voiced' Ian Paisley, is identity-rhetoric at its purest, insisting as it does on the essential nature of Ulster Protestantism as 'bull-voiced bigotry'. The loudest, and least acceptable, manifestation of the tradition is insisted

[5] 'Anglo-Irish Attitudes', in Field Day Theatre Company, *Ireland's Field Day* (London: Hutchinson, 1985), 100.
[6] *Selected Poems* (Oxford: Oxford University Press, 1982), 123.

upon as its most essential expression. Yet there is something itself 'bull-voiced' about such depictions, as can be seen when Montague's poem, written throughout on the auto-pilot of prejudice and 'history', is compared with Derek Mahon's 'Ecclesiastes'. Here, the *status quo* of pre-Troubles Northern Ireland offers a series of temptations to the 'puritan' who may lurk within the poet, offering 'dank churches, the empty streets / the shipyard silence, the tied-up swings', where it is possible to 'close one eye and be king'. The poem's final lines deliver something more devastating than any amount of self-assured condemnation could provide:

> Your people await you, their heavy washing
> flaps for you in the housing estates—
> a credulous people. God, you could do it, God
> help you, stand on a corner stiff
> with rhetoric, promising nothing under the sun.[7]

This clinches something for good, and, as real poetry does, it transforms a source in political reality into a position marked permanently by its distance from the poetic imagination. 'Ecclesiastes' disengages itself from the political stereotypes of Protestant identity by acknowledging both their potency and their inadequacy. Remarkably (by the standards of the more academic instances of 'A New Siege' and its like), Mahon seems to win a freedom for the poetic voice not through a command of historical perspective, but by a rejection of it; where, for Montague and others, history corroborates a shared superiority and contempt, for Mahon the poetic voice, in order to establish itself and to survive, has to work out its own superiority to history.

There is a contrast, of sorts, to be found in some of Tom Paulin's poetry, which comes much closer than Mahon's to servicing the dominant stereotypes of the Northern Irish Protestants. There is much in such an interpretation of Paulin which needs to be qualified, but the initial outlines of the comparison are striking enough. In the poem 'Desertmartin', for example, the following stanza serves up some familiar material:

> It's a limed nest, this place. I see a plain
> Presbyterian grace sour, then harden,

[7] *Poems 1962–1978* (Oxford: Oxford University Press, 1979), 31; *Selected Poems* (Harmondsworth: Penguin, 1993), 28.

As a free strenuous spirit changes
To a servile defiance that whines and shrieks
For the bondage of the letter: it shouts
For the Big Man to lead his wee people
To a clean white prison, their scorched tomorrow.[8]

Here again the historical grip on argument is simple and complete, and the downward trajectory from 'Presbyterian grace' to 'servile defiance' finds its customary nadir in the figure of Ian Paisley (whose presence in Paulin's writing is pervasive). The inhabitants of Desertmartin are assumed in the poem to be indeed 'the butt of the world's derision', and the conclusion, in which a commanding perspective allocates this community a particularly low circle in Hell, has a magisterial tone:

These are the places where the spirit dies.
And now, in Desertmartin's sandy light,
I see a culture of twigs and bird-shit
Waving a gaudy flag it loves and curses.

The assurance of this is remarkable, and there is certainly a note of negative visionary calm here which Paulin expresses in an accomplished way. But there is also a quite breathtaking arrogance—how does the poet know that 'the spirit dies' in places like these? Political condemnation mixes potently with what is finally a religious mode of denunciation (perhaps revealing a deep Paisley influence on Paulin's ways of thinking) and this is, in the end, itself 'stiff / with rhetoric, promising nothing under the sun'. Paulin's particular kind of poetic vision in 'Desertmartin' exists in proximity to the stereotypes and reflex reactions of identity-discourses in which political prejudices are inculcated. It is not entirely surprising, then, to find an English literary critic responding to this poem as an example of Paulin's 'empiricist attitude', calling it a 'fine epitome of Ulster Protestantism', and a 'blend of observation and verified generalization'.[9] 'Verified' here signals an extraordinary confidence, and, with similar trust in Paulin's documentary fidelity, the *Field Day Anthology* notes 'his contempt for the cultural distortions of imperialism', and detects 'a certain elegiac sadness in his studies of a dying

---

[8] *Liberty Tree* (London: Faber & Faber, 1983), 16–17.
[9] Edward Larrissy, *Reading Twentieth-Century Poetry: The Language of Gender and Objects* (Oxford: Blackwell, 1990), 9.

culture'.[10] What Paulin may intend as imaginative engagement is taken for the simple truth, if only because the dominant identity-discourse has outlined the symbols and their interpretation so clearly already.

The poetry of both Mahon and Paulin (it hardly needs saying) is about more than Protestant identity; nevertheless, it is the all-too-ready availability of this identity which has sometimes distorted and limited the poetry's reception. Perhaps, in the case of Paulin, such availability of stereotyped images and ideas has itself had a limiting effect on the poetry's achievement. But for both poets the whole issue of the history which is held to find its culmination and final expression in Protestant identity is a pressing concern, and their differing relations to the idea of history are of central relevance to this. As Paulin's dogged insistence on 'the spirit' in poems like 'Desertmartin' might indicate, and as the ultimately apocalyptic perspectives of much of Mahon's work certainly suggest, the poets' differing concerns for the meaning of history point towards kinds of intensity that are very nearly religious. Given this, the question of Protestant identity changes from one of banal and terminally clichéd cultural or political discourse to something more openly metaphysical in its intent.

Derek Mahon's poetry might seem at first to have effected its escape from the pressures of history with singular grace and efficiency: the poems have always gravitated towards a cold and unpeopled area which exists generally before, or after, anything ordinarily recognizable as historic process. If the particular and pressing contingencies of events upon the individual life are often absent from Mahon's poems, this has to be set against the degree to which those poems come from a clearly recognizable point and persona—one form in which the poet succeeds notably being the verse-letter—and exercise a technical accomplishment and descriptive fidelity which are themselves parts of an altogether more social enterprise. It might be said that Mahon's poetry, while often urgent in its concerns, is never pitched at the level of emergency; the remoteness of Mahon's registers speaks generally of last things, but with an air of equanimity. As he puts it, with precise self-mockery, in 'Another Sunday Morning':

[10] Declan Kiberd, 'Contemporary Irish Poetry', in Seamus Deane (gen. ed.), *The Field Day Anthology of Irish Writing*, 3 vols. (Londonderry: Field Day, 1991), iii. 1406.

> A chiliastic prig, I prowl
> Among the dog-lovers and growl;
> Among the kite-fliers and fly
> The private kite of poetry—
> A sort of winged sandwich board
> El-Grecoed to receive the Lord;
> An airborne, tremulous brochure
> Proclaiming that the end is near.[11]

The lonely extremities of Mahon's perspectives are not put in question by this degree of irony at the poet's own expense, and the accent of emergency remains missing from even his most catastrophic visions. For Paulin, the demands of poetry's contextual situation (largely its Irish surroundings) mean that the formal altitudes of Mahon's work have to be abandoned in favour of a pitch altogether more edgy and urgent. Thus, after his first two volumes of largely conservative, formally ordered and restrained, poetry, Paulin's work in the 1980s evolved towards thickly applied dialect vocabulary, and staccato, open verse-forms. By the time of *Walking a Line* (1994), this had produced a fast-moving, lightly punctuated stream of (generally) three-beat lines. An aesthetic, of sorts, emerges in '51 Sans Souci Park':

> and a voice thrashing in the wilderness
> an unstill enormous voice
> is offering me this wisdom
> *action's a solid bash*
> *narrative a straight line*
> *try writing to the moment*
> *as it wimples like a burn*
> *baby it's NOW!*[12]

This not only promises to push its way through the divisions between writing and action, but anticipates a moment ('*NOW!*') when literary form and the urgent matter to be conveyed reach a point of identification. In terms of its Northern Irish background and conditioning, such a project tries to speak for emergency, or (as it were) to speak history. Paulin's writing, in other words, is increasingly ready to be unapologetically a part of the discourse by which it is surrounded and threatened.

[11] *Selected Poems*, 140.
[12] *Walking a Line* (London: Faber & Faber, 1994), 33–4.

One very important point of reference for both the poetry of Mahon and Paulin and the dominant strands in its critical reception tends to be that of 'community'. Whatever its sociological uses and nuances, the term is sometimes open to considerable distortion in the context of political argument, and to a dangerous inexactitude when imported into the discussion of literature. For all that, the idea of community is of manifest relevance to the writing of both Mahon and Paulin, though in contrasting (and possibly in the end incompatible) ways. Again, the problematic nature of the term for the two poets might suggest some points of contact with the altogether more approachable and comprehensible notions of community upon which much of Seamus Heaney's most influential work has depended; but neither Mahon nor Paulin, it seems, is willing to make use of the certainties of 'belonging' that served Heaney as an aesthetic resource. It is perhaps no surprise in considering this divergence to discover different literary influences at work: where Heaney has been able to use Patrick Kavanagh's writing as a kind of poetic touchstone of community, Mahon and Paulin, in marking out their own imaginative territories, have been closer to the examples of writers like Samuel Beckett and Louis MacNeice, figures who do indeed have clear senses of place and belonging, but are at the same time fundamentally suspicious of both notions. While the absolute zero of metaphysical loneliness is at one (Beckettian) end of the spectrum for Mahon's imagination, his poetry is also vitalized by a feeling for the lives away from which this impulse tends to drive it; in this sense, his writing balances Beckett against what is (on the surface at least) the more gregarious imaginative drive of MacNeice.

Talk of influences in Irish writing is too often a matter of label-sticking, and this is especially true when literary forerunners carry with them hints of political implication. Nevertheless, there remains a clear need to understand the extent and significance of influence from previous generations on Northern Irish poetry, and in this matter the question of MacNeice's stature cannot be either ignored or reduced to a question of crudely cultural or political allegiance. When the nature of Mahon's imagined community in Northern Ireland is investigated, MacNeice looms very large indeed (as he does, in different ways, for Paulin). In Mahon's early poetry, the issues raised can sometimes look comparatively straightforward, as when 'The Spring Vacation' (originally 'In Belfast') plays tricks with the idea of belonging to anywhere:

> Walking among my own this windy morning
> In a tide of sunlight between shower and shower
> I resume my old conspiracy with the wet
> Stone and the unwieldy images of the squinting heart.
> Once more, as before, I remember not to forget.[13]

The poem is indeed one of public 'conspiracy', but it is a conspiracy with the reader against certain perceived imperatives of place and situation. The weight of 'remember' in Protestant Belfast here is finely judged, and just as deftly redirected.[14] It is characteristic of Mahon that, 'Walking among my own' or not, it is the 'wet / Stone' that occupies the foreground of his attention, as the material, mineral reality outfaces the human scenes that are being played out before it. The poet goes on to acknowledge the coldness of this particular comfort:

> We could *all* be saved by keeping one eye on the hill
> At the top of every street, for there it is,
> Eternally, if irrelevantly, visible…

This is of course an extraordinarily watchful poem, but it is also one in which perspectives are always being twisted or forced: 'the squinting heart', 'Eternally, if irrelevantly, visible', and finally 'the cold gaze of a sanctimonious God' blur any clear-sighted vistas. For Mahon, the ability to see straight is essentially a metaphysical accomplishment, and at best it is one with no easy relation to the 'interest' or 'pity' of the human concerns of which his poem takes stock, 'The things that happen in the kitchen-houses / And echoing back-streets of this desperate city'. Again, the language holds tight to loaded words, and 'desperate' carries both its specifically Northern Irish meaning of something comically wrong or inadequate, and the more standard one of being at the end of one's tether in an extremity of suffering. The poet's perspective, for Mahon, is always rigorous, partaking perhaps of the metaphysical accomplishments of seeing straight, and in this sense 'The Spring Vacation' follows its

---

[13] *Poems 1962–1978*, 4.

[14] Cf. John Hewitt's 'Neither an Elegy Nor a Manifesto': 'Bear in mind these dead: / I can find no plainer words. / I dare not risk using / that loaded word, Remember' (*The Collected Poems of John Hewitt*, ed. Frank Ormsby (Belfast: Blackstaff Press, 1991), 188).

model, MacNeice's 'Belfast', by pushing a line of vision into, through, and beyond the suffering of a known community: both poems set the human element against, or into, the mineral, and the cold absolutes of MacNeice's 'basalt' or Mahon's 'wet / Stone'. MacNeice begins with this hard analysis:

> The hard cold fire of the northerner
> Frozen into his blood from the fire in his basalt
> Glares from behind the mica of his eyes
> And the salt carrion water brings him wealth.[15]

MacNeice's poem continues by directing its perspective 'Down there at the end of the melancholy lough', then into the city itself, and finally to a horizon where 'The sun goes down with a banging of Orange drums'. Yet for Mahon, as for MacNeice, the stern conclusions of such ultimate perspectives are far from the whole story.

In a later poem, 'A Refusal to Mourn', Mahon reapproaches the kind of human surroundings which 'The Spring Vacation' so determinedly sees through. The rigour of the earlier poem is still present, but is tempered by being more fully understood. If the perspective has in one way become still clearer and more unrelentingly absolute, in another its human attention has become more surely realized:

> All day there was silence
> In the bright house. The clock
> Ticked on the kitchen shelf,
> Cinders moved in the grate,
> And a warm briar gurgled
> When the old man talked to himself.[16]

The world of the old man in this poem is made up largely of inanimate items, from the things populating this stanza to 'the photographs of his dead / Wife and their six children'. Mahon moves within this framework towards other last things, where the animate must face, accommodate, and finally become the inanimate:

> In time the astringent rain
> Of those parts will clean

[15] 'Belfast', *Collected Poems*, ed. E. R. Dodds (London: Faber & Faber, 1966), 17.
[16] *Poems 1962–1978*, 75–6; *Selected Poems*, 60–1.

The words from his gravestone
In the crowded cemetery
That overlooks the sea
And his name be mud once again

And his boilers lie like tombs
In the mud of the sea bed
Till the next ice age comes
And the earth he inherited
Is gone like Neanderthal Man
And no records remain.

Mahon's stylistic habits work to wonderful effect in this pushing to extremes of the poem's perspective: 'astringent' is clinically impersonal, while the repeated 'And' at the beginnings of lines suggests a process of parataxis in which points of origin recede into a forgotten distance. The old man's profession (in the shipyards of Belfast) means that his name will 'be mud once again', and the MacNeicean ability here to accommodate literal and clichéd uses (the shipyard workers' 'name is mud' in some political discourses, as it is for the *Observer* journalist who can call them 'kings in their own dunghill', while the name of Mahon's subject will, in time, literally be 'In the mud of the sea bed'.) It is worth taking notice of the site where this speeded-up journey away from human history takes place in Mahon's poem. This is 'the crowded cemetery / That overlooks the sea', and it is important for a number of Mahon's poems, as well as a crucial co-ordinate in MacNeice's imaginative geography, where a thinly populated country overlooks a grey and inhospitable sea (poems such as 'Carrickfergus' are set here). It is, of course, a Northern Irish scene, and the stark contrasts which it contains, of a living community on the very edge of a finally ungovernable perspective, are of primary importance for MacNeice, subsequently for Mahon and, after him, for Paulin. In Mahon's 'My Wicked Uncle', this final scene is both real (that is, faithful to an existing location) and literary (in that it has been made possible in this form by MacNeice's imaginative charge on this particular land- and seascape):

He was buried on a blustery day above the sea.
The young Presbyterian minister
Tangled and wind-swept in the sea air.
I saw sheep huddled in the long wet grass
Of the golf-course, and the empty freighters

Sailing for ever down Belfast Lough
In a fine rain, their sirens going,
As the gradual graph of my uncle's life
And times dipped precipitately
Into the black earth of Carnmoney Cemetery.[17]

This does something with MacNeice's example which is entirely
distinctive (and Mahon's last rhyme here converts MacNeice's
habits into a poetic signature of his own), but its local habitation
on which metaphysical dramas might be enacted is indebted to
imaginative discoveries made by the older poet.

When Tom Paulin chooses to single out a poem by MacNeice for
special praise, writing about his 'House on a Cliff', he is also
returning to a central literary image (or complex of images) which
has provided his own work with significant co-ordinates. Indeed, in
Paulin's reading of the poem, the understanding of this crucial
image need not be, or in fact must not be, exclusively a literary
understanding. Instead, it opens up areas of political self-know-
ledge and analysis, just as Mahon's imaginative exploration of the
'empty freighters / Sailing for ever down Belfast Lough / In a fine
rain' (known also to MacNeice) leaves political knowledge behind
in favour of metaphysical extremities. 'House on a Cliff', written
by MacNeice in 1955, is one of the poet's later, complex, return
journeys to the contradictions and paradoxes of a remembered
place:

Indoors the tang of a tiny oil lamp. Outdoors
The winking signal on the waste of sea.
Indoors the sound of the wind. Outdoors the wind.
Indoors the locked heart and the lost key.

Outdoors the chill, the void, the siren. Indoors
The strong man pained to find his red blood cools,
While the blind clock grows louder, faster. Outdoors
The silent moon, the garrulous tides she rules.

Indoors ancestral curse-cum-blessing. Outdoors
The empty bowl of heaven, the empty deep.
Indoors a purposeful man who talks at cross
Purposes, to himself, in a broken sleep.[18]

The reading Paulin gives of this exceptionally subtle poem is a
suggestive one, and it shows how closely MacNeice's images are

[17] *Poems 1962–1978*, 6.   [18] *Collected Poems*, 462.

linked for the younger poet to the problematic and contested idea of community in Northern Ireland. Praising the poem's 'terrible stoic isolation', which might in itself seem to align 'House on a Cliff' with Mahon's points of metaphysical lift-off, Paulin meditates on 'a mysterious openness within or beyond [its] mirror-like reflections of a dead closed universe', and continues:

> If this is one man facing his lonely mortality on the far extremity of an unnamed place, the 'ancestral curse-cum-blessing', the cross purposes and broken sleep, suggest that the house is Ireland.... If this poem fits that baffled and contradictory term 'Irish', it also has an asocial, even a derelict, quality which makes it difficult to place. It subverts any comfortable notion of belonging, and this is true of all MacNeice's poetry.[19]

Paulin's reading here raises questions which trouble and stimulate his own poetry: extremity, loneliness, the asocial and the derelict, and an impossible imperative of 'belonging' to something which, under scrutiny, might cease to exist. If, for Mahon, MacNeice's vision serves essentially as a resource and a starting-point, for Paulin this vision clarifies and expresses problems of place and culture which poetry can try to address.

However, it is possible to notice that Paulin's terms recall the world inhabited by Mahon—in his poem 'Entropy', for instance:

> We are holing up here
> in the difficult places—
> in caves, terminal moraines
> and abandoned farmhouses,
> the wires cut, the old car
> disposing itself for death
> among the inscrutable,
> earth-inhabiting dandelions.[20]

Mahon's transposition of the situation into the terms of the inanimate is characteristic (and his twist to the text of 'Blessed are the meek: for they shall inherit the earth' is, as in 'A Refusal to Mourn', grimly punctilious); the poetic imagination has to find an extremity answering that of its subject. It would not be unreasonable, however, to read 'Entropy' in terms of 'belonging' in 'the far extremity of an unnamed place'. Paulin is often ready in his own poetry to

[19] *Ireland and the English Crisis* (Newcastle upon Tyne: Bloodaxe Books, 1984), 78–9.
[20] Mahon, *Poems 1962–1978*, 49.

name these places, where for Mahon such names are always already erased. In 'The Lonely Tower', Paulin de-Yeatsifies (and de-MacNeiceifies) such residences:

>—John Melly's breezeblock bothie
>in the dunes above Dooey Strand
>a windy look-out post
>from the Emergency
>the Lone Man's House
>at Ballyeriston
>(baled hay in every room
>blank uncurtained windows
>dust sealight bullocks blurping in the fields
>doggy bones on the kitchen floor)[21]

If this more recent poem shows Paulin attempting to break through the imaginative impasses of places at a 'far extremity', and to make them prosaically and literally habitable, it comes after a protracted engagement with no-through roads where the asocial and the derelict took named form. Again, the poem 'Desertmartin' is a significant point of no return, and its first stanza offers an extremity which mixes MacNeice and Mahon at their most desperately bleak:

>At noon, in the dead centre of a faith,
>Between Draperstown and Magherafelt,
>This bitter village shows the flag
>In a baked absolute September light.
>Here the Word has withered to a few
>Parched certainties, and the charred stubble
>Tightens like a black belt, a crop of Bibles.[22]

This 'far extremity' is up for specifically political analysis in the poem, and yet, like MacNeice's house on a cliff, Desertmartin's 'Indoors' and 'Outdoors', its inside and outside, may not be all that easy to tell apart. Although Paulin's poem can be read by blinkered identity-discourses as a factual report on a 'dying culture', it is haunted by the meshed perspectives of MacNeice, and its modes of denunciation are still engaged with the problem of 'belonging', that 'comfortable notion' which MacNeice subverted for good. Like Mahon's apocalyptic projections beyond human history, Paulin's attempts at historical close-up are

[21] *Walking a Line*, 11.   [22] *Liberty Tree*, 16.

shadowed by a sense of the unsatisfactoriness of any clear definition of a community.

These difficulties are important in the testing of notions like
identity, and the specifically MacNeicean cross-play between inside
and outside, self and other, is at the root of this kind of testing in
poetry. Here, the diverging paths of Mahon and Paulin are of some
importance. Where Mahon examines the seemingly empty spaces in
the available scene and the imagination, the gapped areas where the
very notion of a self becomes problematic, as 'places where a
thought might grow', Paulin has attempted to interpret history's
derelict locations in order to clarify the workings of a Northern
Irish Protestant identity, and lay bare its arcane symbolic complexities. This may perhaps be the difference between a *via negativa* and
a direct route; but it turns crucially on the significance of history,
and here Mahon and Paulin are often poles apart.

One facile reaction to Mahon's poetry, from critics in search of
some palpably political 'engagement', is to understand it as somehow beside the point, holding itself aloof in an exquisite (but finally
irresponsible) aestheticism that always looks the other way. The
judgement of the *Field Day Anthology* that Mahon 'writes not just
of, but for, posterities'[23] conceals a subtle deprecatory pressure.
However, Mahon's writing does not opt out from the present, or
from responsibility, if only because poetry cannot, in any meaningful sense, opt *in* to such things. The poem 'Knut Hamsun in Old
Age' faces this squarely:

> Yes, I shook hands with Hitler; knew disgrace.
> But time heals everything; I rose again.
> Now I can look my butcher in the face.
> Besides, did I not once, as a young man,
> Cure myself of incipient tuberculosis
> Inhaling four sub-zero nights and days
> Perched on the screaming roof of a freight train?[24]

The trauma of that freezing 'cure' might stand as a symbol for
Mahon's own imaginative journey into the cold; whatever illusions
Hamsun here may still be labouring under, there is no loss of
sharpness in the recognition of evil ('Now I can look my butcher
in the face' sends shock-waves through the poem), but there is an

---

[23] Declan Kiberd, 'Contemporary Irish Poetry', 1380.
[24] *Selected Poems*, 132–3.

equal, clear-eyed perspective, setting everything at a distance which
is both level-headed and desperate. An extremity like this has no
choice but to set itself apart from society, but it can also serve as a
means of understanding the society from which it is distanced: in
making himself an ostracized outsider, Mahon's Hamsun is able to
look inside and outside at the same time.

Two other poems by Mahon develop the MacNeicean combination of interior and exterior perspectives in ways that have some
relevance for the poet's own position in relation to ideas like community, history, and identity. In 'Nostalgias', Mahon again aligns
the world of the inanimate, and its material links back to aboriginal
substance, with the human community as it clings to the last
guarantee of its identity:

> The chair squeaks in a high wind,
> Rain falls from its branches.
> The kettle yearns for the
> Mountain, the soap for the sea.
> In a tiny stone church
> On a desolate headland
> A lost tribe is singing 'Abide With Me'.[25]

The precisely controlled pathos here knows that nothing will abide,
and senses the plight of the 'lost tribe' facing up to its far extremity.
This 'lost tribe' is not specified, and its ways are not examined, but
its plight is made part of an overarching (and utterly impersonal)
condition of change and impermanence. As usual, Mahon sees
things *sub specie aeternitatis*, and religion itself has to wither under
such a gaze. In '"Songs of Praise"', the last image of 'Nostalgias' is
transposed into the world of middle-class gentility which has provided Paulin with so much of his satirical register. Here, the lost
tribe of 'the outlying parts', on their best behaviour, 'Lift up their
hymn-books and their hearts / To please the outside-broadcast
cameras'. The theme of 'belonging' is summoned again, and again
Mahon's canvas stretches to include more than the passing and
incidental figures of humanity:

> Never look back, they said; but they were wrong.
> The zinc wave-dazzle after a night of rain,
> A washed-out sky humming with stars, the mist

---

[25] *Poems 1962–1978*, 68; *Selected Poems*, 54. I have quoted here the earlier
version of these lines.

> And echoing fog-horns of the soul, belong
> To our lost lives. We must be born again,
> As the gable-ends of the seaside towns insist . . .[26]

The easy religious cliché of being 'born again' is appropriated here
to point towards the 'lost lives' in the midst of which, and possibly
thanks to which, any given 'self' appears to exist. The 'Indoors'
here, the community of 'proud parishioners of the outlying parts'
must face the 'Outdoors'—not just the watching world as represented by 'the outside-broadcast cameras', but the 'lost lives' of
everything which, by being outside the community, enables that
community to define itself. Mahon's readers are obliged to count
the cost of their own identity:

> to look back constantly
> On that harsh landscape and its procreant sea,
> Bitter and curative, as tonight we did,
> Listening to our own nearly-voices chime
> In the parochial lives we might have led,
> Praising a stony god who died before our time.

The outside view asks the viewer to imagine an identification with
what is happening inside, and to accept it as somehow 'our own'.
This is partly to demand a revision of the given conviction of a self,
and to urge that the self should be born again, and then again. It is
no surprise that such a process should be taking place in sight of
'that harsh landscape and its procreant sea', the site of so many of
Mahon's encounters with last things.

'A Disused Shed in Co. Wexford', which is probably Mahon's
best-known poem, is essentially a sustained meditation on 'lost
lives', and a muted, carefully tempered insistence on the self's
having to be 'born again' in order to realize them. The poem's
mushrooms, shut away in 'the grim / Dominion of stale air and
rank moisture', stand between the inanimate and the human as
symbols for both:

> Magi, moonmen,
> Powdery prisoners of the old regime,
> Web-throated, stalked like triffids, racked by drought
> And insomnia, only the ghost of a scream

---

[26] *Courtyards in Delft* (Dublin: Gallery Press, 1981), 17. The lines quoted here
are cut from the version in Mahon's *Selected Poems*, 119.

> At the flash-bulb firing squad we wake them with
> Shows there is life yet in their feverish forms.[27]

The language is that of suffering and efficient brutality; Mahon's exclamation in the poem's last stanza—'Lost people of Treblinka and Pompeii!'—makes explicit a parallel which has already been felt just beneath the surface. The discovery of fungi in a disused shed carries the symbolic weight of all the 'lost lives' that make up history, and that 'lift frail heads in gravity and good faith' into the present:

> They are begging us, you see, in their wordless way,
> To do something, to speak on their behalf,
> Or at least not to close the door again.

This is a plea on behalf of history as well as a testimony to history's destructive cruelty and indifference. It is, however, history in a fuller sense than merely that of the politically accessible and significant; its importance is that of the forgotten as well as the momentous. Again, Mahon does not anatomize a given community when he encounters its plight; rather, he sets that plight deep in a context of change and human isolation. The poem seems to be a vindication of Mahon's determinedly cold and detached perspectives, and his insistence on seeing straight even when it means seeing straight through what we might want to be there.

Tom Paulin has written interestingly about Mahon's 'Disused Shed', in terms which suggest how the poem interacts with concerns important for his own work. In fact, Paulin appears to regard Mahon's poem as embodying a kind of solution to the many problems presented by politics and history in poetry:

Such poems issue from that condition of supremely unillusioned quietism—the wisest of passivities—which is usually the product of bitter historical experience and which is temperamentally different from disillusion. To be politically disillusioned is often to be cynical; to be politically apathetic is usually to be ignorant, but to possess no illusions is to understand a spiritual reality which is religious in its negativity.[28]

This discloses a good deal about the impulses and reflexes of Paulin's own imagination in its dealings with politics, and shows

---

[27] *Poems 1962–1978*, 79–80; *Selected Poems*, 62–3.
[28] Introduction to *The Faber Book of Political Verse* (London: Faber & Faber, 1986), 51.

something of the embattled, threatened nature of his own sense of political context. It is significant that Paulin should feel able to speak of 'a spiritual reality which is religious in its negativity' coming at the conclusion of a process of political 'unillusions'. The path which leads from 'bitter historical experience' towards this spiritual state is Paulin's equivalent of Mahon's metaphysical *via negativa,* and it explains an aspect of his poetry which tends often to escape critics' attention. There are several reasons for this, one being that Paulin has partly disguised the spiritual designs of his poetry by the urgency of the 'bitter historical experience' in which he has found so many of his subjects. Critics otherwise accustomed to Northern Irish poetic habits of obliqueness can be misled by Paulin's directness of style into seeing his aims in exclusively political, or identity-governed, terms; this is a mistake, but it is also a way of reading Paulin's work which has come too close, on occasion, to influencing the way in which the poet has pitched some of his writing. If the free-form excursions in the paths of wayward, directionless, artistic discovery (for which, in *Walking a Line,* Paulin chooses his precedent in the art of Paul Klee) have taken the poet to areas more easily recognized as 'unillusioned' in political terms, much of his writing in the 1980s followed more directly political routes. Here, in volumes like *Liberty Tree* (1983) and *Fivemiletown* (1987), Paulin's urgency and directness bear uneasily the gravitational pull exerted by the 'condition of supremely unillusioned quietism' which he intuits in Mahon's poetry.

The idea of 'lost lives' translates in Paulin's works into terms much more straightforwardly historical than anything which might survive in the atmosphere of Mahon's poetry. It might be argued that the whole volume *Liberty Tree* is an exercise in making history (redefined and reclaimed) part of a contemporary analysis with specifically political consequences. In 'Father of History', Paulin sets up his new curriculum with such an end in view:

> Folded like bark, like cinnamon things,
> I traced them to the Linen Hall stacks—
> Munro, Hope, Porter and McCracken;
> like sweet yams buried deep, these rebel minds
> endure posterity without a monument,
> their names a covered sheugh, remnants, some brackish signs.[29]

[29] *Liberty Tree,* 32.

The special qualities of this hitherto hidden history, these particular 'lost lives' that have been forgotten or neglected, are as foreign to the spiritual wasteland that is Paulin's Ulster as cinnamon or yams might be, and it is these qualities upon which the poet chooses to insist. The dissenting radical tradition, traced back to 1798 and the United Irishmen, is in *Liberty Tree* a tool of fundamental importance for presenting and explaining the perceived shortcomings of a present-day Protestant community, out of touch with the revolutionary and republican elements of its own past. For Paulin's poems, rhetorical presences like Ian Paisley have their 'lost lives' in figures like Henry Joy McCracken. It is of course important to remember that what Paulin is doing is making an imaginative appropriation of history, and creating (or salvaging) symbols from this process of appropriation. As far as the application of these symbols is concerned, Paulin's conception of his audience allows this to be in some ways uncertain. Here, once again, the question of perspective, of the author's being outside or inside his subject-matter, tends to intrude. *Liberty Tree* strikes an uneasy balance in terms of its register, with Paulin's vocabulary stretching from the most abstract and dry of academic terms to the words he hears as Ulster vernacular; on occasion, this balance can be lost altogether, and the poet drops into pretentiousness or palpably fake attempts at the demotic (or, worse still, a combination of both). But Paulin remains capable of an eerie immediacy and sensitivity which comes closer to touching on the quality of experience in Northern Ireland than any amount of strenuously vernacular experiment. In 'Martello', Paulin asks, and answers, his own questions:

> Can you *describe* history I'd like to know?
> Isn't it a fiction that pretends to be fact
> like *A Journal of the Plague Year*?
> And the answer that snaps back at me
> is a winter's afternoon in Dungannon,
> the gothic barracks where the policemen
> were signing out their weapons in a stained register,
> a thick turbid light and that brisk smell of fear
> as I described the accident and felt guilty
> guilty for no reason, or cause, I could think of.[30]

---

[30] Ibid. 55–6.

Far from wheeling out a pre-packaged version of 'history' here, or indulging himself in a lecture on the theoretical problems involved in the concept, Paulin turns away from the methods of definition or explanation, and opts instead for an incident made solid by the everyday contingency of its nature. Here, the police's role as agents of the state is put in the background by mundane routine, and in the midst of this the poetic voice itself is left to make sense of its own bafflement and imponderable fear. In a sense, Paulin finds here an apt image for the situation in which his poetic imagination likes to operate: a condition of total interrogation where guilt is assumed and the individual is answerable to large (and inscrutable) forces. To be 'guilty / guilty for no reason, or cause' is to experience the conviction of sin, and be left to work out the implications of this conviction; as Paulin knows, this situation has a long and distinguished history in those narratives of conversion and conviction which contribute largely to the religious identity of Protestantism. As often in Paulin's writing, Calvinistic religious shadows merge with those cast by immediate political realities, creating a complicated and intricate pattern.

However persuasive the reasons may be for refusing to discuss the conflict in Northern Ireland in sectarian terms, there is no avoiding Paulin's projections of Protestantism into the aesthetic of his writing; indeed, Paulin's politics, in so far as they are dissenting and radical, are made possible by a deep identification with the religious impulses and energies of a Scots–Irish dissenting tradition. For a writer inclined to give his explicit allegiance to the values of Enlightenment republicanism, Paulin is much occupied with the hermetic imagery of harsh covenants and beliefs, the arcane flip-side of Protestantism which is a stylized version of the history of an embattled community, and is grounded in the themes and imagery of the Old Testament. Masonic imagery runs through *Fivemiletown*, along with the sign-systems of the Orange Order: Paulin's concern for emblem and typology means that his presentation of the Protestant tradition comes much closer than Mahon's to being an account of the Lost Tribe in straightforwardly biblical terms. Paulin takes as his context a shared identity in crisis, riddled with bankrupt allegiances, and threatened continually by political betrayal. As such, Paulin's relation to the identity he writes about is one which has to be inside and outside at once, trying to speak with the accent of the community he anatomizes, while also subjecting that community to a scrutiny complicit with the hostility felt towards it by its historic enemies. These contrary impulses can work as paradoxical forces in Paulin's writing, and can also make themselves felt as debilitating intellectual and political baggage. Again, Paulin's balance in such matters is often a precarious one.

Here, the degree of overlap (or collusion) between Paulin's experiments in identity-discourse and the unthinking prejudices of the real thing is an unavoidable concern for any critic alert to the liabilities of such discourse in contemporary writing. In a 1981 interview, Paulin gave an account of Ulster Protestantism in which a frustrated, almost baffled tone mixes with the certainties of a history lesson:

> But what I find at the moment is a real sense of how fundamentally ridiculous and contradictory it is to be an Ulster Protestant. It's a culture which could have dignity, and it had it once—I mean that strain of radical Presbyterianism, which more or less went underground after 1798. I pretty well despise official Protestant culture, and can't now understand how people can simultaneously wave the Union Jack and yet hate the English, as many Protestants do.[31]

Paulin's admission that he 'can't now understand' is not real bafflement, for it appeals to a consensus in which such things are genuinely incomprehensible. This is, in essence, an English consensus, though it operates also in parts of Ireland and further afield. At the same time, the concerns of *Liberty Tree* are taking shape here, with the search into a particular corner of Irish history for a way of 'understanding' an identity which, seen as too far debased for the poet (or any reasonable person) to share, has to be despised. It is this process which is at work in the earnest dialect-peddling of some of the *Liberty Tree* poems, or in other 1980s pronouncements, such as the prologue to Paulin's play *The Hillsborough Script*, with its denunciation of 'that servile, demoralized, parasitic crowd, the Unionist middle class', 'wee provincial philistines in their Orange Free State'.[32] (An identification of Northern Irish Protestants with white South Africans is common as a piece of clichéd—and mendacious—political rhetoric, but is cultivated uncritically in some of Paulin's writing.) In 1984 Paulin developed

---

[31] John Haffenden, *Viewpoints: Poets in Conversation with John Haffenden* (London: Faber & Faber, 1981), 159.

[32] *The Hillsborough Script: A Dramatic Satire* (London: Faber & Faber, 1987), [p. ii].

his thoughts (from the outside?) on 'the experience of growing up inside an Ulster Protestant community':

That community possesses very little in the way of an indigenous cultural tradition of its own and in its more reflective moments tends to identify with 'the British way of life'. Although the dissenting tradition in Ulster created a distinctive and notable culture in the closing decades of the eighteenth century, that tradition went underground after the Act of Union and has still not been given the attention it deserves. This is largely because most Unionists have a highly selective historical memory and cling desperately to a raft constructed of two dates—1690 and 1912. The result is an unusually fragmented culture and a snarl of superficial or negative attitudes. A provincialism of the most disabling kind.[33]

One might ask where exactly Paulin fetches his word 'provincialism' from, and consider its assumptions and implications for Northern Ireland: from whose vantage-point, in fact, is the culture Paulin condemns 'provincial'? Perhaps it is possible to distinguish the 'highly selective historical memory' of this debased community from the poet's own highly selective historical imagination, which clings desperately to one date—1798—and proposes a kind of Ulster dissociation of sensibility at the end of the eighteenth century. At any rate, it is this 'provincialism' which much of Paulin's writing takes on: the questions that remain unsettled (and which Paulin's writing seems to take care not to address) are whether the poet is attempting to redeem or destroy his subject, and whether he is seriously addressing himself to this dissociated culture, or is holding it up to an outside audience for easy ridicule.

This compromised, and perhaps compromising, sense of a Protestant community is strongest in *Fivemiletown*, where Protestantism's totems, its sign-systems and conception of history, are all codes to be cracked. At the same time, the community is seen to be on the very edge of catastrophic historical crisis; politically, Paulin is dealing in last things, and an apocalypse for the Protestant identity. As usual, Paulin takes the more routinely apocalyptic voices from the Protestant community as his important political indicators here. In a short poem, 'The Red Handshake', the poet confronts, or rather unearths, the thing itself:

> Maybe if I could scrape the earth
> from off that ridge where the Third Force

[33] *Ireland and the English Crisis*, 17.

melted out of *The Tain* one Antrim night,
I'd find a man called Bowden Beggs
wrapped in black plastic, like a growbag,
and breathing 'Mind, it can get no worse'?[34]

Here Paulin allows himself to inhabit the metaphorical ground of
Ulster history, as processed through Heaney and Hewitt, discovering the aboriginal Planter, though this figure is not planted all that
deeply in the Ulster soil; where Heaney has to dig, Paulin need only
scrape a little in order to uncover the threatened, resilient, slightly
absurd character. And how ironic in fact is the poem's alignment of
Paisley's early 1980s 'Third Force' (whose proudly displayed pieces
of paper at one nocturnal parade turned out to be, not firearms,
but dog-licences) with *The Tain*? Whatever its ironies, the poem
seems to collude with the cliché of the Protestant Ulsterman as both
tenuously rooted and cheap and nasty, vulgar and wilfully blind to
reality. It is the handshake of just such a figure which *Fivemiletown*
tries, at one level, to accept and understand, but questions about
the acceptability of Paulin's assumptions, and the context in which
they are made, remain troubling. In this volume, as in *The Hillsborough Script*, Paulin presents Ulster Protestants as having been
driven into a corner by events (with the Anglo-Irish Agreement of
1985 prominent amongst these) or, to use the poet's dominant
metaphor, forced up to an open window. 'The Defenestration of
Hillsborough' puts the situation in stark terms:

> Here we are on a window ledge
> with the idea of race.
>
> All our victories
> were defeats really
>
> and the tea chests in that room
> aren't packed with books.[35]

The poem's final point is similarly rough and clear: 'This means we
have a choice: / either to jump or get pushed.' At a similarly decisive
moment in *The Hillsborough Script*, one character actually leads
another through an open window, assuring him that 'we need never
go back', and adding for good measure, '*Tiocfhaidh ar la* ... our day
will come. It will for sure.'[36] The character given these lines, Herby,

[34] *Fivemiletown* (London: Faber & Faber, 1987), 54.   [35] Ibid. 8.
[36] *The Hillsborough Script*, 69.

is a kind of stage-Ulster Everyman: on the surface a gardener who minds his own business, deeper down an undercover agent for loyalist paramilitaries, and deeper still a mouthpiece for republican slogans.[37] The picture given by Paulin is simple in its outlines: the Protestants, presented with a political *fait accompli* by both London and Dublin, will either have to leap into new political thinking or be forced there. Paulin wants to see this as something distinct from obeisance or humiliation: one side pushes, and the other defiantly jumps.

Paulin's metaphorical thinking, like his poetic and critical rhetoric, is not without its weaknesses and liabilities. The problem of the intended audience is an important one, and can be approached by way of Louis MacNeice's recollection of his schooldays in England:

On the Twelfth of July Powys came into my dormitory and said: 'What is all this they do in your country today? Isn't it all mumbo-jumbo?' Remembering my father and Home Rule and the bony elbows of Miss Craig and the black file of mill-girls and the wickedness of Carson and the dull dank days between sodden haycocks and foghorns, I said Yes it was. And I felt uplifted.... But Powys went out of the dormitory and Mr Cameron came in, his underlip jutting and his eyes enraged. 'What were you saying to Mr. Powys?' Oh this division of allegiance! That the Twelfth of July was mumbo-jumbo was true and my father thought so too, but the moment Mr Cameron appeared I felt rather guilty and cheap. Because I had been showing off to Powys and because Mr Cameron being after all Irish I felt I had betrayed him.[38]

What the young MacNeice rejects here is inextricable from the psychic landscape of his poetic imagination (and, of course, of other imaginations after him). At the same time, a complex and difficult sense of the pressure of an audience is formed here, one which seems relevant both to Paulin's direct addresses and denunciations, and to Mahon's relocation of his audience in a post-political future of 'posterities'. If Mahon has perhaps been over-scrupulous in his determination to disengage his poetry from its historical context (as his remarks on the irrelevance of ideas like

---

[37] This republican motto was used in prison correspondence by the loyalist terrorist Michael Stone: see Martin Dillon, *Stone Cold: The True Story of Michael Stone and the Milltown Massacre* (London: Hutchinson, 1992), 227.

[38] *The Strings are False: An Unfinished Autobiography* (London: Faber & Faber, 1965), 78–9.

a 'Northern Irish renaissance' in poetry might seem to indicate),[39] Paulin has often been too quick to identify and embrace what looks to him like historical certainty. Truth-telling in poetry is never easily achieved, and it suffers in translation, especially from one side of the Irish Sea to the other, when it can amount to telling the English what they want to hear, rather than telling one's country-men what they should already know. Paulin has himself asserted that 'the Irish writer who publishes in Britain has a neo-colonial identity', and has identified the 'central question' for such a writer as 'whom am I writing for?' Here the dangers of commitment mirror those of detachment, and Paulin's description of V. S. Nai-paul as 'writing for nothing and nowhere', and being 'simply against certain ghastly elsewheres', which leads to a warning that 'Otherness...can reduce the writer to an entertainer, a media clown',[40] is not without its possible relevance to the poet's own media-friendly excursions into stereotypes of the Northern Irish Protestant identity.

But 'writing for nothing' need not, necessarily, be a futile or valueless activity. In understanding this, Derek Mahon's poetry is constantly in debt to Beckett, and touches on areas of Protestant identity which are much more complex than the politically acces-sible aspects so common in Paulin's writing. In his poem 'Tithonus', Mahon breathes life (of a kind) into Tennyson's mythological fig-ure, condemning him to outlive his own mythology and become a witness to a Beckettian world of post-nuclear catastrophe, as a figure from prehistory who lives through and finally beyond history itself. This produces the longest of all possible perspectives:

> I forget nothing
> But if I told
> Everything in detail—
>
> Not merely Golgotha
> And Krakatoa
> But the leaf-plink
>
> Of raindrops after
> Thermopylae,
> The lizard-flick

[39] See the introduction to Derek Mahon and Peter Fallon (eds.), *The Penguin Book of Contemporary Irish Poetry* (Harmondsworth: Penguin, 1990), discussed in Ch. 7 below.
[40] *Ireland and the English Crisis*, 18.

> In the scrub as Genghis
> Khan entered Peking
> And the changing clouds,
>
> I would need
> Another eternity,
> Perish the thought.[41]

There is an equanimity about this which is both absurd and appropriate; it is history seen both to infinity and to the point of absurdity. In the way of Mahon's unremitting perspectives, what is called into question is the very possibility of a self when it is, at this farthest-fetched of extremes, itself the only thing left to observe:

> I dream of the past,
> Of the future,
> Even of the present.
>
> Perhaps I am really
> Dead and dreaming
> My vigilance?

Again, nothing abides; and yet this is exactly the point, for Mahon's 'nothing' comes to a good deal, and its abiding value is, like Beckett's work, eerily persistent. Questions of identity within an aesthetic like this are inevitably subject to mutation, though the impulse giving rise to this is itself, ironically, indebted to the unforthcoming imperatives of a powerful religious drive, converted by Mahon into (in Edna Longley's phrase) an 'extreme religion of art'.[42]

At this point, Mahon's art (like Beckett's, and certain aspects of MacNeice's) comes close to the 'spiritual' dimension sensed and sought in Paulin's writing. Before the increasing air of urgency and commitment of his 1980s volumes, Paulin's *The Strange Museum* had circled around this dimension, fighting shy of confusing it with a state to be achieved through political analysis or rhetoric alone. 'What is Fixed to Happen' insists on this:

> The eye is such a cunning despot
> We believe its wordless travelogues
> And call them *History* or *Let it Happen*.[43]

---

[41] *Selected Poems*, 168–72.

[42] See Edna Longley, 'Derek Mahon: Extreme Religion of Art', in Michael Kenneally (ed.), *Poetry in Contemporary Irish Literature* (Gerrards Cross: Colin Smythe, 1995), 280–303.

[43] *The Strange Museum* (London: Faber & Faber, 1980), 34.

The poem pursues unrelentingly the consequences of this kind of history, in which ultimately 'Pulped bodies happen / In a charred street', giving birth to 'imprisoned shadows' and 'black plastic shrouds'. The panorama of determinism is depressing and intimately familiar as a well-grounded negative vision. But this is not everything:

> In a scorched space, a broken nowhere,
> A homeless grief beyond all grievance
> Must suffer nature and be free.
>
> It knows true pity is a rarer love
> That asks for neither action nor revenge.
> It wills nothing and serves nothing.

It may be that this poem is more in the nature of a sketch or a diagram than a fully realized piece, but its sense of the weight of 'nothing' brings it into contact with 'a spiritual reality which is religious in its negativity'. The poetry that faces the worst possible thing might (as here) be able to go beyond the identity that loads down its history, and much of Mahon's best writing (as Paulin senses) is able to achieve just this. The consequences of such achievements for the discourses of identity, and the political agendas within which the identity of Northern Irish Protestants is constructed, are considerable. It may be that even politically useful stereotypes of identity, from inside or from outside, might usefully come to nothing in the end.

5
Michael Longley's Homes

Michael Longley's position in relation to the other Northern Irish poets of his generation makes for an interesting (and perhaps a complicated) situation. Born in the same year as Seamus Heaney, and a little older than Derek Mahon, Longley found himself, as an established poet in the 1970s, one of the writers who seemed, to journalistic and much critical opinion at least, in some sense a group of poets of the Troubles. To read Longley's volume of 1973, *An Exploded View*, such a grouping seems not to have been entirely a journalistic fabrication or convenience; dedicated to 'Derek, Seamus and Jimmy' (James Simmons), and containing verse-letters to each of these poets (as well as one to all three together), the book is secure in its contemporary allegiances. Longley's dedicatory verses speak from a dilemma, but it is a dilemma confidently shared:

> We are trying to make ourselves heard
> Like the lover who mouths obscenities
> In his passion, like the condemned man
> Who makes a last-minute confession,
> Like the child who cries out in the dark.[1]

The lover and the condemned man here both utter things that are (strictly speaking) unnecessary, or at least are needless in their contexts—the lover is making love, the condemned man remains condemned. Like these, the child's cry in the dark is a plea for contact (though like these too, it may be a futile one). In this sense, 'We are trying to make ourselves heard' is neither an announcement nor a promise, but a modest explanation, both for what follows and for what does not follow in the volume. Beyond that, perhaps, it implies a more general notion of what poetry can and cannot do in bad times, one which the small circle of poets is understood to share.

[1] *Poems 1963–1983* (Edinburgh: Salamander Press, 1985), 59.

The dedicatory verses in 1973 explain where Longley is coming from (so to speak) in the volume; the scarred and traumatized Northern Ireland of the early 1970s is a shared location, in which the poets leave subtle marks and hints of themselves. 'To Three Irish Poets', with its determination to 'confound / Baedeckers of the nightmare ground', finds ways to frame the poets' reticence:

> Now every lost bedraggled field
> Like a mythopoeic bog unfolds
> Its gelignite and dumdums:
> And should the whole idea become
> A vegetable run to seed in
> Even our suburban garden,
>
> We understudy for the hare's
> Disappearance around corners,
> The approximate untold barks
> Of the otters we call water-dogs—
> A dim reflection of ourselves,
> A muddy forepaw that dissolves.[2]

Longley's poetry here serves as a kind of recommendation of distance, preferring the 'Disappearance around corners' of shy creatures in the wild to the death-dealing hardware to be turned up in the 'mythopoeic bog'. In this, much of the course of Longley's own writing of the 1970s is plotted out, and in particular the conjunction of the 'suburban garden' with a wilder environment maps out the different locations which a great deal of his poetry inhabits. But the strategy of continually disappearing around corners, of finding approximations and dim reflections, was not to prove so immediately successful as the excavation of 'mythopoeic bog' itself, most obviously at the hands of Seamus Heaney. The poetic solidarity of *An Exploded View* is a prelude to Longley's increasing isolation in the 1970s, as his writing continues to disappear around various corners, concentrating its efforts on acts of the most minute (but complete) imaginative fidelity to a complex home ground. Of the four poets, Longley and Simmons remained in Northern Ireland through the 1970s and after, while Mahon's and Heaney's orbits took them elsewhere; by the end of the 1970s however, it was Heaney, above all, who was making himself heard as a Northern Irish poet with something to say about the Troubles. After *The*

[2] Ibid. 77.

Echo Gate in 1979, Longley did not publish another volume of poetry until *Gorse Fires* in 1991; it was this volume which, with its successor *The Ghost Orchid* (1995), made obvious both the deep continuities in Longley's writing career, and the extent to which these had been missed or undervalued by much critical reception and discussion over the years. Essentially, Longley's ability to keep faith with the instincts and intuitions of his early 1970s writing, which probably cost him (in the short term) the kind of recognition won more easily by Heaney, paid rich dividends after the long decade of silence, not least in the convincing complexity of the poet's dealings with his different kinds of home ground.

In the poem 'River & Fountain' in *The Ghost Orchid*, Longley remembers his student life at Trinity College, Dublin, as a writer who finds himself 'walking backwards into the future like a Greek'. The poem's conclusion is emphatic, though unforced:

> Walking forwards into the past with more of an idea
> I want to say to my friends of thirty years ago
> And to daughters and a son that Belfast is our home,
> Prose a river still—the Liffey, the Lagan—and poetry
> A fountain that plays in an imaginary Front Square.
> When snow falls it is feathers from the wings of Icarus.[3]

The delicacy of the final line's allusion to *Icarus* (the literary magazine at Trinity in Longley's time) is—like this poem in its entirety—understood within a context of familial intimacy, and this is literally so when Longley announces 'that Belfast is our home' to his own children. The unembarrassed clarity here records a literal domicile, but it also makes 'home' into an important central point for writing as well as familial intimacies. A similar directness can be heard in Longley's response, in an interview, to the straight question 'Where is home for you?' 'Home is Belfast. Belfast is home. I love the place. The city, the hills around it, County Down, County Antrim. My home from home is in Mayo. But home is Belfast. It has nothing to do with literature.'[4] Although, as Longley goes on to remark, it is true that the city of Belfast itself seldom enters his poetry directly, the resonances of this matter do in fact have a good deal to do with literature, in so far as they affect the ways in which Longley's writing is situated in contemporary Irish and British

---

[3] *The Ghost Orchid* (London: Jonathan Cape, 1995), 57.
[4] Interview with Dermot Healy, *The Southern Review*, 31/3 (July 1995), 559.

criticism, and in which it situates itself between a 'home' and a 'home from home'. The confidence of the poet's location is in part a consequence of the sustained concentration on the whole complexity of 'home' which Longley's poetry has always brought to bear. Behind, or as well as, that confidence, is an awareness of the issues that converge on 'home' for a poet in Longley's position, and which always make it something more—or less—than a fully private place.

T. S. Eliot's phrase from *East Coker*, 'Home is where one starts from',[5] combines directness with difficulty in a way that is suggestive in quite other contexts. 'Home' means a place of origin, and so may be the concrete site in which a poetic voice locates itself; in that sense, it is a word with its own degree of intimacy. But talk of 'home' also amounts often to a statement arising from intimacy: to say that a place is 'home' is to imprint the place with a personal meaning for the purposes of some more public kind of communication. Indeed, Eliot's poem builds upon the fact that its discussion of an ancestral 'home' in rural Somerset is read in the context of the Home Front during the Second World War; its privacies are charged with the energy of a public meaning. Of course, like many potent words, 'home' as often carries overtones of banality, and is thus a word in poetry that brings with it certain risks. The resonance of 'home' in Irish poetry has to do with these risks, and would not be possible without them; this is owing partly to the word's long-running potency in the discourses of sentiment and nostalgia, and its emotional pull on the individual back to something larger than his personal experiences and reactions. For much Irish discourse, 'home' is a word that drives into private reflex the category of defined identity: after all, if 'identity' has its location anywhere, that deep place is surely in the 'home'. The power of this, and the power of resistance to it, are both audible at the end of W. B. Yeats's 'Under Saturn':

> 'You have come again,
> And surely after twenty years it was time to come.'
> I am thinking of a child's vow sworn in vain
> Never to leave that valley his fathers called their home.[6]

The rhyme 'come'/'home' voices a command which the poet cannot obey, at the same time as articulating an imperative which Yeats's

---

[5] *Complete Poems and Plays* (London: Faber & Faber, 1969), 182.
[6] *Collected Poems* (London: Macmillan, 1950), 202.

poetry survives by refusing. 'Home' here is a place and a state left behind, one to which access is possible, but only at the price of self-consciousness. In a similar way, the figure brooding alone at the end of Louis MacNeice's 'The Left-Behind' finds that the location of 'home' is diminishing in significance:

> My glass is low and I lack money to fill it.
> I gaze on the black dregs and the yellow scum,
> And the night is old and a nightbird calls me away
> To what now is merely mine, and soon will be no one's home.[7]

Here, as in Yeats, 'home' is functioning as a problematic and alluring word, one which eludes the attempts of the poetic voice to possess it; this is not because the concept as offered cannot be possessed, but because the price of such possession is, for poetry, far too high. Coming home, in the full sense, is at some level impossible for an imagination that exists by virtue of its difference from what 'home' represents, and by virtue of having resisted the identity which is consolidated there. It is difficult, then, for poets like Yeats or MacNeice to be fully, or simply, 'at home' in poems, even in poems that speak plangently of returning home.

Poetry from Northern Ireland has been understandably haunted by the attractions, and the liabilities, of 'home'. Often, the word occurs at moments of rhetorical intensity, such as the close of Seamus Heaney's 'The Tolland Man' where 'I will feel lost, / Unhappy and at home',[8] or Derek Mahon's 'Afterlives', where a conscience-stricken poet comes back to Belfast:

> Perhaps if I'd stayed behind
> And lived it bomb by bomb
> I might have grown up at last,
> And learnt what is meant by home.[9]

Too much, finally, hangs on that 'Perhaps', for if there is a basic integrity here, there is also a certain element of posturing, or of saying the proper thing in the circumstances; in the same way, Heaney does not really imagine what kind of unhappiness he will feel in the state of being 'at home', but allows the conjunction of 'Unhappy and at home' to make for a too easily ambiguous ending

---

[7] *Collected Poems*, ed. E. R. Dodds (London: Faber & Faber, 1966), 449.
[8] *Wintering Out* (London: Faber & Faber, 1972), 48.
[9] *Poems 1962–1978* (Oxford: Oxford University Press, 1979), 58.

to his poem. In Longley's poetry, the scope of 'home' is widened, and the care with which the word itself is handled means that, while it still has its double edge of the private and the public, and carries certain specifically Irish inflections, it becomes (finally) an enabling concept, a source of both comfort and possibility, which expands the poetic voice rather than dramatizing its predicament. 'Home', eventually, is uncoupled from the agendas of identity. The process is a slow one, and in this sense Longley's comparative poetic silence from 1979 until 1991 is not without its significance for the gradual development of the poet's uses for 'home'.

Longley has been misread by even his admiring critics, or rather the importance of his work has been under-read in their appreciations. Alan Peacock, for example, has praised Longley's poetry about the west of Ireland, noting how 'Questions of identity... do not seem relevant', since the poet 'simply takes his place in a given world.'[10] The deceptiveness of such simplicity, however, is indicated in the critic's concluding parallel between Longley and MacNeice, where the similarity resides in the poet's being able to draw 'naturally and instinctively on a wide range of fully assimilated literary, cultural, and historical periods', but 'Unlike MacNeice... he knows in the last analysis where he belongs.'[11] The false note struck here makes plain a deficiency in the critical framework within which Longley is being appreciated, and the elevation of the notion of 'knowing where you belong' (itself as much a cliché as 'in the last analysis') to an evaluative criterion aligns even this appreciation with the kinds of critical deprecation Longley's work has sometimes provoked. An instance of this occurs in the 'Contemporary Irish Poetry' section of the *Field Day Anthology*, where Declan Kiberd instructs readers on where Longley belongs:

Longley may have more in common with the semi-detached suburban muse of Philip Larkin and post-war England than with Heaney or Montague. His self-effacing courtesy, his dry good humour, and his addiction to off-key closures, all align him with British post-modernism, as is manifest in his homage to L. S. Lowry. And yet the very fact that he should apply these techniques to the Belfast of the 'Troubles' indicates also his sustained attempt to widen the traditions of modern Irish poetry. With Derek

[10] 'Michael Longley: Poet between Worlds', in Michael Kenneally (ed.), *Poetry in Contemporary Irish Literature* (Gerrards Cross: Colin Smythe, 1995), 272.
[11] Ibid. 279.

Mahon, he represents a strand of Ulster that identifies itself as British and asserts its right to the English lyric.[12]

The anxiety to pin down where exactly Longley is coming from casts around for pigeonholes with mounting comic effect, settling eventually for 'British post-modernism' (Longley's poem 'After Horace' has the final word on the appropriateness of this particular category). However, the 'post-war England' and 'British' count for more than the wobbly sense of aesthetic fashion here, and the poet's supposed representativeness is insisted on, as usual in terms of identity-politics. But the critic's difficulty in thinking for himself, besides necessitating the customary aids of identity shorthand and anti-English prejudice, means that the critical observation itself parrots a poetic text by a higher authority. The allusion to Heaney's lines (addressed to Seamus Deane), 'Ulster was British, but with no rights on / The English lyric',[13] puts Longley very firmly in his place. Heaney, it appears, in even the most minor of his verbal felicities, has foreseen and foresuffered all. Given the nature of Longley's achievement, and its utter distinctiveness in the contexts of both Irish and British contemporary poetry, an assessment like this (self-consciously situated as it is in a canon-defining exercise) reads as the kind of sustained insult which its critical vacuousness cannot quite excuse.

It is an implication of judgements such as that enshrined in the *Field Day Anthology* that Longley's sense of his home (or homes) is either mistaken or under-analysed, and that critical understanding of cultural identity can read this more accurately than the poet himself is willing (or perhaps able) to do. In this context, to say 'Home is Belfast. Belfast is home' without adding a gloss on whether or not it 'identifies itself as British' is, on Longley's part, almost a gesture of defiance. Once the word 'home' is in the air, public agendas mean that some kinds of 'home' will turn out to be superior to others—will, that is, be clearer about their identity, and more explicit about their historical meaning. In a 1995 'Diary' written for the *London Review of Books*, Tom Paulin gives an account of meeting an old man who can recite the Ulster Scots words for different species of bird; a list of these is followed by an

---

[12] 'Contemporary Irish Poetry', in Seamus Deane (gen. ed.), *The Field Day Anthology of Irish Writing*, 3 vols. (Londonderry: Field Day, 1991), iii. p. 1375.
[13] Seamus Heaney, *North* (London: Faber & Faber, 1975), 65.

apparently gratuitous reference to Longley which is, nonetheless, indicative of much:

> it's a relief to listen to this old man standing on the moss and reciting a list of bird names in Ulster Scots: whap (curlew), skert (shag), parr (tern), mossie (meadowpipit), cooterneb (puffin), chitterling (swallow), yellayorling (yellowhammer), chittyran (wren), cran (heron).
>
> When he's finished, I ask him does he feel at home in the language? 'I do, aye,' he says. 'My soul sings in it.' I recall there's a poem packed with Ulster Scots words in Michael Longley's new volume, *Ghost Orchid*. Maybe the poet is wanting to ruffle his deft parnassian or to raise certain readers' hackles? For there's a calculated over determined quality to the language that makes it more like a piss-take.[14]

It is, doubtless, the length and richness of the list of birds which takes Paulin from his old man of the hills to a new book of Michael Longley's poems, since lists are of consuming importance for a great deal of Longley's writing, and constitute one of its most distinctive stylistic traits.[15] But the contrast between this oddly Yeatsian user of Ulster Scots and Longley turns on how far they 'feel at home in the language', and Paulin's view of Longley's 'calculated over determined quality' (there is nothing over-determined, one presumes, in the old man's 'My soul sings in it') means that both his use of words from Ulster Scots and his more usual 'deft parnassian' are found wanting. The implication seems to be that Longley is insufficiently 'at home' in his poetry, and is condemned therefore to an ultimate inauthenticity in whatever language he adopts. If the critical judgement is askew here, so is the assumption that there is a state of unproblematic authenticity in language, of being uncomplicatedly 'at home' in it, which can be identified through its cultural manifestations and declarations of allegiance. Paulin's old man of the hills is co-opted as a living link with eighteenth-century Presbyterian republicanism, and that particular historical 'home' is used as the guarantee of the authenticity of *his* use of certain words. A lot depends on the matter of

---

[14] *London Review of Books*, 24 Aug. 1995, p. 25. In a letter published in the same journal on 5 Oct. 1995, Jim Fenton of Newtownabbey, Co. Antrim, identified himself as the 'old man' of Paulin's encounter, adding that 'the words "my soul sings in it" have never, I swear by Saint Patrick, been uttered by me' (p. 4). Fenton suggested alternative sources for the Yeatsian outburst, and for Paulin's confusion.

[15] See John Lyon, 'Michael Longley's Lists', *English*, 45/183 (Autumn 1996), 228–246.

having the right 'home', and Longley's unsatisfactoriness in that respect is perhaps unsurprising.

From early on, 'home' has been a word given special prominence in Longley's poetry. Alongside this, or part and parcel of it, the poet's range of subject-matter (especially in his work up to 1979) has been relatively narrow, much of it being accounted for by poems on aspects of landscape, flora, and wildlife in the west of Ireland, a kind of pastoral (or sometimes georgic) mode which opens up to include love poetry and (occasionally) poetry relating obliquely to more public themes. In doing this, Longley made use both of the physical aspects of possible home grounds, with particular relish for the various nomenclatures involved in describing these, and the familial elements in a concept of 'home', those which mark it as a place for love of the living and remembrance of the dead. In this sense, Longley's 'love' poetry and his 'nature' poetry tend towards common points of origin, just as they share their destinations. A short poem from *An Exploded View*, 'The West', shows how Longley complicates the idea of 'home' at the same time as allowing it apparently simple, physically precise, expression:

> Beneath a gas-mantle that the moths bombard,
> Light that powders at a touch, dusty wings,
> I listen for news through the atmospherics,
> A crackle of sea-wrack, spinning driftwood,
> Waves like distant traffic, news from home,
>
> Or watch myself, as through a sandy lens,
> Materialising out of the heat-shimmers
> And finding my way for ever along
> The path to this cottage, its windows,
> Walls, sun and moon dials, home from home.[16]

The self-consciousness of this is the opposite of self-importance; the significant activities here are listening and watching, accumulating evidence of two homes, one distant and the other immediately present. 'News from home' and a 'home from home' are balanced at the end of each stanza, but both of these 'materialise', whether from 'atmospherics' or 'heat-shimmers', in becoming subjects for the speaking voice. As in much of Longley's poetry, the standpoints of the resident and the holidaymaker are brought together, but not artificially resolved, by means of precise description. It is just this

[16] *Poems 1963–1983*, 94.

element of description, and its development in the process of naming, which is crucial for the success of Longley's poetry. At the same time, it is also one of the principal risks taken by the poet, for much of the ground on to which he ventures is not unqualifiedly 'his own' until made so by the poetry—and even then, the poetry's characteristic sense for delicacy and fragility, for things that 'powder at a touch' (which has increased steadily throughout Longley's career), seems to resist models of imaginative possession of the world it observes. The poet does seem to be often a figure 'materialising' in the landscape of the west of Ireland from another point of origin, a home in Northern Ireland, to which the poetry itself obliquely relates: there is a proper absence of the rhetoric of rootedness here. It is in the light of this that Longley's poems need to be read: their pastoral serenity, their sure-footed excursions into natural history or folklore, and their pervasive feeling for the buoyancy of love and the gravity of death, all rely on the exploration of a 'home from home' where origins and destinations have become relative and, perhaps, of secondary importance.

As a place to 'watch myself', Longley's West always tends to unsettle or in some way alter the self that has come to visit. This results in the prominence of the first-person voice in so much of the poetry, which speaks, not for a settled and rooted identity, finding images of itself in everything, but for a self absorbed in, and maybe also in the process of being absorbed by, its surroundings. In 'Landscape', where 'my imagination / Tangles through a turfstack', the first-person voice loses its contact with physical stability:

> I am clothed, unclothed
> By racing cloud shadows,
> Or else disintegrate
> Like a hillside neighbour
> Erased by sea mist.[17]

In this 'place of dispersals', the voice, and the observing self behind it, are drawn closer and closer to a landscape that 'rips thought to tatters'. By the end of the poem, the distance between observer and observed has been reduced almost to nothing:

> Melting into water
> Where a minnow flashes:

[17] Ibid. 126.

> A mouth drawn to a mouth
> Digests the glass between
> Me and my reflection.

How far this is a poem about landscape, and how far it is a poem about 'me', is difficult to determine. However, the process here is not one of quasi-Romantic projection of the self into nature, or finding the self prefigured by nature, but of an incursion of the natural world into the stable, self-recognizing perspective of identity. The nature poet, or the poet of place (in critical convention at least) is a kind of celebrant: in recent Irish poetry the earlier work of Seamus Heaney might come to mind as a good example of how exploration and celebration of 'home' can contribute to a solidly defined sense of identity. The power of Heaney's early pastoral, in books like *Death of a Naturalist* (1966) and *Door into the Dark* (1969) has fixed a certain kind of nature poetry as something recognizably 'Irish' (its debts to English poets like Ted Hughes being often discounted), and has made for a common notion of the link between place, poetic description or celebration, and grounded individual poetic identity. Yet for Longley, the 'home from home' of the West offers a way of *undoing* the settled nature of an identity rooted in its own place of origin.

It is important to stress that this tendency in Longley's writing has been apparent from the beginning, and that it continues to develop further in his most recent volumes. Above all, it is the result of a habit of concentration, a characteristic set of angles of approach to the natural world, and not in itself anything resembling a strategy or a programme. Indeed, the resonances which Longley's dealings with 'identity' in his nature poetry might have acquired in critical reception are unlikely to have been sought by the poet, and remain in certain important ways irrelevant to the processes of his writing. Nevertheless, one question which inevitably arises with regard to Longley's dealings with the West, and with the identity of the inhabiting (or visiting) self there, is that of a possible relation between this poetry and Longley's origins in the Protestant community of Northern Ireland. The question works from certain assumptions which are themselves questionable (not least the idea that Longley's familial origins are in any simple way in that 'Protestant community', for his parents were English and, as his memoir 'Tuppenny Stung' records, his early relations with

Protestant Belfast were in some ways strained).[18] In the terms of
such a question, the seemingly uprooted, homeless poetry of Derek
Mahon, or perhaps even that of MacNeice, makes for a neater
solution than does Longley's comparatively neutral, precise, and
faithful approach to the West. However, the question may be mistaken in its implicit assumption that a secure sense of 'home'
necessarily follows from, or gives rise to, a stable feeling of identity—and, indeed, that identity can always be so easily identified.
As has been suggested above, the whole discourse of 'home' in Irish
writing insinuates that identity is a means of making the private
realm publicly accessible, and in doing so it brings in certain
already fixed meanings and responses. Gerald Dawe, writing on
Mahon and Longley together, senses that 'home' is at the heart of
the matter, but fails to grasp the implications of Longley's work in
this respect:

It is, one feels, a question of acceptance and rejection similar to that which
MacNeice experienced. Longley, I would suggest, has accepted his past (the
Protestant city, the cultural 'duality', the shaky identity) whereas Mahon
has rejected his. MacNeice's spiritual sons have gone their different ways:
one has remained at home, the other has left.[19]

In fact, Longley's work makes terms like these difficult to sustain.
'Acceptance and rejection' can never be so clear-cut as this, at
least not at the point of writing poetry as opposed to making
political or cultural statements. There is nothing uniquely 'shaky'
about Longley's 'identity'; instead, Longley is aware of how shaky a
concept 'identity' is in poetry. Once terminology such as this is
disowned or undermined, of course, poetry runs the risk of
losing its immediate attractiveness in a critical world that needs
to 'place' or otherwise identify its subjects in clear terms. Longley's
poetry, though it has never gone short of respect, has yet to work its
way into the discourse of those cultural critics for whom Irish
writing occupies a central position. His writing almost never
addresses the problem of the supposed crisis of identity of the
Protestant writer in Northern Ireland, but this is not a sign of
evasion on his part, for there is nothing here to evade. Rather, the

[18] See Michael Longley, 'Tuppenny Stung', in *Tuppenny Stung: Autobiographical
Chapters* (Belfast: Lagan Press, 1994), 15–29.
[19] 'Icon and Lares: Derek Mahon and Michael Longley', in Gerald Dawe and
Edna Longley (eds.), *Across a Roaring Hill: The Protestant Imagination in Modern
Ireland* (Belfast: Blackstaff Press, 1985), 227.

poetry helps to provide angles from which 'home' can be re-
approached without the encoding of tribal claims to certain territories, and perhaps without the imperatives of identity pressing in
on both response and imagination.

The element that is missing from Longley's homes, at first sight at
least, is that of community. The landscapes of the West are sparsely
populated at best, while the Northern 'home' tends to be peopled
almost exclusively by the poet's immediate family. Typically, Longley is drawn to what MacNeice called 'island truancies': islands in
the West, or places on the very edge of the ocean, are the counter-
parts to a family origin islanded in history. In the poem 'The Island'
(from *An Exploded View*), Longley creates a place where 'Visitors
are few', and 'we' build up a place to live from bric-à-brac that
arrives by chance:

> Our ship continues to rust on the rocks.
> We stripped it completely of wash-hand basins,
> Toilet fitments, its cargo of linoleum
> And have set up house in our own fashion.[20]

This community is on the edge of everything, self-marginalizing
and finally slipping out of view altogether:

> We count ourselves historians of sorts
> And chronicle all such comings and goings.
> We can walk in a day around the island.
> We shall reach the horizon and disappear.

The reader of 'The Island' is put in the visitor's position, unable to
enter the community that is observed, and in the end unable to
share the home. The attempted objectivity of 'Linguists occasionally, and sociologists' is defeated because it asks the wrong questions, and takes up the wrong angle of approach. This wariness in
the matter of access is significant, and Longley's subsequent writing
continues to take it seriously, never claiming for the poet any
special insight into the community (or at least the human community) of the landscape he visits. Longley is in fact not very concerned
with entering the West on such terms, preferring to let the places he
describes provide him with the physical material from which a
personal—and lonely—environment can be put together. The sense
of distance being maintained between himself and others is impor-

---

[20] *Poems 1963–1983*, 93.

tant even in poems that record friendship, as in 'Between Hovers' in *Gorse Fires*, where Longley commemorates a neighbour in Mayo:

> His way of seeing me safely across the duach
> Was to leave his porch light burning, its sparkle
> Shifting from widgeon to teal on Corragaun Lake.[21]

This is distance becoming benign in quite a literal way, though the good nature of the reticence which the poem begins by recording ('And not even when we ran over the badger / Did he tell me he had cancer') has its own distance, to which Longley is reconciled. In many poems, Longley acknowledges that, as 'Washing' puts it, 'All the washing on the line adds up to me alone'.[22]

Such communities as Longley does allow himself to inhabit are made up as much of concrete bits and pieces, and of flora and fauna, as of people. In 'Detour', the poet's imagined funeral 'Down the single street of a small market town' takes him past shops with 'such names / As Philbin, O'Malley, McNamara, Keane', but the non-human inhabitants are also listed:

> A reverent pause to let a herd of milkers pass
> Will bring me face to face with grubby parsnips,
> Cauliflowers that glitter after a sunshower,
> Then hay rakes, broom handles, gas cylinders.
> Reflected in the slow sequence of shop windows
> I shall be part of the action...[23]

The poet makes little or no impression on this community, moving through its streets 'Behind the only locked door for miles around'. Again, the relation between the poet and this other home is an oblique one, which does not express itself directly in any statement of place or 'belonging'. An earlier poem, 'Ghost Town', takes a more interventionist approach to the 'place of interminable after-noons, / Sad cottages, scythes rusting in the thatch':

> Since no one has got around to it yet
> I shall restore the sign which reads CINEMA,
> Rescue from the verge of invisibility
> The faded stills of the last silent feature—
> I shall become the local eccentric...[24]

---

[21] *Gorse Fires* (London: Secker & Warburg, 1991), 5.   [22] Ibid. 3.
[23] Ibid. 7.   [24] *Poems 1963–1983*, 99.

Again, however, the first-person voice is subject to irony here, exposing its own determination to use this place for its own purposes ('Already I have retired there to fill / Several gaps in my education'). The poem ends with the voice plotting a course for itself which relies on separation from its origins in the familial 'home':

> Indeed, with so much on my hands, family
> And friends are definitely not welcome—
> Although by the time I am accepted there
> (A reputation and my own half-acre)
> I shall have written another letter home.

In striving to impose itself on a community, the voice in this poem in fact ensures its own isolation. The difficulty lies perhaps in the desire to be accepted rather than the ability to accept, in imagining that 'family and friends' have to be left somewhere else to wait for news of the poet's experiment in self-education.

Longley's poetry is engaged in 'writing home' in a richer sense than that suggested at the end of 'The Island'. The writing often serves to articulate careful observation, listening and watching, by providing the names proper to the environment. Getting the names right is, in fact, crucial to the way these poems work, and Longley's increasingly frequent lists of names serve, in part at least, to record accurately what exists quite apart from its appropriation in a poem. The accuracy of virtuoso acts of naming, such as the catalogue of 'all the wild flowers of the Burren / I had seen in one day' in 'The Ice-Cream Man'[25] matters in Longley's writing, since it bears witness to something which is beyond the reach of self-interested distortion; significance here does not reside in what the names tell us about the poet's sense of himself. The creation of a 'home from home' in poetry is for Longley an act of naming, and it is this act, in turn, which reshapes the vocabulary and tone of the poetic voice. There are any number of possible precedents here, such as Edward Thomas's 'Adlestrop' which allows a place name to expand in meaning until it encompasses an entire countryside, 'all the birds / Of Oxfordshire and Gloucestershire'.[26] Closer to Longley's own favoured landscapes, Patrick Kavanagh's 'Kerr's Ass' allows the

---

[25] *Gorse Fires*, 49.
[26] Edward Thomas, *Collected Poems*, ed. R. George Thomas (Oxford: Oxford University Press, 1981), 25.

particularity of a name to resonate, with 'the God of imagination waking / In a Mucker fog'.[27] Deriving from these, and in parallel with Longley, is Seamus Heaney's use of place names which, in influential poems such as 'Broagh', makes naming an act loaded with potential political significance. Indeed, Heaney reads Longley's acts of naming in implicitly political terms when he writes of Longley's 'The Linen Industry' that 'here Edward Thomas's English naming-poems rather than Joyce's riddling prose are the sponsoring presence', adding (a little disingenuously) that this is 'a sponsorship with just as much political significance as we want to assign it'.[28] In Longley's poetry, the voice in solitude is left to list the names that are, in fact, the real community in the midst of which it must exist—a situation which may not be 'political' at all, in Heaney's sense. In the sequence of short poems entitled 'Fleadh', for example, different musical instruments are taken in by the poet as parts of a rural environment. The pipes, the last items on Longley's list, do not just sound like the natural world around them, but are in fact parts of it:

> One stool for the fireside
> And the field, for windbag
> And udder: milk and rain
> Singing into a bucket
> At the same angle: cries
> Of waterbirds homing:
> Ripples and undertow—
> The chanter, the drones.[29]

Longley's device of letting nouns drop free at the end of a poem (later to develop into his characteristic closing lists) can be seen here to be an act of naming, or rather of allowing the voice to accept names as adequate to the full range of its observations. A main verb would seem out of place in such an arrangement, being altogether too blatant an intervention in the settled (perhaps static) collage of objects and images. Another sequence, 'Carrigskeewaun' (itself named for the place which has served as the poet's particular 'home from home' in the West) begins by bringing one home into

[27] Patrick Kavanagh, *Complete Poems* (Newbridge: Goldsmith Press, 1984), 254.
[28] 'Place and Displacement: Reflections on Some Recent Poetry from Northern Ireland', in Elmer Andrews (ed.), *Contemporary Irish Poetry: A Collection of Critical Essays* (Basingstoke: Macmillan, 1992), 142.
[29] *Poems 1963–1983*, 125.

contact with another through naming the elements that are missing. Here, it is the family 'home' that is named in the stern solitude of a mountain landscape:

> This is ravens' territory, skulls, bones,
> The marrow of these boulders supervised
> From the upper air: I stand alone here
> And seem to gather children about me,
> A collection of picnic things, my voice
> Filling the district as I call their names.[30]

This is the other side of Longley's naming process, one which colonizes the new place with a 'voice / Filling the district'. The irony of a poem like 'Company', where 'we are living in the country / In a far-off townland' under constant observation by the local populace, undercuts any attempt the poet might make to claim direct authority over the adopted place:

> As I sit late beside a tilley-lamp
> And try to put their district on the map
> And to name the fields for them, for you
> Who busy yourself about the cottage,
> Its thatch letting in...[31]

This version of pastoral, which sets out to impose something on its subject, is undermined by the slow seeping-in of rain, like a neighbour 'leaning against the half-door', which provides the 'Watermarks under all that we say'. The attempt 'to name the fields for them' is not adequate to the local conditions, and is grounded in the wrong kind of ambitions: if the concerns of 'home' are to find a place, they will have to be able to accommodate the 'watermarks' of a different environment. The pastoral fantasy here is far removed from Longley's actual practice; it is prepared for, however, by the first half of the poem, in which the speaking voice imagines an urban future for itself, where:

> Love has diminished to one high room
> Below which the vigilantes patrol
> While I attempt to make myself heard
> Above the cacophonous plumbing...

This other home is shrunken too, and shadowed by violence. In both parts of the poem, Longley foresees a kind of failure, and in

---

[30] Longley, *Poems 1963–1983*, 96.   [31] Ibid. 140.

each case the figure of the poet is at a remove from the surrounding place.

The degree to which the poet, who brings with him the elements of his own home, enters and affects the landscape he describes is carefully judged in Longley's work; the balance between one home and another, though often delicate, is never lost. In his earlier work, Longley tends to dramatize the self in a new landscape: in 'Leaving Inishmore', for instance, he speaks for himself and a companion whose 'holiday' perspective means that 'we left too soon / The island awash in wave and anthem'. However, the poet's stance is perhaps too secure, too confident in finding the names for its surroundings:

> Summer and solstice as the seasons turn
> Anchor our boat in a perfect standstill,
> The harbour wall of Inishmore astern
> Where the Atlantic waters overspill—
> I shall name this the point of no return...[32]

This remains the visitor's perspective, which approaches a place in a self-interested spirit: Inishmore, in fact, merely provides Longley here with images of peace and escape, a far point on a mental horizon. In this, Longley is closer to MacNeice's West, or to the numerous points of no return to which Derek Mahon's poetry returns obsessively. The change in Longley's angle of approach informs his verse-letter, 'To Derek Mahon', which recalls a trip to Inisheer:

> That was Good Friday years ago—
> How persistent the undertow
> Slapped by curraghs ferrying stones,
> Moonlight glossing the confusions
> Of its each bilingual wave—yes,
> We would have lingered there for less...
> Six islanders for a ten-bob note
> Rowed us out to the anchored boat.[33]

Once the 'anchored boat' has been left for actual contact with the island, for 'confusions' rather than the 'perfect standstill' of 'Leaving Inishmore', the self-centred perspective is no longer adequate. The poem carries its own 'undertow' of reference which partly

---

[32] Ibid. 54.   [33] Ibid. 83.

explains the lack of integration with the island, 'Our ears receiving then and there / The stereophonic nightmare / Of the Shankhill and the Falls'. The bringing together of homes is threatened by the hostility of one place and its concerns to those of another: the poem understands that there are no easy escapes to be made from this situation.

Of course, the point of intersection between Longley's different homes is bound in part to be a violent one; it is also, however, one coloured by intimacy and love. What Longley brings to the West from 'home' is 'My children and my dead', love and grief that expand from their customary locations within the family out into a larger society. 'In Mayo' is a love poem in which the significance of the visiting lovers for the district is weighed up:

> Though the townland's all ears, all eyes
> To decipher our movements, she and I
> Appear on the scene at the oddest times:
> We follow the footprints of animals,
>
> Then vanish into the old wives' tales
> Leaving behind us landmarks to be named
> After our episodes, and the mushrooms
> That cluster where we happen to lie.[34]

Love is the act of most significance with which Longley, as visitor, associates himself: the ambition to enter folklore as 'landmarks' associated with love indicates the centrality of intimacy to the poet's self-projection. Similarly, in the poem 'On Mweelrea' the lovers find themselves absorbed in the landscape, finally perhaps becoming that landscape:

> Behind my eyelids I could just make out
> In a wash of blood and light and water
> Your body colouring the mountainside
> Like uncut poppies in the stubbly fields.[35]

Love poetry is in fact very close to the centre of Longley's concerns: in his writing, it expands to fill, not only the district, but the entire range of concerns the poet comprehends. As the most obvious kind of intimacy at work in the situation of the home, love seems to mark an area of the utterly private, and sexuality itself appears to be a realm which it is difficult for an 'outside world' to disturb.

[34] Longley, *Poems 1963–1983*, 118.   [35] Ibid. 178.

Nevertheless, Longley's love poetry is not an attempt to seal off a private sphere, any more than his location of it in a 'home from home' is without awareness of the ironies and liabilities that may be implicit there.

The large-scale pun involved in seeing the body as landscape is pervasive in Longley's work: it is less the land which is sexualized than the body which is landscaped. This landscape of the body is the scene of much of Longley's love poetry, and his work is distinctive in the degree to which it allows this place to be coloured by both delight and grief. The processes involved in both 'nature' and 'love' poetry are very similar in Longley, each necessitating a reverential exploration of new territory, and a consequent mingling of 'homes'. The difference between the human and the pastoral landscapes, however, involves the recognition of mortality. In 'Love Poem', from *Man Lying on a Wall*, Longley explores 'your magnetic lines, / Your longitudes, latitudes' in the hope of a complete absorption in the loved one, a total immersion, and loss, of the self. But the poem is in the conditional voice:

> If my ears could hear nothing
> But the noise of your body's
> Independent processes,
> Lungs, heartbeat, intestines,
> Then I would be lulled in sleep
> That soothes for a lifetime
> The scabby knees of boyhood,
> And alters the slow descent
> Of the scrotum towards death.[36]

The lover here becomes both enfolding landscape and enveloping mother, but the poem itself does not quite escape from the conditional voice in which it is cast. The balance which Longley achieves here does succeed in holding in equilibrium mortality and comfort, and acknowledging the relation between death and love. Like inanimate landscape, and the creatures that populate it, the lovers embody 'processes', elements in flux and on their way somewhere else. In 'Meniscus', from *The Echo Gate*, Longley observes the body as moisture:

> You are made out of water mostly, spittle, tears,
> And the blood that colours your cheek, red water.

[36] Ibid. 115.

> Even your ears are ripples, your knuckles, knees
> Damp stones that wear the meniscus like a skin.
> Your breasts condense and adhere, drops of water.[37]

Again, body and landscape are brought together, the mortality of
the one colouring, and being coloured by, the resilience of the other.

In achieving this balance in his love poetry, Longley often uses
images of breasts to combine associations of eroticism and the
maternal, both making sense within a context of mortality. Two
lines in MacNeice's early poem 'Mayfly' seem to have influenced
Longley profoundly here, and to have had a talismanic function in
his approach to love poetry: 'But when this summer is over let us
die together— / I want always to be near your breasts'.[38] In these
lines, which, Longley has claimed, 'disclose the nucleus of Louis
MacNeice's imagination',[39] there is already some blurring of the
line between lover and mother. A tiny poem, 'Couplet', in Longley's
The Ghost Orchid notes how 'When I was young I wrote that
flowers are very slow flames And you uncovered your breasts often
among my images';[40] and indeed, in 'No Continuing City', the poet
starts by contemplating 'My hands here, gentle, where her breasts
begin', and ends by welcoming the lover's arrival 'To eat and drink
me out of house and home'.[41] The injunction in 'The Linen Industry' to 'be shy of your breasts in the presence of death'[42] develops
beautifully from MacNeice's lines, reluctant to abandon the breasts
to mortality. The lover–mother combination in Longley's use of the
image is made explicit in 'Icon', from *Gorse Fires*, where the poet
'on the day my mother died' is 'protected' by the lover's 'shoulders
and hair':

> Your tears fell from the ceiling on to my face.
> I could not believe that when you came to die
> Your breasts would die too and go underground.[43]

Going underground, entering the landscape at a more intimate level
than the visitor, takes the lover literally into the world of nature

[37] Longley, *Poems 1963–1983*, 176.
[38] MacNeice, *Collected Poems*, 14.
[39] Introduction to *Louis MacNeice: Selected Poems* (London: Faber & Faber,
1988), xxii.
[40] *The Ghost Orchid*, 27.
[41] *Poems 1963–1983*, 34.
[42] Ibid. 179.
[43] *Gorse Fires*, 36.

poetry. Sometimes the tension between the two modes, the poetry of nature and that of love, can be felt in Longley's work, as in 'View', where the loved one threatens to slip away and become the shoreline:

> I have put my arms around her skeleton
> For fear that her forearms might unravel
> Like hawsers, ligaments stiffening to kelp
> That keeps ocean and boulders in their places,
> Weights on the heart, ballast for the ribcage...[44]

As in a great deal of Longley's love poetry, the setting and the subject are difficult to distinguish from one another. The 'view' in question is one of mortality at the same time as it is a more conventional 'view' of the landscape from 'the same cottage on every island'.

Love poetry deepens the tone of Longley's West by bringing to it the desires and griefs associated with 'home'. This is true of two different aspects of the process, the private, familial area of memory, and the public domain of history. Of course, these aspects of Longley's approach are often combined, but both are altered by their projection on to a 'home from home'. A short poem, entitled simply 'Love Poet', marks a point in Longley's work at which the whole enterprise of love poetry begins to assume a new darkness, as private and public tinges of mortality converge. The eight lines, which appear in a 'New Poems' section at the end of Longley's *Poems 1963–1983* mix the surreal and the quotidian:

> I make my peace with murderers.
> I lock pubic hair from victims
> In an airtight tin, mummify
> Angel feathers, tobacco shreds.
>
> All that survives my acid bath
> Is a solitary gall-stone
> Like a pebble out on mud flats
> Or the ghost of an avocado.[45]

The poet's role as preserver and custodian of things is strangely inflected here, and his voice becomes aligned, perhaps, with that of the 'murderers'—'my acid bath' allows this voice to be heard as either that of the murderer or of the victim. The love poet has become the ultimate maker of inventories and preserver of details,

---

[44] *Poems 1963–1983*, 187.   [45] Ibid. 193.

who has also seen too literally the skull beneath the skin (or at least
the stone within the avocado) in the process of his concentration.
The strong resonance of Longley's first line, 'I make my peace with
murderers', persists through his later writing, and perhaps comes
back again most powerfully in 'Ceasefire' from *The Ghost Orchid*,
but here its imaginative liabilities seem to be stressed. The stability
of the first-person voice is left uncertain, and this slight blurring of
identity makes both murderer and love poet parts of a problematically shifting 'I'. Both activities, murder and love poetry, have to do
with death.

The location of Longley's love poems, then, is unlikely to be a
very stable kind of home. Here again, Longley's principal resource
lies in the candour of the first-person voice he employs: a good deal
of autobiographical material is filtered through the poems, while
references outwards to points in more public history are always
particular rather than general. Whereas Longley's perspectives on
the West are almost always set outdoors, the poems relating to the
familial 'home' are domestic affairs, in which it is the house which
contains everything of significance. In 'The Linen Industry', the
'bleach-green' on which the lovers find themselves is in fact 'our
attic under the skylight', while in the elegy 'The Third Light' the
poet turns his parents' grave into a house:

> Where I kneel to marry you again,
> My elbows in darkness as I explore
> From my draughty attic your last bedroom.
> Then I vanish into the roof space.[46]

This sense of domestic space is always open to distortion in Longley's work, and can also be seen as restricting or limiting. In the
short poem 'The Lodger', a novel-writing lodger in the attic with
'the run of the house' 'occupies my mind as well', and threatens the
freedom of the family space:

> A hundred noons and sunsets
> As we lie here whispering,
> Careful not to curtail our lives
> Or change the names he has given us.[47]

Similarly, in 'Check-up' the self as a body becomes cramped and
closed, so that finally 'There's no such place as home'.[48] More

---

[46] Longley, *Poems 1963–1983*, 200.   [47] Ibid. 111.   [48] Ibid. 111.

distortion is evident in 'Second Sight', where Longley follows a
course back to his father's 'home' in London, another domestic
space which opens to include the Irish 'home', so that the poet's
grandmother would 'see right through me and the hallway / And
the miles of cloud and sky to Ireland'. In this poem, however, the
ability to see beyond 'home' is also a way of perceiving nightmare:

> Flanders began at the kitchen window—
> The mangle rusting in No Man's Land, gas
> Turning the antimacassars yellow
> When it blew the wrong way from the salient.[49]

'Home' both is and is not private in this respect: it is a place where
past and present are liable to fold into one another, and into which
death can enter. In the elegy for his father, 'In Memoriam', Longley
remembers how 'Death was a visitor who hung about / Strewing
the house with pills and bandages'.[50]

When the Troubles enter Longley's poetry, the dominant perspectives are domestic ones. In 'Wounds', the bus-conductor is 'shot
through the head / By a shivering boy who wandered in / Before
they could turn the television down / Or tidy away the supper
dishes'.[51] Similarly, 'The Civil Servant' (in the sequence 'Wreaths')
'was preparing an Ulster fry for breakfast / When someone walked
into the kitchen and shot him'.[52] Death's disruption of the domestic
space happens either violently, as here, or through more 'natural'
causes; Longley, however, sometimes attempts to bring these
together, as in the short 'Kindertotenlieder', where new lodgers
arrive to live 'unrestricted' in the family home:

> There can be no songs for dead children
> Near the crazy circle of explosions,
> The splintering tangent of the ricochet,
>
> No songs for the children who have become
> My unrestricted tenants, fingerprints
> Everywhere, teethmarks on this and that.[53]

The poem, like all of Longley's poems about the Troubles, refuses
to be a statement of anything, or indeed to make violence into a
narrative; what the poem achieves, on the other hand, is an
uncanny relocation of 'home', along with the associations of that

---

49 Ibid. 151.   50 Ibid. 49.   51 Ibid. 86.
52 Ibid. 148.   53 Ibid. 87.

idea, in a poetic imagination which is itself situated on the edge of 'the crazy circle of explosions'. Once again, it is necessary to emphasize that the poet is not setting out to evade issues that sometimes appear both pressing and clear, but is instead attempting to experience them in a different way, to let them sink in to the deepest level of personal concern at 'home'. Longley has expressed himself clearly on the issue of 'Troubles poetry' on several occasions, but the implications of his statements for his own poetry are perhaps more complex, since they involve bringing violence and catastrophe into the 'home' which the writing inhabits. Longley has written, for example, of how 'I find offensive the notion that what we inadequately call "the Troubles" might provide inspiration for artists; and that in some weird *quid pro quo* the arts might provide solace for grief and anguish',[54] and has spoken of how 'You have got to bring your personal sorrow to the public utterance', since otherwise 'you are in deadly danger of regarding the agony of others as raw material for your art', resulting in 'Atrocities of the mind'.[55] To bring material like that thrown up by the Troubles fully home to the imagination in poetry is a process fraught with difficulty for other poets besides Longley, of course; but he remains unusual in not having written *about* that difficulty, and not having made it seem, therefore, in some sense a dramatic resource. A statement Longley made in 1979 is important, not just for his own writing, but as a way of understanding (and perhaps evaluating) the ways other poets have dealt with the Troubles:

I would insist that poetry is a normal human activity, its proper concern all of the things that happen to people. Though the poet's first duty must be to his imagination, he has other obligations—and not just as a citizen. He would be inhuman if he did not respond to tragic events in his own community, and a poor artist if he did not seek to endorse that response imaginatively. But if his imagination fails him, the result will be a dangerous impertinence. In the context of political violence the deployment of words at their most precise and most suggestive remains one of the few antidotes to death-dealing dishonesty.[56]

The prominence given here to imagination is notable, and Longley's insistence on the need to make imagination central to an artistic

[54] *Tuppenny Stung*, 73.
[55] Interview with Dermot Healy, 560.
[56] *Tuppenny Stung*, 73–4; the statement was made on the occasion of the Poetry Book Society's choice of his collection *The Echo Gate* in 1979.

response is unambiguous. This puts the apparent surrealism of poems like 'The Linen Workers' in context, perhaps, but it also indicates just how completely Longley demands that the individual poetic imagination should accommodate the hard matter of the Troubles. 'Words at their most precise' remains the only general strategy here, one that challenges a reciprocal attentiveness and subtlety from the reader.

The pastoral side of Longley's writing does not exist in isolation from violent disruptions, any more than his love poetry isolates itself from the burden of mortality. The poet does not set out to establish some kind of equivalence between one 'home' and the other, but he does allow the violence of one to shadow the peace of the other. A sequence of short poems in *The Echo Gate*, 'Lore', straightforwardly records items of practical wisdom from the countryside, but certain images recur within the sequence: those of binding and tying, of cutting and bleeding, and finally of healing. Gauging the resonance of the final section, 'Finding a Remedy', is an extremely delicate business:

> Sprinkle the dust from a mushroom or chew
> The white end of a rush, apply the juice
> From fern roots, stems of burdock, dandelions,
>
> Then cover the wound with cuckoo-sorrel
> Or sphagnum moss, bringing together verse
> And herb, plant and prayer to stop the bleeding.[57]

The precision involved in the act of naming here is coming close to the more subtle sense of invocation and charm; no further meaning need be assigned than that which is already provided in the title, but 'Lore', like many of Longley's poems, seems to gesture towards an unspoken relation between its subject and the unvoiced injuries comprehended at home. Naming, once again, is the soothing act, one which cannot be dramatized or overstated. 'The Greengrocer' (in the sequence 'Wreaths') provides an example of naming, or listing, giving the poet a voice which can remain uninfected by rhetoric in addressing violence:

> Astrologers or three wise men
> Who may shortly be setting out
> For a small house up the Shankhill

[57] *Poems 1963–1983*, 158–9.

> Or the Falls, should pause on their way
> To buy gifts at Jim Gibson's shop,
> Dates and chestnuts and tangerines.[58]

The focus on the particular at the end of this poem is the very opposite of frivolous; it ensures the maintenance of Longley's characteristic *gravitas*, which is essentially the seriousness of a complete imaginative fidelity to the immediate. The nouns are meant to soothe, though they cannot (and do not) pretend to console. The *tour de force* of botanical listing which concludes 'The Ice-Cream Man', and the unspoken compassion that prompts this oblique angle, show Longley's style adopting a delicacy which seems to resist the formulas of explanation or consolation. The fundamental respect for the particular in Longley's poetry is a legacy of his 'home from home', since it is in his poems about the west of Ireland where it develops, and where the demands it makes on a descriptive voice and vocabulary are first met; it is here that the poet learns to name things, and to give them the right names, not with any ulterior motive ('name the fields for them'), but as the work of humility and love. One instance of this can be seen in the sequence of short verse-units that makes up the poem 'Ghetto' in *Gorse Fires*, with its imaginative reception of the raw data of disaster, and its fidelity to the precision of lists (including at one point a list of potato varieties) in the light of its subject-matter's ultimate and terrible lists ('Your last belonging a list of your belongings').[59] Another instance occurs in the short poem 'The Fishing Party', where resistance to 'Atrocities of the mind' means that Longley's attention must focus on the individual peculiarities of fly-fishing and insect life when accommodating in the imagination the kind of killings which seem to be utterly at odds with the pastoral calm suggested by the poem's setting. The image of Christ 'walking on the waters of Lough Neagh' glances back at the Christ whose 'teeth ascended with him into Heaven' at the beginning of 'The Linen Workers', but is now developed to show a creator of insects (several of which Longley lists), and, like fishermen, of artificial insects:

> Until about his head swarm artificial flies and their names,
> Dark Mackerel, Gravel Bed, Greenwell's Glory, Soldier
> Palmer, Coachman, Water Cricket, Orange Grouse, Barm,

[58] Longley, *Poems 1963–1983*, 148.   [59] *Gorse Fires*, 40.

Without snagging in his hair or ceasing to circle above
Policemen turned by gunmen into fishermen for ever.[60]

The poem is one of the most extreme examples in Longley's work of
the parallel development of symbolic imagination and literal fidelity. Although the poem's religious overtones are atypical, its conjunction of violent death with a kind of particularity and precision
so pronounced and prolonged as almost to stop the lyric in its
tracks is in keeping with tendencies visible in much of his earlier
poetry.

There remains a sense in which the scope of 'home' within the
confines of the lyric poem, even given the special pressures exerted
on Northern Irish poetry by both violence and the cultural and
political expectations generated by violence, is inevitably limited.
Longley's writing, in his three volumes of the 1970s, goes perhaps
as far as is possible in complicating 'home' for lyric poetry in the
first person, without giving in to pressures which would force the
poet to dramatize his own difficulties and hesitations in the face of
disaster. It may be indicative of a certain increase in reticence that
Longley's dedicatory verse to *The Echo Gate* (addressed to Michael
Allen and Paul Muldoon) looks towards a place of complete
absence, a holiday spot so remote that it will remain perpetually
unvisited:

> I have heard of an island
> With only one house on it.
> The gulls are at home there.
> Our perpetual absence
> Is a way of leaving
> All the eggs unbroken
> That litter the ground
> Right up to its doorstep.[61]

The 'Disappearance around corners' of 1973 has become here an
idea of 'perpetual absence', and the preservation of fragile things is
now to be achieved by staying away from them, allowing them to
live on in the imagination (and undisturbed actuality) alone. Perhaps the difficulties that contribute to Longley's comparative poetic
silence in the 1980s are detectable here; the poem's miniature scale
leaves room for very little in the way of argument, but its success as
a lyric depends partly on that very constriction, for imagining the

[60] *The Ghost Orchid*, 42.   [61] *Poems 1963–1983*, 143.

place where 'the gulls are at home' entails an answering delicacy of
form which will frame satisfactorily the kind of ultimate reticence
Longley is suggesting. By this point, Longley's sense of place in lyric
poetry has become so refined (and so acutely aware of its contextual liabilities) as to be in formal terms a sense of reticence,
restraint, and silence.

In an interview at the time of the publication of his *Poems 1963–
1983*, Longley reflected on the fact that he had written 'practically
nothing for the last three years', and mentioned tentatively his sense
of having come up against an impasse of sorts:

> It may have something to do—and this is an intuitive, mysterious thing—
> with the feeling I had when I was putting the four books together with the
> little coda of new poems, that I'd come full circle, that there's some kind of
> formal impasse and that I've got to break out of the circle that I've care-
> fully, over 20 years, inscribed around myself.... In a religious sense I
> believe that my present silence is part of the impulse and sooner silence
> than forgery.[62]

It was to be another six years before the publication of *Gorse Fires*.
The question of how far Longley's protracted silence can, indeed,
be understood as a 'part of the impulse' of his poetry is a complex
one, but its implications for the reception of other poets from
Northern Ireland may be considerable, since the whole 'impulse'
of Longley's work touches on the conditions of poetry, and poetry's
subject-matter, which the poets have in common. In an original and
perceptive study of Longley's early poetry, Michael Allen has noted
the significance of another break in the compositional history of the
writing, from 1968 until 1970, a period after which changes at
deep rhythmic and stylistic levels begin to make themselves felt in
the poems.[63] The breaking of the later, and longer, silence which is
represented by *Gorse Fires* marks a significant shift in Longley's
dealings with 'home', and at the same time the opening up of his
lyrics to elements of narrative epic, in translations from Homer.
Including in the volume seven poems drawn from passages in the
Odyssey, Longley finds in the narrative of Odysseus' return to his
home in Ithaca the new element which is needed to enlarge and

[62] Interview with Robert Johnstone, *The Honest Ulsterman*, 78 (Summer 1985),
27.
[63] See Michael Allen, 'Rhythm and Development in Michael Longley's Earlier
Poetry', in Andrews (ed.), *Contemporary Irish Poetry*, 214–34.

confirm his own imaginative involvement with different kinds of
home ground. At the same time, the (generally very short) poems
set in the west of Ireland 'home from home' gain a confidence in
their own procedures and idiosyncrasies which is (arguably) missing from earlier poems; it is as though Longley no longer needs to
explain himself in quite the ways which were necessary earlier on.
(Indeed, there may be some question of overconfidence in the
achieved voice by the time of *The Ghost Orchid*, where poems
occasionally risk bathos when Longley's voice makes itself too
readily at home in perilous registers and subjects.) The transposition of 'home' in *Gorse Fires* through the matter of translation,
however, was what enabled the more confident, and expansive,
poetic voice to emerge; it is the emergence of what one might
almost call a distinctive poetic identity.

The figure of Odysseus had been waiting to return in Longley's
writing for some time. *No Continuing City* gestures frequently
towards this literary or mythic paradigm of home and homeless-
ness, as the Homeric figure wanders at sea in his attempts to return
to Ithaca. The poems 'Odyssey' and 'Circe' both concentrate on the
erotic element of these wanderings, 'all new areas / Of experience'.
The imagery here, of islands and shores, of love and landscape,
prefigures that of much of the poet's later work. Odysseus comes
bringing both his 'home' and his 'dead' along:

> And, going out of my way to take a rest,
> From sea sickness and the sea recuperate,
> The sad fleets of capsized skulls behind me
> And the wide garden they decorate.[64]

Each of Odysseus' 'Ladies' represents only a temporary stop on his
journey, though each might also be in her own way significant,
'Your faces favourite landmarks always, / Your bodies comprising
the long way home.' Circe, one of their number, in her turn expects
'Out of the night, husband after husband'.[65] In fact, Odysseus'
wanderings represent a series of quasi-familial relationships that
foreshadow the real thing, his return to his actual wife Penelope in
Ithaca. Throughout *No Continuing City*, Longley uses the sea as a
place of chance encounter and exile: the 'ocean icebound when the
year is hurt' in 'Leaving Inishmore' is part of 'the curriculum / Vitae

---

[64] *Poems 1963–1983*, 30–1.   [65] Ibid. 32.

of sailors and the sick at heart'.[66] The long and formally elaborate poem 'The Hebrides' negotiates a course between dizzying land-scapes and a sense of identity, 'My journey back from flux to poise, from poise / To attitude'. This journey, in a poem locked into tight verse-form almost as if testing its own resources of determination, carries further overtones of Odysseus' voyage:

> For these are my sailors, these my drowned—
> In their heart of hearts,
> In their city I ran aground.
> Along my arteries
> Sluice those homewaters petroleum hurts,
> Dry dock, gantries.[67]

There is the suggestion here that all is not well in 'homewaters' which could be close to Belfast Lough as well as Ithaca.

In *Gorse Fires* Longley revisits the odyssey motifs of his first book, this time in a series of translations from Homer, in which episodes in the actual homecoming of Odysseus are rendered into free-standing lyrics using long lines. The hero's return is inter-preted by Longley primarily as a return to the family, to his father and his nurse, as well as to a waiting wife; but it is also, of course, a return for revenge upon the suitors and unfaithful servants. These versions of passages from the *Odyssey* mark a deepened sense of 'home' as a place of both reunited family and the most brutal horror. Again, the moments of reconciliation are made points of lyrical intensity; Longley's translations approach Homer in search of such moments, cutting away as much as possible of the broader narrative context. Odysseus encounters his father, in the poem 'Laertes', in 'a goatskin duncher', 'So old and pathetic that all he wanted then and there / Was to kiss him and hug him and blurt out the whole story'. The moment of recognition comes like a gift cast up from the sea:

> Until Laertes recognised his son and, weak at the knees,
> Dizzy, flung his arms around the neck of great Odysseus
> Who drew the old man fainting to his breast and held him there
> And cradled like driftwood the bones of his dwindling father.[68]

In the context of the concerns of much of Longley's writing, this episode takes on a personal charge as a father, who has always been

[66] Longley, *Poems 1963–1983*, 54.   [67] Ibid. 41.   [68] *Gorse Fires*, 33.

'buried' in Longley's poems, is allowed to meet his returning son. And yet, in this reading, one might want to know what 'the whole story' is, and where Longley (as opposed to Odysseus) is returning to. Writing about 'The Linen Workers', Michael Allen has seen 'Longley's grotesquely awakened father...sitting up, determined to see out the Ulster Troubles',[69] and this degree of overlap between the Homeric material and Longley's autobiographical motifs is important in establishing the complex resonances of Odysseus' homecoming. The material in the *Odyssey* comes to Longley with a difficult undertow of both content and associations: Odysseus' emotional reunions with his family are part of a narrative in which he (along with his son) will engage in wholesale slaughter of suitors and servants; Longley's heightenings of episodes in this story bring him to areas of his own family history which seem charged with some pain, and aspects of more public experience in Northern Ireland which remain sorrowfully intense. 'The Butchers', with which Longley concludes *Gorse Fires*, does not flinch from the details of the massacre in its translation:

> Odysseus, spattered with muck and like a lion dripping blood
> From his chest and cheeks after devouring a farmer's bullock,
> Ordered the disloyal housemaids to sponge down the armchairs
> And tables, while Telemachos, the oxherd and the swineherd
> Scraped the floor with shovels, and then between the portico
> And the roundhouse stretched a hawser and hanged the women
> So none touched the ground with her toes, like long-winged thrushes
> Or doves trapped in a mist-net across the thicket where they roost,
> Their heads bobbing in a row, their feet twitching but not for long...[70]

This stays close to Homer—the similes are his—but Longley is still able to 'use words at their most precise and suggestive' by declining (beyond his title, 'The Butchers') to summon any specific parallels. As in many of the Homer versions, the translator is notable for his absence—his 'Disappearance around corners' perhaps. Moments of direct contact with Longley's biography are few, but the poems read, nevertheless, with the intense charge of any first-person lyric. At one point of direct crossover, in the meeting with Eurycleia, Odysseus' nurse, Longley draws a parallel with his own childhood nurse and 'surrogate mother' who features prominently in the

---

[69] 'Rhythm and Development in Michael Longley's Earlier Poetry', 216.
[70] *Gorse Fires*, 51.

memoir 'Tuppenny Stung'. There, 'I began by loving the wrong woman',[71] and in the version of Homer:

> I began like Odysseus by loving the wrong woman
> Who has disappeared among the skyscrapers of New York
> After wandering for thousands of years from Ithaca.[72]

This rare note of explicit identification is sounded in a more subdued way in the translations from the *Odyssey* of *The Ghost Orchid*, where the figure of Odysseus appears in a gentler mode, either foreseeing his own death ('The Oar'), or preparing for sleep, ('A Bed of Leaves'). Here, Odysseus' ability to make himself a home from home is celebrated, and Longley's similes (while again they are Homer's) seem to look across to much of his own poetry, and its guarded sense of isolation:

> As when a lonely man on a lonely farm smoors the fire
> And hides a turf-sod in the ashes to save an ember,
> So was his body in the bed of leaves its own kindling
> And sleep settled on him like ashes and closed his eyelids.[73]

An identification with Odysseus is, as Longley knows, an identification with a figure who is (in the Greek) *polymetis*, able to turn his hand to anything, a master of disguise and dissembling, a changer of identities who retains, despite it all, an unrelenting sense of purpose in his determination to come home. As Louis MacNeice's 'Day of Returning' (chosen by Longley for inclusion in his 1988 selection of MacNeice) puts it:

> But even so, he said, daily I hanker, daily
> Ache to get back to my home, to see my day of returning
> After those years of violent action—and these of inaction.[74]

Such an identification, and such a 'home', are far from simple matters.

In breaking the silence of the 1980s, Longley's new work broke out of a constraining context in which expectations of both 'voice' and 'place' were continuing to exert pressure on the individual poet. The translations, and the emphasis on extraordinary feats of sentence-control and the pacing of verse, all go to make *Gorse Fires*

---

[71] *Tuppenny Stung*, 15.
[72] *Gorse Fires*, 31.
[73] *The Ghost Orchid*, 33.
[74] MacNeice, *Collected Poems*, 315; *Selected Poems*, ed. Michael Longley, 117.

and *The Ghost Orchid* volumes with form in the foreground; they might well be seen as putting into practice a kind of classicism. Bernard O'Donoghue, comparing Longley with Heaney, contrasts Heaney's ability to learn from a 'freestyle poetic' to 'the classicism (which can seem unbending) of his most distinguished Northern contemporaries, Mahon and Longley'.[75] Leaving Mahon aside, the notion of Longley's classicism as 'unbending' is off the mark; it expects that something will give, that 'classicism' is a technique to be bent to a poet's purposes. Longley's work does something quite different from this. John Lyon has written of 'Longley the classicist often finding his own voice by inhabiting the voices of others', and noted how the 'wonderful, politically reticent Homeric poems... modestly establish a creative space at some distance from Longley's own immediate political or historical moment'.[76] The nature of the 'creative space' opened by Longley's classicism is important: what is *not* there is, in a literal sense in the Homeric poems, the poet's first-person identity; it is also, in a broader sense, the whole con-textually shadowed matter of 'identity' in Northern Irish poetry. Instead, Longley uses the 'space' to develop an independent voice, one which combines openness to the particular and the actual with a determined commitment to the imagination and its separateness. As Lyon goes on to phrase this (in its 'political' application), 'Longley knows that poetry is never mere politics, nor is poetry merely apart from politics'.[77] An understanding of Longley's 'space' entails some critical imagination of the spaces around, apart from, or overlooking the given sites of the 'political'; by the same token, it necessitates an effort to think one's way around ideas like 'home' and 'identity'.

The delicacy and apparent fragility of Longley's poetry are not, therefore, signs of self-marginalizing ambition: its miniatures are not minor things, but in their way formidable challenges to a number of assumptions about what constitutes substantial poetry. Poetry's substance, for Longley, always sets the agenda, and this means that notions of what poetry *should* be doing (or meaning) are always liable to be disappointed or undermined. The achieved poetic voice, therefore, has no real need to look for an identity, or

[75] *Seamus Heaney and the Language of Poetry* (Hemel Hempstead: Harvester Wheatsheaf, 1994), 118.
[76] 'Michael Longley's Lists', 236,232.
[77] Ibid. 233.

offer it for mass consumption, since its business is somewhere else entirely. The eight lines of 'Birdsong' provide a beautifully resonant instance of this happening in a poem. Longley's subject is 'a very old (Scottish) relative who suffers from Alzheimer's disease',[78] and the poem is able to imagine this loss of identity by offering lucidities of its own:

> 'Where am I?' Consulting the *Modern School Atlas*
> You underline Dalkey in Ireland, in Scotland Barrhead.
> 'What day is it?' Outside the home, house-sparrows
> With precision tweetle and wheep under the eaves.
>
> Although you forget their names, you hear the birds
> In your own accent, the dawn chitter, evening chirl,
> The woodpigeon's rooketty-coo and curdoo. 'Who
> Am I? Where am I?' is what a bird might sing.[79]

The poem's language draws its own map of Ireland and Scotland, and the birdsong modulates into questions like 'Who / Am I?' with extraordinary effect. In this place (a 'home' in one sombrely accurate sense) places blur, and identity resolves itself into richly mimetic language; the delicacy of the whole, and its precision that answers to that of the 'house-sparrows', do something original to place and identity, and happen within a poetic space which has no pressing interpretations to urge. Questions like 'Who / Am I?' and 'Where am I?' sound often in the various 'homes' Longley has projected, and do so with a terrible insistence in the Irish rhetoric of 'home'; the eight lines of 'Birdsong' change such questions in a permanently valuable way. As usual in Longley's best work, even the hard words are at their most suggestive when they are at their most precise.

---

[78] Michael Longley, in a letter to the *London Review of Books*, 7 Sept. 1995, 4.
[79] *The Ghost Orchid*, 51.

6

Paul Muldoon and the Windlass-Men

> ...none will,
> I trust, look for a pattern in this crazy quilt
> where all is random, 'all so trivial',
>
> unless it be Erasmus, unless
> Erasmus again steel
> himself as his viscera are cranked out by a windlass
>
> yard upon 'xanthous' yard;
> again to steel himself, then somehow to exhort
> the windlass-men to even greater zeal.
>
> (Paul Muldoon, *The Prince of the Quotidian*)

I

The centrality of form to poetry, from the point of view of a critic, is always shadowed by its potential for apparent critical triviality. For the writing poet, on the other hand, the matter of formal constraint seems overwhelmingly serious; a rhyme missed, like a fluffed cadence or a clumsy repetition, looms much larger than a line's critical 'meaning' in the process of composition. Yet for a critic only to analyse poems at this level would be, eventually, tedious beyond bearing, and would also deny readers access to much of what we understand by interpretation. Although we often choose not to ask ourselves the question of how important it is, the significance of poetic form in interpretation is central to what readers and critics do with poetry.

However, any discussion of form in poetry tends to be waylaid by ironies before it can properly begin: in the first place, critical pondering over 'form' is already employing a metaphor to describe—in abstract terms—a phenomenon (or, rather, a condition) of being a poem; and a poem is something which, whatever else might be said about it, is not an abstract thing. Some awareness of such liabilities might issue in difficult questions: does a poem *have* a form, for example, or *is* every poem a form in (or unto) itself? And there are further problems: critical language about poetic form—even at theoretically 'formalist' extremes—cannot be *purposelessly* descriptive, and mapping operations will not persist long without some evaluative function, however obscurely expressed. More awkwardly still, the kinds of literary criticism which set out to tell the reader something about a poem—or a poet—cannot afford to engage with form much beyond the point where it delivers up the necessary material for the interpretation being advanced: what a critic has to say about the form of a poem is generally (and perhaps inevitably) in the nature of an illustration of his or her argument. In this sense, strictly, we are all bad critics and bad readers, for we understand (and produce) interpretations of poems in which form has a subordinate, illustrative function—in which, as it were, form is processed as critical information. Merely acknowledging that this is the case does not go far towards amending matters (though to whom, or to what, might amends in fact be made here?). Beyond the point at which form—in itself—ceases to serve the needs of our interpretation, does it become, in some ways, a gratuitous phenomenon? And is 'gratuitous' to mean here something perversely excessive, or the unexpected, unlooked-for gift? At its best, perhaps, criticism of poetry registers the intellectual discomfort that arises with respect to form, and takes the measure of its own, necessarily metaphorical, dealings with the complex actual structures of its subjects.

Where demand on the 'content' of poetry is particularly pressing, 'form' is likely to be neglected altogether—or at least to be regarded as simply a mould into which a poem's interpretable meaning is poured. It is easy and conventional enough to say that this is a fallacy, but again such admissions have to work hard to become something other than token gestures in critical practice. The fallacy is one which is both persistent and attractive, especially in relation to poetry from Northern Ireland, where 'content' (like 'meaning') crosses over with such apparent immediacy to newsworthy and shallowly 'relevant' aspects of the poetry's contextual situation. In the light of this, the four lines of Michael Longley's poem 'Form',

with which he opens *The Ghost Orchid*, offer an important complication:

> Trying to tell it all to you and cover everything
> Is like awakening from its grassy form the hare:
> In that make-shift shelter your hand, then my hand
> Mislays the hare and the warmth it leaves behind.[1]

Longley (who is alluding to Yeats's 'Because the mountain grass /
Cannot but keep the form / Where the mountain hare has lain'[2])
makes use of a precise meaning of 'form' (*OED*, *sb* 21a., 'The nest
or lair in which a hare crouches') in order to suggest a pun in the
poem's title, though no more than this. Just as Longley's poem does
not quite make the pun whose possibility it raises (a pun on what
the *OED* calls—with inevitable imprecision—'Style of expressing
the thoughts and ideas in literary or musical composition, including the arrangement and order of the different parts of the
whole' (*sb*. 9)), so it takes the measure of something absent in a
suggestive—though actually an unoccupied—shape. The distance
between poem and title is uncertain, and a lot depends on how the
word 'its' in the second line is voiced (stressing the word brings the
title back, for a moment, into the poem—*its* 'form', and not that
other 'Form'). Nevertheless, 'Form' remains a poem in which an
awareness of what has escaped conditions the very attempt to 'tell
it all to you and cover everything'. The effort to 'cover' itself
undergoes a change in nuance, and a more immediately human
kind of covering follows, as two hands explore the hare's 'make-
shift shelter', feeling out the contours of what is no longer there.
The poem's delicacy is betrayed by the proposition that Longley is
making a point of 'content''s necessarily uncatchable relation to
'form': like other poems in *The Ghost Orchid*, 'Form' possesses a
fragility which is, in part, defensive. At the same time, Longley is
registering in these four lines an awareness both that what poems
say is inextricable from how their language disposes itself, and that
the very attempt to 'cover it all' on such issues is always (so to
speak) behindhand in its relation to the way poems work.

Despite its originality, Longley's short poem shows signs of
indebtedness beyond the Yeatsian allusion: both the profusion of
hands, and the single, muted rhyme of 'behind'/'hand' indicate that

---

[1] *The Ghost Orchid* (London: Jonathan Cape, 1995), 1.
[2] 'Memory', *Collected Poems* (London: Macmillan, 1950), 168.

Longley has, like many other poets, been able to learn from the example of Paul Muldoon, in whose work such casually deployed felicities (and imagery) abound. It may be that at another level 'Form' engages with the kind of pressures and conditions which Muldoon's poetry has both encountered and generated: the demand for 'content' in poetry that comes from the Troubles, and the insistence on poetic form as something with its own sometimes inscrutable rules; most of all, perhaps, the primacy and unpredictability of language and chance in the workings and designs of poems. Muldoon's writing (especially his poetry since *Meeting the British* (1987)) has brought these areas of critical discomfort into increasingly sharp focus, and it should be no surprise that poets like Longley, whose own work has encountered similarly difficult expectations, might profit from Muldoon's strategic example.

Muldoon's poetry begins by courting the interpretations it will finally reject, and the issue of form has been brought into his work in this spirit. One aspect of Muldoon's attitude to his own writing has always been to equate its artificiality with a degree of impersonality: thus, in interviews and other such statements, the poet is often concerned to distance himself from the first-person personas of his poetry. In maintaining that 'I've no sense of what a poem by this person Paul Muldoon might be like', there has often been a strong element of ironic humour which has led the poet to point out how formal aspects of his writing can be 'a debunking thing... playful in their comments on their own procedures':

But that isn't the main point, it's just a little part of what I was trying to do. Of course I sometimes make little jokes and I do, quite often, engage in leading people on, gently, into little situations by assuring them that all's well and then—this sounds awfully manipulative, but part of writing is about manipulation—leaving them high and dry, in some corner at a terrible party, where I've nipped out through the bathroom window.[3]

The elusiveness of an authorial identity pervades Muldoon's writing, and it has become more and more associated with the impersonal constraints of form. Indeed, Muldoon's enormous poetic narrative of 1990, 'Madoc: A Mystery' is a work of complex and precise—though arcane—systems of formal arrangement; before this, and especially in *Quoof* (1983), the profusion of

---

[3] Interview with Clair Wills, Nick Jenkins, and John Lanchester, *Oxford Poetry*, 3/1 (Winter 1986/7), 19.

sonnets (or, at least, fourteen-line poems and verse-units) had given Muldoon's writing an air of formal rigour; more recently, in the long poem 'Yarrow', there are 149 sections, and Muldoon's comments on the formal arrangement strike a characteristically detached and humorous note: 'I wonder how useful it is for me to describe the poem as "a series of twelve intercut, exploded sestinas"? Not too useful, I suspect, more likely to clear a room than anything else.'[4] But as well as this there is Muldoon's declaration that 'I'm interested in formal challenges that coincide with challenges of content',[5] and these 'formal challenges' go to the heart of the poet's work. They also, increasingly, constitute challenges for the reader, who is left to interpret, or make the best of, their gratuitous workings in the poems themselves.

Poetic form does something to a poet's 'identity' (and, it may be, form does something *for* that identity in the process); the constant changing of one thing by the terms of its expression in something other—a poet, after all, is not the same thing as a poem—presents those in search of stable patterns of poetic meaning and blueprints for identity in poetry with considerable problems. In Muldoon's case, the elusiveness of the authorial identity is implicated deeply with the continual bringing to the surface of questions of form. One, ideal, extreme is that at which the authorial self vanishes altogether in the poem's perfect formal system. In 'Toxophilus', an uncollected poem of 1984, Muldoon dwells on the art of archery as a possible instance of this kind of achieved formalism:

> 'The right art', the Master told Herrigel,
> 'is purposeless, aimless.
> The shot must fall from the archer
> like snow from a bamboo leaf.
> *It* shoots. *It* hits.
> At last the bowstring has cut through you.'[6]

Here art not so much transcends the artist as obliterates him, effecting its own version of T. S. Eliot's 'extinction of personality' as if it were a force of nature. Yet this vanishing-point of artistic will and identity may be illusory: Muldoon frames the anecdote

<hr>

[4] 'Between Ireland and Montevideo', the first Waterstones Lecture, delivered on 29 May 1994 at the Hay-on-Wye Festival of Literature, in typescript.
[5] Interview with Lynn Keller, *Contemporary Literature*, 35/1 (Spring 1994), 15.
[6] 'Toxophilus', *Times Literary Supplement*, 10 Feb. 1984, 137.

with two others, the first of which features someone who 'ended as a wet-job / on a Third-Avenue sidewalk' as a result of selling 'a "state of the art" / micro-chip / to the Japanese', and the second of which ends the poem with a portrait of lovers who 'set each other up as statues / to Eros, see, and Aphrodite'. In both cases, whether as a result of 'a teeny-weeny poison dart' or of Cupid's arrows, human agency and decision are involved, producing both actual harm and apparently harmless fantasy. Framed in this way, the Master's advice on 'the right art' seems slightly evasive in its mysticism ('*It* shoots. *It* hits' is not an argument which will stand up in court, after all), and the attractiveness of the ideal submission to formal discipline is undercut, or complicated, by the continuing contingencies of wilfulness and accident. Nevertheless, the point at which 'the bowstring has cut through you' is a significant one in Muldoon's writing, and gestures towards (though it cannot, of course, actually achieve) an ideal abandoning of identity.

At another pole, however, Muldoon's poetry is drawn towards the autobiographical, with numerous poems mapping the territory of childhood and adolescence in County Armagh, and many others referring with apparent accuracy to the adult poet's career, relationships, and places of residence. Here, the Muldoon of the interviews is constantly at pains to remark on his own distance from the material: he has spoken of even a poem like 'The Soap-Pig' in terms which leave room for its artificiality, and has qualified a remark on 'the first poems to have something of "me" in them' with the observation that 'I hesitate to say "of me" because I don't know if "I" exist'.[7] In speaking about his own poetry, Muldoon's characteristic position is that of 'just another reader', one subject to (or, indeed, able to benefit from) a reader's occasional sense of bafflement. The first-person poetry is often teasingly intimate with the life of Paul Muldoon, but this is a matter of holding back as much as revealing the nature of such intimacy. The 'Gypsy' (Rose-Lee) of '7, Middagh Street' expresses this on the level of showbiz know-how:

> I've no time for any of that unladylike stuff.
> An off-the-shoulder shoulder-strap,

   [7] Interview with Kevin Smith, *Gown Literary Supplement* (1984), [4]; on 'The Soap-Pig', see Muldoon's interview with Kevin Smith, *Rhinoceros*, 4 (n.d. [1991]), 85.

> the removal of one glove—
> it's knowing exactly when to stop
> that matters,
> what to hold back, some sweet disorder...
> The same goes for the world of letters.[8]

A continually changing distinction between the dancer and the dance remains a distinction, and Muldoon's poetry also maintains a distance between its apparent confidences and the formal matrices within which they are expressed. When Muldoon's voice seems to be at its most frank or confiding, it is also likely to be engaged in a ramifying series of formal moves: in the most immediate sense, these concern the particular paths of connection between words and phrases opened up by rhyme, while larger patterns of interconnection—of words, references, or images—are also made between the particular poem and other poems in its volume. Thus, for example, in 'Aisling' Muldoon concludes a poem which has featured goddesses alongside hunger-strikers with a first-person visit to a hospital:

> A lick and a promise. Cuckoo-spittle.
> I hand my sample to Doctor Maw.
> She gives me back a confident *All Clear.*[9]

The effect of this as a coda is disarming, for it raises questions which the poem does not make it its business to answer: why is the speaker in a hospital? Is this the same hospital (Belfast's Royal Victoria) in which 'the latest hunger-striker' has just 'called off his fast'? Why Doctor *Maw*? As it happens, there is a Belfast consultant called Maw, but this is a man, not a woman: Muldoon's decision (if that is what it is) to alter the gender here links the doctor with the various goddesses earlier in the poem ('Was she Aurora, or the goddess Flora, / Artemidora, or Venus bright, / or Anorexia'), while the name itself, and the line that follows it, rhymes with a couplet eleven lines earlier ('Her eyes spoke of a sloe-year, / her mouth a year of haws'). Prospects of autobiographical content become even more far-fetched as an echo of 'Maw' makes itself felt, this time from the first poem in the volume, 'Gathering Mushrooms':

---

[8] *Meeting the British* (London: Faber & Faber, 1987), 44.
[9] *Quoof* (London: Faber & Faber, 1983), 39.

And you were suddenly out of my ken, hurtling
towards the ever-receding ground,
into the maw
of a shimmering, green-gold dragon.[10]

The reference back is to a moment of loss of identity (mushroom-induced, this time), and it brings to bear on the autobiographical-feeling material a sense of impersonal design, and of associations made (and made possible by being) beyond the scope of the self's factual experiences. In Muldoon's writing, then, the loss or abandonment of identity in the formal game of art tends to be shown as itself an illusion; by the same token, the presentation of personal identity is generally exposed as artifice, cut through and transformed by its formal constraint and occasion.

There are consequences here for the larger arguments about poetry's capacity to distil and contain a sense of identity, and in particular for the Northern Irish inflections of these arguments. To read Muldoon with a sense of his 'formal challenge' is to allow for the possibility that the poetry, instead of discovering, cultivating, or triumphantly proclaiming a certain kind of identity, will make notions of identity (whether personal, local, or national) much more difficult to imagine. Especially in his work since *Madoc* (1990), Muldoon has allowed formal patterns to become more pronounced, and their bearing on the poetry's 'meaning' to become increasingly problematic.

II

Muldoon's short book of 1994, *The Prince of the Quotidian*, makes a point out of something which has been inherent in much of his poetry from the beginning: the quotidian, the unpredictably various data from 'everyday' experience, has always been subject to imperious heightening in the poems, so that (for example) the Moy and its environs have become charged, in sometimes apparently random detail, with powerful significance. For *The Prince of the Quotidian* Muldoon embarked on an especially gratuitous course, resolving (in the words of the book's jacket note) 'in the New Year, 1992, to write a poem each day', producing a "January journal"'. The nod in the

[10] Muldoon, *Quoof*, 8.

direction of MacNeice's *Autumn Journal* perhaps marks the literary provenance of even the most clearly autobiographical material contained in the book's short poems, but *The Prince of the Quotidian*, like 'Incantata' and 'Yarrow' in Muldoon's major volume of 1994, *The Annals of Chile*, is nevertheless unusually direct in its use of first-person material. Treated with due caution, the 'journal' might provide Muldoon's readers with a record of certain pressures and preoccupations important for a sensitive reading of his work.

Of course, the 'record' is not always immediately accessible, and the details of any quotidian existence remain inevitably 'private' in many ways. Muldoon's life in 1992 in the hinterlands of Princeton, his weekend break in New Orleans, and visit to a first night at the Met. in New York are about as meaningful in themselves as Louis MacNeice's commuting to work in London in 1938: these things are the routine accidents and circumstances of a particular life, which offer themselves, in the context of their artistic use, as material for transformation. The conversion of random detail into un-random detail implies design and (however inconspicuously) the imposition of form. Muldoon's short book (consisting of thirty-one poems, thirteen of which are sonnets) does not allow all its details to remain random, however 'quotidian' their origins, and patterns of echo and association are established between poems which bring to the material the feel of some order and arrangement (albeit finally of an opaque nature). The apparent triviality of the particular events, like the seeming gratuitousness of the undertaking itself, is a part of the poet's pushing to an extreme of the question of form in writing.

The Prince of the Quotidian's air of domestic cosiness goes together with an unusually confrontational attitude to the climate of the poet's own critical reception. Thus, the direct engagement with a statement by Seamus Deane (on Muldoon's being 'in exile' in Princeton), or a coolly scornful account of 'the casuistry / by which pianists and painters and poets are proof / that all's not rotten in the state', or a treatment of the Field Day enterprise as 'balladeers and bards' who 'add up to so much less than the sum of its parts / like almost every Irish stew', all make for a sense of Muldoon's speaking, *in propria persona*, against the various distortions and political presumptions of the cultural intelligentsia.[11] Yet Muldoon's answer

---

[11] *The Prince of the Quotidian* (Oldcastle: Gallery Press, 1994), 35.

to the different kinds of error is not a series of counter-arguments, but the alternative discipline of the quotidian itself, with its right to apparent triviality. In one sonnet (part of which is quoted as an epigraph to this chapter), Muldoon writes of how 'none will, / I trust, look for a pattern in this crazy quilt / where all is random, "all so trivial" ':[12] the quotation-marks around this last phrase are important, for they recruit to the poem a casually dismissive remark which the poem itself will go to work on, and which will be subject to significant transformation as a result of the formal pressures exerted on it by both poem and volume. In a much earlier interview, Muldoon spoke of his interest in allowing poems, and elements within different poems, to glance at, and thus subtly alter, one another:

I've become very interested in structures that can be fixed like mirrors at angles to each other—it relates to narrative form— so that new images can emerge from the setting up of the poems in relation to each other: further ironies are possible, further mischief is possible. I hope the mischief I make is of a rewarding kind, not that of a practical joker, and will outline the complexities of being here.[13]

This structural principle of poems 'like mirrors at angles to each other', which may be seen operating to powerful effect in volumes like *Why Brownlee Left* and *Quoof*, has always been a productive source of 'mischief' for Muldoon; increasingly, the extent of this has gone beyond 'images', and has come to include other levels of poetry's language and workings. It is worth remembering that the mirror is an icon of identity, and that response to Muldoon's ways with mirroring structures will depend (as the poet says elsewhere) on 'whether you feel lost or enlarged in a hall of mirrors'.[14] Muldoon's poetry (in this, perhaps, again taking certain cues from MacNeice) tends to enlarge casual language and cliché to reveal its determined purposes and designs. In ' "all so trivial" ', the mirror principle is applied to real effect, so that triviality is made a strange and troubling poetic property.

Muldoon's way of 'enlarging' words owes something also to Seamus Heaney's example, in that it often makes use of etymo-

---

[12] Muldoon, *The Prince of the Quotidian*, 19.
[13] John Haffenden, *Viewpoints: Poets in Conversation with John Haffenden* (London: Faber & Faber, 1981), 136.
[14] Muldoon, interview in *Oxford Poetry*, 14.

logical methods to lay bare unfamiliar (and metaphorical) strata. Unlike Heaney, however, Muldoon tends to allow such explorations to complicate and make strange the given words, rather than to produce an originary, deeply rooted meaning for them. *The Prince of the Quotidian* includes the discipline of etymological rigour as part of a surreal or comic focus on the everyday: when, for example, the speaker is accosted by various figures who have 'careened towards us' and have surrounded his car at traffic-lights, one tells him to ' "try not to confuse *carrus*, a cart, / with *carina*, a keel..." '.[15] Later in the book, 'a small green finch' instructs the poet to 'try not to confuse your "cor" with your "Corinna".'[16] In the case of 'trivial', Muldoon encourages the reader to pursue the word back to two distinct stages: in the first place, by mentioning 'Erasmus' (who is revealed, a couple of lines later, to be in fact *Saint* Erasmus and not the more immediately familiar humanist scholar), the 'trivium' lurking within 'trivial' is for a moment coaxed out; in a later poem, further (and darker) origins are sounded:

> amid the cheers and the cries of 'Bravo'
> I hear the howls of seven dead
>
> at a crossroads between Omagh and long Cookstown.
> The 'trivial' happens where 'three roads' meet.
> Does Saint Augustine
>
> 'trivialise' the sack of Rome?[17]

Here, the sudden irruption into the poem of Northern Irish violence is followed immediately by an etymological explanation of 'trivial', one which hints at the ominous overtones of a place where 'three roads meet' (it was in such a location, for example, that Oedipus murdered Laius, not knowing him to be his father— an apparently random incident which proved to be part of a larger design). Saint Augustine's ability to 'trivialise' the sack of Rome (by Alaric in 410) issues in *The City of God*, a text which was to be profoundly influential in the Middle Ages, and which itself, arguably, enacts its own Christian 'sack' of the classical world; here again, the 'trivial' is made complex and difficult as an idea, for it bears traces of both the contingent and the designed: an accident is something over and above an accident, and details are something other than random. Muldoon's etymological *excursus* does not try to settle the

---

[15] *The Prince of the Quotidian*, 11.   [16] Ibid. 37.   [17] Ibid. 35.

matter, but does bring the 'three roads' (in clichéd terms, perhaps answering to contemporary talk of historical or cultural cross-roads) into close contact with their apparently unrelated consequence in the Middle Ages of Augustine's legacy to Erasmus in the *trivium* (grammar, rhetoric, and logic), as well as the modern understanding of the merely 'trivial', with its rash confidence in the immediately-perceived significance of things.

Of course, the liabilities as well as the possibilities of the 'trivial' are particularly apparent in attempts (like the present one) at a critical interpretation of Muldoon's uses of such things. More could be said—that is, one might push on further, conscious of the seeming unreasonableness of the farther- and farther-fetched material. In praising Muldoon's transformative allusions and counterallusions, one is also, to some degree, praising his folly. Yet it is not, after all, the Erasmus of *The Praise of Folly*, who transformed European notions of grammar, rhetoric, and logic to whom Muldoon alludes, but quite another Erasmus; the poem in question does hesitate, however, before making this clear, for a moment (perhaps) encouraging our mistaken identification:

> unless it be Erasmus, unless
> Erasmus again steel
> himself as his viscera are cranked out by a windlass
>
> yard upon 'xanthous' yard;
> again to steel himself, then somehow to exhort
> the windlass-men to even greater zeal.[18]

This is St Erasmus, also known as St Elmo, who was martyred at sea by the mechanical means Muldoon describes. His repeated ability to 'steel himself' against (or into) these circumstances is matched by the poet's determination to be precise about things, and to court the 'trivial' in achieving such precision. The quotation-marks that emphasize ' "xanthous" ' are signs of this determined risk of pedantry, Muldoon's own way of steeling himself into the coldness of formal constraint. The ' "xanthous" ' viscera are again trivially linked with linguistic events elsewhere in the volume, so that the word itself is a place where poetic roads meet. In the penultimate poem, the poet is confronted by a talking horse's head (alluding back to Swift certainly, but also to earlier work by

[18] Muldoon, *The Prince of the Quotidian*, 29.

Muldoon himself, such as 'Gathering Mushrooms' in *Quoof* where 'my head had grown into the head of a horse / that shook its dirty-fair mane / and spoke this verse'[19]):

> 'But nothing: you know it's dross;
> you know that "Erasmus" stuff is an inept
> attempt to cover your arse;
>
> leave off your laundry-lists and tax-returns
> and go back to making metaphors...'
> Something in that 'go back' reminds me of Xanthus.[20]

The confrontation is humorous, for it brings the reader as well as the poet up against the all-too-obvious limitations of the 'trivial'; but Muldoon takes care to contain its humour, and the last word here is charged with all the allusiveness of 'that "Erasmus" stuff', sounding its own echo with the earlier ' "xanthous" ' of St Erasmus' viscera. As to the identity of Xanthus, Muldoon allows only guesses: this could, perhaps, be one of the horses of Hector in the *Iliad*, named for his fair colouring—and in this case, an injunction to the reader to 'go back' in the poem might lead him to the name of a pub earlier in the book ('Now everything turns on a pub; / "The Lion's Head", "McKenna's", "The White Horse" '.)[21] Yet the purpose of such allusions remains obscure; roads meet, but a pattern in this randomness is still beyond immediate reach. The poet's ability to 'steel himself' into this kind of risky determination is at issue in the poem itself, and is in part what *The Prince of the Quotidian* is about, gambling as it does on the formal pattern to be coaxed out of apparently random events and allusions. The possibility that this boils down to 'an inept / attempt to cover your arse' is kept in play by Muldoon as a further level of the risk inherent in aiming for more than just 'making metaphors'.

Who, then, are the 'windlass-men' whose 'zeal' St Erasmus stoically exhorts, and whose attentions Muldoon seems also to court? One poem in the volume has the poet consort with 'umpteen / ex-colleagues from the BBC' who 'huddle / in the bar with a dozen

---

[19] *Quoof*, 8.

[20] *The Prince of the Quotidian*, 40.

[21] Ibid. 11. The list of pub names is something upon which, evidently, some intertextual allusion turns: in section XII of Derek Mahon's sequence 'The Hudson Letter', 'I... / who, once a strange child with a taste for vorse, / would lurch at 3.00 a.m. through drifting snow / to the Lion's Head, McKenna's, the White Horse' (*The Hudson Letter* (Oldcastle: Gallery Press, 1995), 62).

off-duty windlass-men'; these may be the kind of cultural opera-
tives who give rise to 'the casuistry / by which pianists and painters
and poets are proof / that all's not rotten in the state',[22] and as such
may represent the kinds of demand for 'meaning', and imposition
of significance, which Muldoon (like other Northern Irish poets) is
obliged to keep in view. There is something here more complex
than outright rejection of unwanted attention, for Muldoon seems
to register the attentions of the 'windlass-men' as inevitable, and
their demands as in themselves elements of what a poem has to steel
itself against. The 'windlass-men' are almost necessary, in so far as
they force poetry back to an insistence on its formal distinctiveness;
its answers to their questions are not statements or propositions but
the rhymes, mirroring images, and patterned echoings of allusions
which inhere in poetic form. Questions of will ('what is the poet
trying to achieve here? what does the poem *mean* in the light of the
political situation?') draw out poetry's resources of the apparently
wilful. Just as, in one poem, Muldoon finds a rhyme for 'windlass'
in 'relentless', so the kinds of involvement with form which his
writing undertakes, or steels itself into, are often of a certain
impersonal relentlessness. Muldoon's involvement, then, with the
various 'windlass-men' of his critical reception and, beyond that, of
the cultural and political climate in which he is read, is essentially a
matter of his insistence upon form (though not in any narrow sense
of 'formalism' or 'New Formalism'). Furthermore, it is this insistence which gives Muldoon's poetry its actual distinctiveness, and
which is central to some of its most notable successes.

Muldoon's wilfulness in the matter of form begins at the level of
the microcosm, in the particular verbal and stylistic details of his
lines. Here, the strangeness and originality of his rhyming practice
has always been a defining characteristic. In an interview, Muldoon
has claimed to have 'rather loose notions of what a rhyme is, since
many of mine are assonantal',[23] but this looseness is in fact more
a flexibility that permits extraordinary acrobatic feats. Often,
Muldoon seems to allow his rhymes to dictate line-length, so
that a short line will tend to point up its formal burden, drawing
attention to its rhyme, sometimes without establishing itself as a
rhythmic unit. In 'Cauliflowers', for example, the highlighting of
rhyme-words produces:

[22] *The Prince of the Quotidian*, 35.   [23] Haffenden, *Viewpoints*, 141.

> More often than not he stops at the headrig to light
> his pipe

And, later:

> All this. Magritte's
> pipe
> and the pipe-
> bomb. White Annetts. Gillyflowers.[24]

Here, the rhythmic identity of the 'pipe' lines is minimal, seeming
even to be wilfully denied in the interests of the recurring rhyme
figure. This putting into the foreground of a poem's formal properties is common in Muldoon's writing, and it is in fact one of the
poet's most impressive technical accomplishments to manage to
combine this so often with rhythmic arrangements that have their
own kind of felicity. An obvious example of this comes at the
conclusion of 'Why Brownlee Left':

> They had found all abandoned, with
> The last rig unbroken, his pair of black
> Horses, like man and wife,
> Shifting their weight from foot to
> Foot, and gazing into the future.[25]

The delicacy and pervasiveness of enjambment in these lines is
crucial to the effect of the closing rhyme; the barely detectable
rhyme effect of 'with'/'wife' prepares the way for the final couplet's
rhyming against its own enjambment (read aloud conversationally,
the 'foot to'/ 'future' rhyme will remain largely subliminal). The eye
dwells on (and delights in) the formal balance which, for the voice
and the ear, remains implicit in the sentence. That the subject of the
lines itself is balance adds a further element of daring to the formal
achievement. In successes like this, the apparently arbitrary is
reclaimed as the designed, and accidents become arranged felicities.
In a third instance, the wilfulness of the procedure is again
acknowledged at the same time as it pays its dividends, this time
by a poem's seizing on the word 'arbitrary' itself:

> I ought to begin with Evelyn Waugh's
> 'How old's that noise?'

---

[24] *Madoc: A Mystery* (London: Faber & Faber, 1990), 10–11.
[25] *Why Brownlee Left* (London: Faber & Faber, 1980), 22.

> when you wander arbi-
> trarily into *Le Déjeuner sur l'herbe.*[26]

Is the line-break here arbitrary? The rhyme it makes possible is, certainly, an original one, and the enjambment appears to play out the gratuitous process the lines describe. Once again, Muldoon's gratuitousness in these matters (like his use of the 'trivial') is double-edged, and carries design along with chance.

Muldoon's formal procedures in rhyming, then, tend to make obvious the wilfulness of their own design. One critic, Clair Wills, has seen this formal side of Muldoon as an indicator of some rather over-specific 'content' to his work (his questioning 'the opposition between Enlightenment rationalism and Romantic notions of community'); Wills's remarks on this are not untypical of many critical attempts to deal with Muldoon:

Having dispensed with the notion of the intrinsic value of a thing, all events and objects may be substitutable, all of equal worth (a process which is suggested formally by the tendency for Muldoon to allow the seeming arbitrariness of rhyme and word association to direct his poems).[27]

The cranking of the critical windlass is audible here, most notably in Wills's assumption that the 'process' she interprets can be 'suggested formally' in the poems, whose formal processes are, it seems, obedient to the poet's meaning. In search of the determinable, Wills and other critics are liable to be wrong-footed by Muldoon's indeterminacies, and his poetry's way with the 'arbitrary'. Indeed, in the poem which Wills cites as a footnote to her parenthesis, 'Something Else', Muldoon's subject is, in part, the connectedness which the 'arbitrary' brings about. Again, wilfulness here answers the over-determination of cause and effect, form and content expectations. The poem itself begins with strongly foregrounded rhyme:

> When your lobster was lifted out of the tank
> to be weighed
> I thought of woad,
> of madders, of fugitive, indigo inks,[28]

---

[26] 'Bears', *The Wishbone* (Dublin: Gallery Press, 1984), 11.
[27] Clair Wills, *Improprieties: Politics and Sexuality in Northern Irish Poetry* (Oxford: Clarendon Press, 1993), 197.
[28] *Meeting the British*, 33.

The 'weighed'/'woad' rhyme carries the explicit 'I thought of' as its explanation, and this level of personal association continues, immediately producing a literary reference to Gerard de Nerval, who 'was given to promenade / a lobster on a gossamer thread'. As the poem progresses, the connections of rhyme with rhyme come increasingly to be ways of considering different kinds of connection, and the 'gossamer thread' issues in another kind of lead, this time the 'length of chain' with which Nerval hangs himself:

> how, when a decent interval
>
> had passed
> (*son front rouge encor du baiser de la reine*)
> and his hopes of Adrienne
>
> proved false,
> he hanged himself from a lamp-post
> with a length of chain, which made me think
>
> of something else, then something else again.

The brutal 'length of chain', which is intimate through rhyme both with Nerval's own words and with the name of his mistress, becomes itself a link in the chain of rhymes ('something else, then something else again') which the poem's speaker is able to produce. The poem's formal composure is crucial to its handling of the apparently arbitrary: Muldoon allows a decent interval to pass, for example, in the enjambment of 'when a decent interval / had passed', just at the point where a sonnet would turn from octave to sestet. The poem's last line, in fact, is set apart so that it appears to be surplus to requirements, the rogue fifteenth line spilling over from a sonnet. The 'gossamer thread' and the 'length of chain' may seem to be at opposite extremes of delicacy and crudeness, but the poem has connected them, and in the process dwelt on the processes of connection: one thing leads to another, but not in an 'arbitrary' way. The poem itself is also hooked up to other pieces in its volume: the piece which precedes it in *Meeting the British*, 'Paul Klee: *They're Biting*', besides referring to an artist known for his notion of 'taking a line for a walk', features 'caricature anglers' who 'have fallen hook, line and sinker' for the fish, and has at its centre the line 'At any moment all this should connect'.[29] Seafood

---

[29] Ibid. 32.

abounds too in the poem which follows 'Something Else', 'Sushi', a *tour de force* of rhyming connections in the course of which the reader glimpses 'a woman in a leotard / with a real leopard / in tow'.[30] Further on in the book, in '7, Middagh Street', the monologue for 'Salvador' (Dali) begins with 'This lobster's not a lobster...'.[31] All of these connections, whether they are in the nature of gossamer threads or lengths of chain, seem to make artistic capital out of their apparent gratuitousness; they are certainly not means of 'formally suggesting' any determinable or paraphrasable meaning.

The apparent marks of arbitrariness in form, like his poems' courting of triviality, are defining characteristics of much of Muldoon's writing. On a larger scale than the local effects of rhyme and line-length, Muldoon's way with formal structure displays a similar willingness to provoke and tease the windlass-men in search of clear connections between form and content. The pervasiveness of the sonnet in Muldoon's poetry is a case in point: here, the question of the significance of a recurring formal pattern (albeit one subject to sometimes drastic kinds of mutation) seems as pressing as it is undecidable. The proliferation of fourteen-line units in Muldoon's poetry began with the volume *Mules* (1977), in which various configurations of the sonnet are present, leading to the closing 'Armageddon, Armageddon', seven poems arranged as a sonnet sequence. Although they share a number of images and preoccupations, such as the districts around Armagh or the constellations in the sky, these pieces make up a peculiar kind of sequence, one characterized more by *non sequitur* than connection. Elements of narrative are present, but remain unresolved and ambiguous (the slightly coy account of Oisin's return to Ireland in the second poem, or the splicing of Frost and Faulkner in the domestic drama of the sixth). Although there is a general sense of a vaguely Symbolist concern with apocalyptic transformation of the ordinary, and hints of violence lurking in the vicinity, 'Armageddon, Armageddon' does not constitute a narrative, nor is it a series of poems 'related' in any narratively comprehensible way. Bernard O'Donoghue has written of how these poems are 'connected less by thematic than by formal recurrences', and has seen in this a foreshadowing of Muldoon's subsequent practice in 'the disruption of the expectations of

[30] Muldoon, *Meeting the British*, 34.   [31] Ibid. 49.

the fourteen-line form.'[32] While it may be truer to say that any disruption in 'Armageddon, Armageddon' is less in the structure of individual sonnets than the disruption of readers' expectations of what a sonnet *sequence* will do, O'Donoghue's observation is an acute one. The sequence is, as a whole, determinedly out of kilter with itself.

The conclusion of the final poem, in which the speaker has hidden in a stream and is breathing through a hollow reed, watches a 'black beetle' ('Like a blood-blister with a mind of its own') make its way across the authorial hand:

> My hand might well have been some flat stone
> The way it made for the underside,
> I had to turn my wrist against its wont
> To have it walk in the paths of uprightness.[33]

This elegant readjustment suggests, perhaps, the priority of the seemingly contingent detail over the apparent centre of attention: a poem which has featured the speaker taking desperate refuge concludes by concentrating—and having the speaker also concentrate—on the fortunes of a wandering black beetle. To achieve this, 'I had to turn my wrist against its wont', and there is a sense in which the poem too, considered as a sonnet, has been turned 'against its wont', divided as it is into three sections of four, six, and four lines respectively. Once a decision has been taken to ignore the conventional 'turn' in a sonnet's structure, between an octave and a sestet, then one can ask whether in any new configuration conformity to the fourteen-line limit is not in some way a barren gesture. If, that is, a sonnet is fourteen lines long because of the eight-line/six-line balance, a structure subdivided in a different way has no *inherent* reason to continue for the same fourteen-line duration. In an interview in 1994, Muldoon has seemed to endorse an almost organic view of the sonnet's structure (helped on his way here by the interviewer):

The sonnet, though it's an Italian form initially, of course, came into English, as you know, and there's something very appealing about the sonnet. I remember reading somewhere about the way the thought process

---

[32] Bernard O'Donoghue, '"The Half-Said Thing to Them is Dearest": Paul Muldoon', in Michael Kenneally (ed.), *Poetry in Contemporary Irish Literature* (Gerrards Cross: Colin Smythe, 1995), 408.

[33] *Mules* (London: Faber & Faber, 1977), 59.

of the sonnet [Interviewer: 'You mean, with the turn?'] Exactly. You establish something, then there's a slight change. And how that way of looking at the world still obtains. The fact that it's such a common form, I think, is no accident...[34]

This enthusiasm does not quite match the actual structures to be found in 'Armageddon, Armageddon' (where only two of the seven poems share the same stanzaic divisions, and none is divided into octave and sestet), and still less those accounting for the bulk of Muldoon's subsequent sonnets. It may be more in the spirit of Muldoon's actual writing in this form to see his favoured structures as divisions within an arbitrarily accepted limit, again bringing to the foreground the problems of artificiality which are latent in all formal composition. Indeed, Muldoon goes on to consider the 'organic' view of the sonnet from a number of angles in the interview:

Now, many people of course think of formalism, so-called, as somehow imposed on the language, rather than being organic. I don't see it as being anything but natural to the language. So this just happens to be the way a lot of these poems come out. ... I believe in the poem writing itself, through the medium of the writer. As writer I'm somehow determining how it comes out. Of course there are dangers that too early in the process one can think, 'This is likely to be a sonnet.' After all, though I argue for it being an organic form, the sonnet is not what one sees in nature. So the fact that I am predisposed to write in these conventional forms is an element in why so many of the poems come out that way, even though I would argue that every poem determines its own form.

What is at stake here is clear enough, even if Muldoon's own position in the argument becomes increasingly ambiguous; the poetic form is allowed its own identity, as it were, which can in some senses use the writer as its 'medium', and thus take priority over any narrowly conceived notions of self-expression. Muldoon, as has become characteristic, downplays his role in the process of composition (speaking of 'Yarrow', he has remarked that 'though I was the medium through which this poem was written, I'm now just another poor, dear reader...');[35] at the same time, he understands the problematic nature of 'organic' ideas of poetic form—'the sonnet is not what one sees in nature'.

[34] Interview in *Contemporary Literature*, 25.
[35] 'Between Ireland and Montevideo'.

The profusion of fourteen-line units in Muldoon's poetry, how-ever, is 'not an accident', even given that it is always difficult to be sure of the meaning of the accidental in the context of his writing. Bernard O'Donoghue's remarks on 'Armageddon, Armageddon' note that the form is 'one that Muldoon has used relentlessly ever since', and there is a justice to his 'relentlessly' that makes good what is (in literal terms) an exaggeration. To detect something 'relentless' in a formal habit is to take the measure of form's impersonal pressure on writing (and reading), and Muldoon's prac-tice in a volume like *Quoof* does indeed push the idea of the son-net towards relentless, or apparently obsessive, extremes. Here, thirteen of the twenty-eight poems are sonnets, and a further three are made up of sonnet-length stanzas; most notably, the long narrative poem, 'The More a Man Has the More a Man Wants' consists entirely of fourteen-line stanzas (forty-nine of them, plus a one-word coda, of 'Huh'). Edna Longley has written that '*Quoof* as a whole stretches the elastic of sonnet-sequence...although "sequence" seems too serial a term for a set of relations more akin to a Rubik cube'.[36] Longley's sense that the sonnet form in 'The More a Man Has...' 'is mutating under brutal pressures' and that 'its architecture is being determined by fault-lines' responds to the kinds of alteration made to sonnet form in Muldoon's work, assign-ing it (however tentatively) a meaning within the context of the violence with which the poem—like the collection—is filled. Inter-pretations such as this leave undecided questions of the arbitrari-ness of Muldoon's practice; Muldoon himself in interviews steps back from these questions in declaring himself the 'medium' through which the form emerges (or mutates), thus leaving open a number of possibilities. Is there purpose to Muldoon's formal vio-lence, or is it random? A 1986 interview includes an interesting reflection on the degree to which Muldoon's practice can actually be interpreted:

A lot of poems do end up with a sort of sonnet shape: 'deconstructed sonnets' is what Edna Longley called them once—perhaps she meant 'destructed sonnets'. There was a guy at the University of Saskatchewan who did an analysis of my sonnets...One of the things he was saying was that he felt that I think that I might be taking the sonnet as an archetypally

[36] *The Living Stream: Literature and Revisionism in Ireland* (Newcastle-upon Tyne: Bloodaxe Books, 1994), 196–7.

'English' structure and breaking it up, almost as an anti-British thing—which I remember saying to someone at the time, is worth thinking about for about as long as it takes to think it, but not that much more. The whole of irony is very difficult. A difficult thing to talk about or to engage in.[37]

The line between 'deconstruction' and 'destruction' is not really one which Muldoon sees it as his business to draw; it is a distinction in the secondary realm of critical interpretation, and as such it has consequences for (and perhaps sources in) arguments from which the poetry itself stands at a distance. Muldoon's detachment from the crudely 'anti-British' interpretation of his formal habits, which is expressed here as a sceptical *reader*'s detachment, rather than the outright rejection of a poet confident in his own authority, leads him to reflect on the difficulty of discussing 'the whole of irony'. As Muldoon may suggest here, such a 'whole' is present in the poems, but necessarily missing from any single interpretation of them; like distinguishing between the random and the purposeful, telling the difference between 'deconstruction' and 'destruction' is a process fraught with liabilities.

How important, then, is it that Muldoon interferes with received ideas of the shape of a sonnet, or that he should employ the sonnet length with such apparently obsessive regularity? The framing of this very question, of course, falls considerably short of 'the whole of irony'. Nevertheless, there are reasons to pursue the problem. In *Quoof*, Muldoon divides the sonnet in unorthodox ways: each division has its logic and local effectiveness, but its relation to the overall limit of fourteen lines remains inevitably obscure. An extreme position is reached in a poem such as '*from* Last Poems', where the fourteen lines are divided into four units, each with a roman numeral as title: the first, four lines long, is 'IV', the second, three lines long, is 'VII', the third, consisting of five lines, is 'IX', and a last couplet is titled 'XIV'. In all but the third case, the roman numeral corresponds to the number of lines to which that stanza brings the sonnet as a whole. The third stanza's departure from what looks like a pattern is also a departure from the grim tone of the rest of the poem ('Not that I care who's sleeping with whom / now she's had her womb / removed...':[38]

---

[37] Interview in *Oxford Poetry*, 19.   [38] *Quoof*, 31.

IX

I would be happy in the knowledge
that as I laboured up the no-through-road
towards your cottage
you ran to meet me. Your long white shift,
its spray of honesty and thrift.

This 'knowledge', as the poem makes plain, is more in the nature of
a fantasy, and the numbering of the stanza as 'IX' (rather than the
expected 'XII') perhaps serves to draw attention to what is in fact
the whole poem's ninth line, and its 'no-through-road'. The reader's
ability to detect a logic to the (at first sight) random numbering of
the stanzas is also pulled up short here, and when the apparent
pattern re-emerges in the final couplet, it is with a significant irony:

XIV

Ours would be a worldly wisdom, heaven-sent;
the wisdom before the event.

To find an interpretation for the apparently random is its own kind
of 'worldly wisdom, heaven-sent', and, like any 'wisdom before the
event', it runs certain risks. As against such wisdom, there is the
constant possibility of the 'no-through-road'; it is here, perhaps,
that the limits of interpretation block off the ambitions of critical
'wisdom before the event', just as Muldoon's pervasive irony comes
into play as soon as definite significances are assigned to particular
formal features of his writing. It is important, however, that Muldoon tends to lead his readers up such no-through roads, and
provides instances of the 'knowledge' to be found there.

The formalism of *Quoof* is often as chilling as it is intellectually
bracing, and in this the volume foreshadows an increasingly prominent aspect of Muldoon's writing. As far as the sonnet is concerned, similar formal innovation is present in *Meeting the British*,
and in the short interim collection *The Wishbone*, where a poem
like 'Pandas' subdivides into four, unequal stanzas:

The shuttlecock had lain in your lap
like the barely perceptible
birth of a panda.

*

C'mon, you said. For half an hour
we thwacked it to and fro

across the imaginary badminton-net
rigged up in our back entry.

*

C'mon, you said. Then it got spirited
over the wall, into the bamboo
of Friar's Bush cemetery.

*

Impossible bamboo. The cholera-mound,
the graves of so many
prominent men, their would-be children
in pantalettes: sea-squirt, anemone.[39]

The points of division are important in this poem (rather like the
'fault-lines' in Edna Longley's description above), precisely because
they are places where the poem breaks off from itself, suggesting
lines of development which may, or may not, turn out to be no-
through roads. If the poem possesses a formal 'turn', it comes after
the third stanza, once the shuttlecock has gone over the wall into
Friar's Bush cemetery (a long-closed site near Belfast's Botanic
Gardens, and near to Muldoon's address of the time in Landseer
Street). The various simplicities of the imagery and diction of
'Pandas' are deceptive, since they are counterpointed with the
asterisk-divisions, with their quizzical hints at connection. The
comparison, for example, between a shuttlecock and the 'barely
perceptible / birth of a panda' leads to 'bamboo', almost at once redefined as 'Impossible bamboo', and the distance covered here
from simile to a first literal, then seemingly metaphorical, image
is in a sense made legible in the marked-out gaps between the
stanzas. The poem's concluding concentration on other, now
'barely perceptible' births in the historic cemetery with its
'cholera-mound' resolves abruptly into 'sea-squirt, anemone', final
images which relate only obliquely to anything that has come
before. The sonnet's 'turn' has been, as it were, turned again in an
unexpected direction, and may not now be the 'turn' that matters.
Both the sea-squirt, with its hard outer coat, and the sea-anemone,
with its tendency to close against intrusion, are defensive as well as
delicate forms of life, and might offer apt images for the poem's

[39] *The Wishbone*, 12.

own tendency to resist too certain an interpretation. They might, also, give instances of the sudden resistance which form puts up to the free development of the poem's constitutive elements. In fact, the significance of the sonnet form here seems principally to be its limitation on length, which results in an imposition of reticence, as though the gaps between stanzas had finally been allowed to take over altogether in the ending of the poem. The apparently arbitrary can create, and guard, a life of its own.

Muldoon's poetry, marked as it is by its emphasis on the (sometimes arbitrary) properties of rhyme and the (sometimes bewildering) determinacy of formal units like the sonnet, is often engaged in formal disciplines of a larger-scale nature. Both '7, Middagh Street' in *Meeting the British* and 'Madoc: A Mystery' are undertakings in which the shape of the poetic narrative has a crucial (though not always an immediately clear) role to play in its interpretation. The constituent monologues of '7, Middagh Street' make verbal contact with one another, the last line of one being taken up or completed by the first line of the next, with the final monologue (that of 'Louis') referring back to, or leading up to, the opening quotation of the first (belonging to 'Wystan'). This circular structure, imitating that of the Renaissance *corona* of sonnets, such as Donne's 'La Corona', means that, as Edna Longley puts it, 'the poem has its tail in its mouth', and is a device which enables Muldoon to make different kinds of certainty relative to each other, where 'the fate of all expression depends on incalculable twists and turns'.[40] Longley's remarks indicate that, for a circumspect reader, the poem makes use of the larger forces of form to shadow the seeming immediacies of the details it contains—details which include discussions of art's relation to contemporary politics; here, as she goes on to say, 'form imitates the ceaseless engagement between flux and pattern', for each moment of apparent standstill, or achieved statement, is also, in the light of the poem as a whole, a moment open to mutation and arbitrary change. Nobody, in '7, Middagh Street', can have the last word, and again the effect of this is akin to a hall of mirrors, or an echo-chamber, in that the attempt to find a definitive centre or point of origin is doomed to failure. Given the nature of much of the discussion in the poem, '7, Middagh Street' almost sets out to tempt readers into a number of no-through roads

[40] *The Living Stream*, 265–6.

on the subject of art and commitment (or indeed of Muldoon's own indebtedness to actual literary precursors); yet these apparent subjects are themselves subject to the encircling, recurring form in which they occur. In the end, '7, Middagh Street' uses form to frustrate the search for a 'meaning' that can be translated out of poetry, or transported away from it, and even its most naturalistic ventriloquism is laid bare as an artificially conditioned (and determined) gesture.

The requirement that the reader should be simultaneously— and perhaps uncomfortably—aware of 'content' and 'form' applies in rather more stark terms to 'Madoc'. In this, Muldoon's most ambitious narrative, two formal co-ordinates, so to speak, remain constantly in view: that of the narrative itself, with its characters, events, and locations, and that of the superimposed classification from South (the figure from whose disintegrating retina the narrative is being retrieved—or perhaps lost—in the poem's science-fiction framing device). The shape made by the poems on the page bears the mark of this superimposition, since the fragments carry over them square-bracketed titles, each the name of a philosopher, running in chronological sequence from '[*Thales*]' to '[*Hawking*]'. The (often very tangential) relations between philosopher and poem contribute much of 'Madoc''s comedy, but they also keep in view, however subtly, the presence of South, who can safely be assumed to be, as Muldoon has said, 'very philosophical and scientific in his concerns'. If it is South who gives the narrative his kind of coherence, then it is also South whose coherence makes the narrative—in a more conventional sense—so oblique, wayward, and difficult of access. For readers attuned to the explanations, descriptions, and causes and effects of much conventional narrative, the structure of 'Madoc' means that difficulty and bewilderment are— in a curiously literal sense—built into the poem. Muldoon's remarks on this acknowledge the possible problems:

I like to think of the philosophers' names in *Madoc* as film sub-titles, which disappear almost as one sees them but which one takes in subliminally. One risk is that the poem is burdened by this structure—as if the scaffolding were still around the building, or the crane had never been dismantled. And some readers might feel exasperated looking for a connection.[41]

---

[41] Interview with Blake Morrison, *Independent on Sunday*, 28 Oct. 1990, 37.

There is in fact a great deal of difference between an interest in the subliminal and the (unconvincingly postmodern) gesture towards leaving the paraphernalia of construction all around the building. Does Muldoon hope that this aspect of his poem's form will be intrusively visible, or problematically out of sight? It is often a mistake, as Muldoon hints, to look for a 'connection' between philosopher and narrative fragment, or at least to concentrate on this 'connection' (which will often be fortuitous, depending on a turn of phrase, a chance allusion, or an apparently trivial moment of resemblance). To read the poem in this way would be to marginalize its narrative content altogether in favour of a particularly extreme (and possibly arid) categorical formalism. And yet, the poetic form of 'Madoc' is in fact that of a series of lyric fragments over which South makes his 'subliminal' mark; this formal marking—as well as the fragmentation itself—disrupts the elements of conventional narrative by its constant imposition on the narrative material.

To read any section of 'Madoc', then, is to read a piece of the 'story', to make sense of the information as a fragment which requires to be connected with other fragments, and to experience the episode in relation to the scheme belonging to the character South. As well as all this, a page of 'Madoc' also looks and behaves very much like a separate poem with, of course, all of Muldoon's characteristic stylistic traits fully in play. Whether this lyric medium contributes more to 'Madoc''s narrative or to its meta-narrative is a difficult question, for it could be argued that Muldoon's style tends to impede conventional narrative by imposing its own principles of detail, formal analysis, and quibble. The poetry is, unsurprisingly, often of a principled and rigorous triviality, as when, in '[*Hobbes*]', Coleridge 'can no more argue from this faded blue / turtle's splay... to a universal / idea of blue':

> than from powder-horns, muskets,
> paddles, pumpkins,
> thingums, thingammies,
> bear-oil against mosquitoes,
>
> hatchets, hoes, digging-sticks,
> knives, kettles,
> steel combs, brass tacks,
> corn-husk masks or ceremonial rattles

to anything beyond their names. The silent drums.
The empty cask of trade-rum.[42]

'Madoc' is packed to the gunwales with the 'thingums, thingam-
mies' of its narrative, but their significance, like that of any trivia in
Muldoon, is often a matter of abstruse, if not ironic, import. In
terms of the writing itself, catalogues like the one above are both
playful, with their frequent arabesques of connectedness, of everything leading to 'something else, then something else again', and
impediments to the flow of conventional narrative: their quibbles
and quiddities come, perhaps, from South, but their effect is also to
set the various shocks and surprises of Muldoon's lyric style *against*
the design of a story: the foreground of style and sheer virtuosity is
so wildly patterned and engrossing that the background of 'story
and event' seems often to vanish. In this sense, it is poetry which
gets in the way of things happening, which holds them up, or puts
itself in between them; it is poetry which fixes an intricate formal
grid over all-too-raw material, and which holds up a past-tense
narrative in a series of kaleidoscopic present moments, each of
which creates a new level of contingency and complexity for any
simple line of 'content'. Thus, as the poem concludes, the reader is
told that 'It will all be over, de dum, / in next to no time';[43] yet it is
narrative 'time', in fact, with which the poem has continually
interfered, and to such an extent that form has been perceptible
throughout as something which makes time and temporal relations
fraught with complexity.

III

One way of understanding form in poetry is to think about poems
as mechanisms for repetition; the ways in which repetition is varied
in poems (most obviously, rhythm and rhyme) are elements of the
writing in which the expected and the unexpected are played off
against one another, and in which the random is made into the un-
random. As well as this, form is a pattern imposed on a poem's
inescapable progress from its beginning to its end; in some sense,
every poem has its own duration, and it is poetic form which, as it
were, measures the time taken and the time left in the shapes it

[42] *Madoc: A Mystery*, 92.   [43] Ibid. 261.

creates through various kinds of recurrence and recapitulation. Aspects of poetry like rhyme and rhythmic pattern are points of near-identity that include difference; always identifiably similar, they are never exactly the same. By the same token, their differences are always grounded in their aspects of similarity, so that identity and difference shadow each other.

In this way, it might be possible to think of form as the element of poetry which says 'something else, then something else again' in the duration of a poem; but the new thing always carries the old thing with it, for development remains an aspect of duration. The 'again' in 'something else again', with its apparent openness to novelty, can also mark the inevitability of 'again and again', a phrase which repeats through Muldoon's long poem 'Yarrow' to record the finally unalterable:

> The bridge. The barn. Again and again I stand aghast
> as I contemplate what never
> again will be mine:
>
> 'Look on her. Look, her lips.
> Listen to her *râle*
> where ovarian cancer takes her in its strangle-hold.'[44]

Here, 'again and again' sets down the finality of 'never / again', and its repetition is the repetition of loss. 'Yarrow', along with Muldoon's other major poem in *The Annals of Chile*, 'Incantata', is marked by elaborate formal patterning, and uses this relentless formalism to extraordinary effect. Form, duration, and inevitability are what these poems are about, as well as being prominent elements in their construction. Both poems seem to turn on personal history, and are free with the first-person voice: 'Incantata' is an elegy for the artist Mary Farl Powers (to whom *The Wishbone* had been dedicated in 1984), while 'Yarrow' comes back to Muldoon's childhood and adolescence near the Moy, and includes prominently the figure of his mother, who died in 1974. Despite this, the two poems go further than much of Muldoon's earlier work towards the point where 'At last, the bowstring has cut through you'; that is, their aspect of autobiography is transformed by the formal matrices into which it is fed, and the matter of loss, like the reality of duration, becomes in these poems something against which the

---

[44] *The Annals of Chile* (London: Faber & Faber, 1994), 175.

voice has to steel itself in the repetitive rigour of poetic form. Time, as it is experienced in the conventionalized narratives of personal identity, is altered in the windlass-operations of a relentless poetic form; perhaps the most remarkable aspect of Muldoon's achievement in these poems is his success in bringing together an apparently unconstrained voice and a formal environment of the most extreme constraint. The consequences of this artistic success for received notions of a poet's 'identity' in poetry are far-reaching.

The densities of 'Yarrow''s structure, with its elaborate intercutting of repeating lines and rhymes, are foreshadowed in Muldoon's libretto of 1993, *Shining Brow*. Here, working with the American composer Daron Aric Hagen, Muldoon creates a series of exchanges and monologues rich in repetition; each leitmotif can recur with variations, and the text as a whole relies heavily on the echo-chamber effect of such recapitulations. It is tempting to say that *Shining Brow* thus makes each of its parts integral to the whole, and that it establishes a self-contained and self-coherent textual world, but this is to fall into a trap, for it is Frank Lloyd Wright, Muldoon's protagonist in the libretto, who most believes in the virtues (and the possibility) of the fully 'integral' design:

> Be it mud hut, mansion or mosque
> a Mineatree
> earth-lodge, a cabin with the antlers of an elk
> gracing its eaves—
> be it the chapel of the Holy Grail—
> they should all be somehow integral.[45]

In purely architectural terms, Wright's notion of the 'integral', that 'form and function are one', means that 'Each room opens into the next...like the chambers / of the heart'. As the simile shows, of course, there are no such things as purely architectural terms, and Wright's confidence regarding his own organic understanding in architecture of 'the prairie of men's hearts' is utterly misplaced. Wright's belief is one with costs attached, and its application to life rather than architecture leaves a trail of victims. As Edwin Cheney, the client with whose wife Wright conducts an affair, puts it:

> I know, I know, I know; I know
> only too well the features of the 'prairie house'—

---

[45] *Shining Brow* (London: Faber & Faber, 1993), 26.

> its walls of rain, its window-panes of ice,
> its door of wind, its roof of hard-packed snow,
> and, at its core, a vast emptiness.[46]

As the piece concludes, the 'prairie house' is a burnt-out shell, Cheney's wife Mamah is dead, and Wright is left alone to contemplate the panorama of ruin. Even here, Wright is able to make some kind of coherence out of the chaos, and his closing monologue repeats and reapplies phrases and words from elsewhere in the text. Wright's compulsion to see form in everything (in which he imagines he follows the native American tribes who 'all perceived the intricate / order in even a pine-cone') leads him to the rhetorical assertion 'That Mamah's dead and gone / is itself a grand illusion'. Of course this is not so, but the libretto's recurring 'would that...' optative construction helps Wright's rhetoric on its way:

> I will fill her plain pine box
> with wild
> flowers and marjoram
> and mulberry leaves.
> Would that she might take me in her arms.
> Would that I myself
> might fill her unmarked grave.
> Why mark the spot where desolation began
> and ended?[47]

Wright's utterances are marked by the formality of their occasion, and the fact that they are repetitions of the libretto's recurring verbal formulas is important in establishing the character's enduring allegiance to the 'integral'. The problematic distance between formal arrangement (and, indeed, self-composure) and the fact of loss is made especially clear in *Shining Brow*, and the text's satisfyingly complete patterns of repetition and variation are set against the 'vast emptiness' in the human relations, and losses, over which they are applied.

The repetitions of lines, words, and phrases through *Shining Brow* bring into Muldoon's work the kind of formalized recurrence which had previously been mainly present in the form of rhyme, or the repetition and alteration of certain images. The poem

---

[46] Ibid. 22.   [47] Ibid. 86.

'Cauliflowers' in *Madoc* had experimented with the repetitive energies of the sestina, but *Shining Brow* brought into Muldoon's writing a new intensity of repetition, which was to be developed much
further in 'Yarrow'. In this 150-page poem, the repetitive principle
of the sestina is enlarged and multiplied, resulting in (according to
Muldoon's own account) 'a series of twelve intercut, exploded
sestinas'.[48] This intercutting, or scrambling, along with the sheer
size of the canvas in 'Yarrow', means that the sestina-patterns
themselves would probably remain undetected without the poet's
mentioning their existence. What would remain perceptible, however, would be the degree of repetition involved in the poem, and it
is to this, more than to the mathematical details of his design, that
Muldoon has drawn readers' attention:

At least two things may be said in favour of the sestina, though: firstly,
there's an inherent force in the repetitions and returns of the form that is, in
its strictest sense, magical; secondly, and relatedly, the sestina is the perfect
embodiment of obsessiveness and obsessiveness, particularly sexual obsessiveness, along with violence and death, drugs and rock and roll, may justly
be said to be a 'subject' of 'Yarrow'.[49]

Muldoon's passing remark on the relatedness of the magical and
the obsessive is important; both sides of the coin, as it were, are
visible at the same time in 'the repetitions and returns of the form'.
This observation might apply equally to Frank Lloyd Wright at the
end of *Shining Brow*, whose vision of the 'integral' involves a
relentless obsessiveness. Interestingly, Wright begins to look into
the sources of his own obsessions in his last monologue:

> Through winter and summer, spring and fall,
> we will—we must—endure.
> Would that the Osage, bows in hand,
> the Ostrogoths under Theodoric,
> might come sweeping back across the land...
> It all goes back to those cowboy books
> my mama gave me as a child.[50]

There are points of contact between this and the world of 'Yarrow',
not least in terms of expression (Muldoon makes 'Would that...'
one of the poem's recurrent phrases). The Osage, who consort

---

[48] 'Between Ireland and Montevideo'.   [49] Ibid.
[50] *Shining Brow*, 85–6.

oddly with the Ostrogoths and Theodoric here, would be at home in 'Yarrow''s collection of historical and fictional tribes, along with the various heroes and villains of the 'cowboy books', while their 'sweeping back across the land' foreshadows the yarrow 'that fanned across the land' before which 'All would be swept away' (another of the poem's recurring verbal motifs). Wright's 'we will— we must—endure' voices a determination that 'Yarrow' (itself, like 'Incantata', much concerned with both duration and endurance) renders problematic, part-magical and part-obsessive. As regards what is to 'endure', there may be some relevance to 'Yarrow' also in the fact that Wright's lines (quoted above) which follow this recollection ('I will fill her plain pine box...') may refer either to his mother or to his mistress, to mama or Mamah. Such ambiguities, or continually blurring lines between time, memory, and the self, are a central principle of 'Yarrow'.

Several different time-schemes seem to be involved in 'Yarrow' (which in this sense develops and complicates the future/past double perspectives of 'Madoc'): the poem's first-person speaker, in a contemporary present in America, channel-surfs through the small hours; he remembers events in the year 1963 when he (like Muldoon) was 11 years old, living outside the village of the Moy with a market-gardener father and a schoolteacher mother; he narrates incidents from ten years after this, when he and a woman referred to as 'S——' are lovers, deep in both the 'drugs and rock and roll' mentioned by Muldoon above, and in the fast-souring political radicalism of the early 1970s. These three periods are spliced in the poem, so that it is not always easy to be sure which one is in play at any one time—often all three appear to be operating simultaneously. Further overlapping occurs between the speaker's memories of 1963 and 1973, in the fate of S—— and the fatal illness of his mother, the former coming to grief through worsening heroin addiction, the latter succumbing to cancer. Points of contact between these different layers of narrative abound in the poem, and include characters from boys' adventure-stories and medieval romance, references to the Irish language and Irish culture (admonitory and improving from the mother, would-be revolutionary from S——), and literary tags or longer quotations (most insistently from *King Lear*, which is even glimpsed, at one point, in a Spanish-language production with 'Cordelia's smart-ass *nada*'). In such a complicated textual terrain of interrelation, the large-scale repetition involved in 'Yarrow''s form is of special importance.

The speaker's contemporary perspective is a mixture of abandoned openness to television's images ('I zap the remote control: that same poor elk or eland / dragged down by a bobolink')[51] and a determined, inescapable vision of how 'All would be swept away' in the physical sites of his memory. It is here, perhaps, that the equivalent to Frank Lloyd Wright's 'spot where desolation began / and ended' is to be found:

> All would be swept away, all sold for scrap:
> the hen-house improvised from a high-sided cattle-truck,
> the coils of barbed wire, the coulter
>
> of a plough, the pair of angle-iron
> posts between which she'll waver, one day towards the end,
> as she pins the clothes on the clothes-line.[52]

The slipping of tenses here is reproduced often in 'Yarrow' ('All would be ...', 'she'll waver'), and even here, very early in the poem, the matter of the end is already the burden of the beginning. The interweaving of memories from different points in time results in the deliberate mixing of tenses here and elsewhere (a stylistic decision alluded to most openly in Muldoon's 'César Vellejo: *Testimony*' elsewhere in *The Annals of Chile*, with its opening declaration that 'I will die in Paris, on a day...I can even now recall').[53] However, the most important analogue to this in terms of the poem's form is the use of the 'intercut sestinas', which give Muldoon's material a complexity and depth to which it would not otherwise have access. Any page from 'Yarrow' would not, considered alone, carry much weight, and the poem's mixtures of reference and register are, in isolation, often lacking in coherence. It is in the poem's larger design, though, that Muldoon's most original effects make themselves felt, in their deepening of the motif of 'Again and again' for the contemplation of 'what never / again will be mine'.

Formal recurrence in 'Yarrow' is a matter both of rhyme (in Muldoon's customarily innovative sense of the word) and repetition, where identical verbal forms repeat with different semantic functions. Because of the 'intercut' nature of the sestina structures the poet works with, such rhymes and repetitions can often be

[51] *The Annals of Chile*, 47. [52] Ibid. 42. [53] Ibid. 32.

remarkably for apart. Muldoon's operations here are best explained by example: the poem's third section has the following words at the ends of its lines: 'Pharaohs', 'Tutankhamen', 'ring', 'Ali Baba', 'Morgiana', 'jars', 'senators', 'rush', 'Charlemagne'. In the twentieth section, words like 'ring', 'jar', and 'rush' turn up again, while 'Cayman' answers to the earlier 'Tutankhamen'; the thirty-ninth section has 'jar' and 'rush' again, along with 'C'mon' to rhyme with 'Cayman' and 'snatters' to echo 'senators'; by the sixty-first section 'Alan Quatermain' appears, as well as 'Umbopa' (picking up on 'Ali Baba' from fifty-eight pages before); cognate clusters of rhymes occur in the eighty-ninth section, the hundred and twelfth, hundred and thirtieth, and hundred and forty-seventh. Thus, any one of these sections is related formally to any other, and its shape on the page is in part determined by such relations:

> For the time was now ripe, S—— had vowed, to 'make a *Sendero Luminoso* of our *Camino*
> *Real*': along with the tattoo, she'd taken to wearing a labiaba-
> ring
> featuring a salamander, a salamander being the paragon
> of constancy; it was twenty years to the month the water-main
> froze
> on Fitzroy Road and the *T.L.S.* had given the bum's rush
> to *The Bell Jar.*[54]

The isolation of words like 'ring' and 'froze' here is a sign of their formal interaction with other parts of the poem through repetition or rhyme ('froze' is answering to 'furze' in the eighty-ninth section, and foreshadowing 'thuriferous' in the hundred and thirtieth). Such relations are not, of course, the audible relations of close rhyme in a lyric poem, but are implicated instead in the aspect of repetitive form which Muldoon has characterized as 'magical' (and has also understood as 'obsessive'). Given that 'Yarrow' as a whole is structured according to intricate and far-fetched formal principles of recurrence, the question which arises from a reader's experience of the poem is that of the meaning of such formal insistence. Moreover, the first suspicion to arise in connection with the question is one of technical perversity, as if Muldoon had constructed

---

[54] Ibid. 150. For a clear and helpful account of the rhyming form of 'Yarrow', and of the extent to which 'the second half of the poem is a mirror image of the first half', see Tim Kendall, *Paul Muldoon* (Bridgend: Seren Books, 1996), 228.

not a poem, but a maze or a crossword-puzzle. Referring simply to the kinds of reference contained in 'Yarrow''s multiple allusions, Edna Longley has warned that 'There may be a point at which the mock-academic slides into the academic', and has sensed that here 'a tease becomes institutionalised' in Muldoon's form of 'sexy mystification'.[55] It is easy to imagine similar wariness with regard to Muldoon's use of poetic form in 'Yarrow'; like numerological pattern in some Renaissance poetry, Muldoon's virtuosity of design might appear to be for the eyes of God (and the ingenious) only.

Such objections are not to be lightly dismissed, but neither can they be casually laid against the poem: Muldoon's own caution in speaking about 'the whole of irony' needs to be exercised in trying to come to grips with the problems, and the possibilities, of 'Yarrow''s formal design. That the elaborate patterns involved in the poem's composition are unlikely to be apparent in all their detail to even an exceptionally dedicated reader is part of the difficulty which is Muldoon's subject: the imaginative effort to achieve a coherent version of memory, or a transcendent compensation for loss, fails in the poem at every turn. Even in the concluding *tornada*, when the poem's rhymes and repeated phrases roll all their strength into one ball, Muldoon finds only that 'I can no more read between the lines...than get to grips with Friedrich Hölderlin / or that phrase in Vallejo...', while the final lines ponder 'something...I've either forgotten or disavowed'.[56] Just as the speaker's mother is allowed to speak in terms of warning and reproach, so S—— launches accusations that cannot be answered directly:

> All I remember is a lonesome tu-whit tu-whoo from the crate
> and her bitter, 'What have *you* done for the cause?
> You're just another Sir Pertinax
>
> MacSycophant,
> brown-nosing some Brit who's sitting on your face
> and thinking it's, like, really cool.'
>
> She brandished a bottle of Evian;
> 'Thing is, *a Phóil*, your head's so far up your own fat butt
> you've pretty much disappeared.'[57]

[55] 'Irish Bards and American Audiences', *The Southern Review*, 31/3 (July 1995), 770.
[56] *The Annals of Chile*, 189.
[57] Ibid. 163.

This more earthy transposition of 'At last the bowstring has cut through you' suggests, perhaps, how far Muldoon's formal enterprise is mocked from within. Like the reproach in 'Incantata' ('you detected in me a tendency to put / on too much artificiality, both as man and poet, / which is why you called me "Polyester" or "Polyurethane"'[58]), this registers a level of ruefully acknowledged cost in the context of Muldoon's formal determinations. The terms of S——'s reproach here, however, are themselves shadowed by the tendencies of her other enthusiasms; all of her certainties are addictive and, finally, destructive (in this, S—— may have some affinities with the goddess-figure in 'Aisling'), while it is the speaker who has survived to remember her sexual, narcotic, and political appetites. If the speaker in 'Yarrow' has, indeed, 'pretty much disappeared', he has disappeared into the poem's formal matrix, to have his identity endlessly reformulated and altered in the medium of its repetitions and temporal confusions. The meaning of the poem's form, then, in which every line is ghosted by other lines far away, and key phrases gather and shed connotations as rhymes mutate and return with unlikely accuracy, is perhaps that 'All would be swept away' until everything, and not least the speaker's own identity, has 'pretty much disappeared'.

Such a reading of 'Yarrow' is, undoubtedly, a sombre one, and neglects much in the way of the poem's literary (and not-so-literary) humour. Nevertheless, the relentlessness of formal imposition does, in the end, answer to material which has a grim bearing on Muldoon's writing; the destructiveness of sexual obsession, or the damage done in relationships cut short by death, have long been themes in the poetry. With 'Yarrow', and its contemplation of 'what never / again will be mine', a knowledge which the poem insists upon 'Again and again' in its labyrinth of repetition and variation, Muldoon makes form the principle of both memory and loss, the transcendent and the untranscendable, the magical and the obsessive. The form of the poem, like the windlass against which Erasmus must 'steel himself', seems to insist on its own kind of meaning, as though it possesses (to use a misleadingly vital metaphor) a life of its own. At that point, however, talk of the 'meaning' of form has to cease, just as the poem itself faces up to the inevitability of what it has not transcended. Jorge Luis Borges, whose

[58] Ibid. 17.

work Muldoon has adduced in relation to *The Annals of Chile*, provides a suggestive analogue for this point at which form *seems* to have something to communicate:

...we might infer that *all* forms possess their virtue in themselves and not in any conjectural 'content.' This would accord with Benedetto Croce's thesis; and Pater had already, in 1877, asserted that all the arts aspire to the condition of music, which is pure form. Music, states of happiness, mythology, faces scored by time, certain twilights, certain places, all want to tell us something, or told us something we should not have missed, or are about to tell us something. This imminence of a revelation that does not take place is, perhaps, the aesthetic fact.[59]

The shape made by 'Yarrow''s large panorama of intercut sestinas seems to gesture towards a 'pure form' in which transformation of loss into recovery will be 'imminent'; 'something else' will become 'something else again' as the wheel turns. At the same time, the form means that one line is immanent in another, and everything that will happen has, in a sense, happened already or has already been laid down; the same losses will come 'Again and again' as the wheel turns full circle. The directions of withershins and deasil (to use Muldoon's terms), or anticlockwise and clockwise, return to the same point on the circuit.

The subject-matter of 'Incantata' brings with it a similar inevitability, for elegy, although as poetry it does something *with* the facts of loss, can do nothing about such facts. Again, Muldoon here makes use of the most extreme formal constraints in shaping his poem, and again these constraints are also central to the poem's business. At first sight, 'Incantata' makes a show of its conventionally stanzaic form (the stanza is the *aabbcddc* taken from Cowley by Yeats for 'In Memory of Major Robert Gregory'), but Muldoon's forty-five stanzas also contain further layers of formal arrangement. Here, the long-distance effects are akin to those of 'Yarrow', and the significance of form is similarly pronounced. Briefly, Muldoon sets up rhyming relations between the first stanza of 'Incantata' and the last, between the second stanza and the penultimate one, the third and the pre-penultimate, and so on: each of the first twenty-two stanzas, therefore, rhymes with its matching stanza counted back from the end. The pivotal stanza in this arrangement is the twenty-third, which occupies the centre of the poem:

> The fact that you were determined to cut yourself off in your prime
> because it was *pre*-determined has my eyes abrim:
> I crouch with Belacqua
> and Lucky and Pozzo in the Acacacac-
> ademy of Anthropopopometry, trying to make sense of the '*quaquaqua*'
> of that potato-mouth; that mouth as prim
> and proper as it's full of self-opprobrium,
> with its '*quaquaqua*', with its 'Quoiquoiquoiquoiquoiquoiquoiq'.[60]

The stanza's music is that of rhymes reduced to their sound alone, and the mouth imagined in a potato-cut is the source of only an apparently nonsensical voice, though one which alludes to specific moments in both Beckett and Joyce. But from this point onwards, 'Incantata' recomposes itself, and each of the twenty-two remaining stanzas, as well as corresponding through rhyme with its partner in the first half of the poem, is governed by the phrase 'That's all that's left of . . .'. As a technical feat, in both metrical and stylistic terms, Muldoon's achievement here is extraordinary, imposing as it does on the vast list of the minutiae and intimacies of shared lives an overarching design and completeness in which every detail, no matter how random and individual it may seem, has its precise part to play. As each rhyme comes round in the answering stanzas of the poem's second half, its fortuitousness is also, so to speak, '*pre*-determined' by its position in the overall shape. Like 'Yarrow', 'Incantata' ends by coming full circle, and the 'Inca / glyph for a mouth' of the first stanza is met by 'my own hands stained with ink'.[61]

The details of Muldoon's formal design in 'Incantata', like the quotidian details in the material to which they apply, are implicated in issues of chance and purpose. As an elegy, one of 'Incantata''s most distressing burdens is Mary Farl Powers's decision to refuse standard treatments for cancer, and concentrate instead on unorthodox herbal treatments and remedies. Behind this, as the poem admits, lies a painful fatalism, and Muldoon's concentration on this gives an acute edge to the formalities operating in the overall shape of 'Incantata'. In the first half of the poem, Muldoon alludes to Mary's explanation of Minnesota as 'sky-tinted water',

---

[60] *The Annals of Chile*, 20.   [61] Ibid. 28.

and the idea 'that the sky is a great slab / of granite or iron ore that might at any moment slip / back into the worked-out sky-quarry'; this leads to the last stanza of the first half, which dwells again on the way things are determined:

> To use the word 'might' is to betray you once too often, to betray
> your notion that nothing's random, nothing arbitrary:
> the gelignite weeps, the hands fly by on the alarm clock,
> the 'Enterprise' goes clackety-clack
> as they all must; even the car hijacked that morning in the Cross,
> that was preordained, its owner spread on the bonnet
> before being gagged and bound or bound
> and gagged, that was fixed like the stars in the Southern Cross.[62]

Followed as it is by the apparently meaningless noises of the potato-mouth in much of the poem's pivotal twenty-third stanza, this can be seen to be the point at which determinism, like determination, is at its most impersonal. The idea that in fact 'nothing's random, nothing arbitrary' in language or in life seems here to be almost cruel, and the long catalogue which is to ensue, taking up all of the rest of the poem, might be seen at first as a huge and eloquent refutation of the 'preordained' by the miscellaneous, distinct, and unrepeatable comings and goings of actual experience. In this reading, Muldoon's model might be Louis MacNeice's elegy 'The Casualty', in which the final seven stanzas are filled with separate incidents and situations from the subject's life, governed by 'Look at these snapshots...', and with the repeated formula of 'Here you are...' ('Here you are gabbling Baudelaire or Donne, / Here you are mimicking that cuckoo clock...').[63] If this is indeed a model for Muldoon's long catalogue, it is also one which the poet in fact transforms into something much more complex, moving, and problematic in the course of 'Incantata''s protracted and meticulous formal return to its beginnings.

One effect of Muldoon's extended catalogue of the details of his and Mary's time together is to bring to the forefront of a reader's attention the idea of duration itself; each stanza adds another set of particulars to the recollection, one thing on top of another, but with

---

[62] Muldoon, *The Annals of Chile*, 20.
[63] MacNeice, *Collected Poems*, ed. E. R. Dodds (London: Faber & Faber, 1966), 247.

no indication of order, of what happened first, or what happened next. What does govern each stanza, however, is the 'Of' with which it begins, extending the 'That's all that's left of . . .' construction, with the result that the reader remains aware of finality, of the fact that everything being presented is at an end, even as fresh details, seemingly at random, continue to emerge. Here, Muldoon's resources of rhyme mean that novelty follows novelty, as though the possibilities were indeed endless:

> Of the 'Yes, let's go' spoken by Monsieur Tarragon,
> of the early-ripening jardonelle, the tumorous jardon, the jargon
> of jays, the jars
> of tomato relish and the jars
> of Victoria plums, absolutely *de rigueur* for a passable plum baba,
> of the drawers full of balls of twine and butcher's string,
> of Dire Straits playing 'The Sultans of Swing',
> of the horse's hock suddenly erupting in those boils and buboes.[64]

All this invention, this capacity to become 'something else, then something else again', seems almost to suspend duration in the poem, or rather to postpone its ultimate resolution in the conclusion of the list. But these random details are not entirely random in terms of poetic form, since each stanza in this second half of the poem is plotted against its corresponding stanza in the first half: thus, 'plum baba' is developed from 'the Christ you drew for a Christmas card as a pupa', while 'jargon', like 'Tarragon', can indeed be traced directly 'to those army-worm dragoons' that end the sixth stanza. In fact, with each stanza that 'Incantata' comes closer to its conclusion, the formal patterning used by Muldoon means that the proximity of that ending is measured: in this case, the fortieth stanza, because it corresponds to the sixth in its rhymes, indicates that five stanzas remain before the poem can be at an end. Like the complexities of arrangement in 'Yarrow', the formal disciplines of 'Incantata' are hardly visible; but their importance consists perhaps in this very hiddenness, and in the uncanny analogue it provides to 'your vision of a blind / watch-maker' and 'your fatal belief that fate / governs everything'.

In MacNeice's 'The Casualty', the understanding of death in terms of time is acknowledged to be fraught with irony and difficulty, and the subject's sudden end (Graham Shepard died in a

[64] *The Annals of Chile*, 26.

torpedo attack) is imagined as freezing everything in the present tense:

> How
> You died remains conjecture; instantaneous
> Is the most likely—that the shutter fell
> Congealing the kaleidoscope at Now
> And making all your past contemporaneous
> Under that final chord of mid-Atlantic swell.[65]

'Incantata' allows the illusion to develop that all the past is indeed, in the catalogue of the poem, to be contemporaneous; at the same time, however, it builds in to this catalogue the rigidly mathematical structures of a form which counts its way down to the end. This is a harsher version of the kinds of double-take effected by 'Yarrow', and it finds its most powerful expression in the poem's last two stanzas, where the 'That's all that's left of . . .' construction gains a subsidiary construction in 'of the furrows from which we can no more deviate / than they can from themselves'. This 'no more than' (itself remotely governed by 'That's all that's left of . . .') governs the poem's conclusion:

> than that this *Incantata*
> might have you look up from your plate of copper or zinc
> on which you've etched the row upon row
> of army-worms, than that you might reach out, arrah,
> and take in your ink-stained hands my own hands stained with ink.[66]

Both form and syntax seem to be achieving two things at once: the form of the rhymed stanza, in itself, appears to be launching out afresh when it is in fact returning to a predetermined set of rhymes; the 'no more than . . .' allows the reader to imagine what is in literal terms being denied. It is as though Muldoon's poetry is giving with one hand what it takes away with the other.

In some ways, the excellence of 'Incantata' (which has claims to be Muldoon's best single poem), like the weight and power of *The Annals of Chile* as a whole, establishes Muldoon as the Northern Irish poet whose work matters most in the continuation of the debate on poetry and identity in Northern Ireland. Dreary and familiar as the contours of that debate may be, the attractiveness of notions of identity, which cross over between political and

---

[65] MacNeice, *Collected Poems*, 245.   [66] *The Annals of Chile*, 28.

academic spheres, is put in question by Muldoon's achievements. It may be that his developing enagagement with the demands of form in poetry is seen as leading to what appears a mandarin remoteness, some vaguely decadent disavowal of 'life' in favour of 'art' when what is required is a visible solidity of content, or what the early 'Lunch with Pancho Villa' calls '*How It Happened Here*'.[67] But those interests keenest on 'content'—and who have their own, rather precise, ideas about what exactly that 'content' has to be—have much to learn as a result of being outraged by 'form', with all its seeming irresponsibility and impersonality. Ideas impatient of the 'trivial' and the random, or unable to be surprised by the 'arbitrary', for all the designs they may have on art, or the certainties and stabilities they may want art to deliver, are finally inimical to what art really does and makes possible. The degree to which Muldoon's poetry has failed to deliver reson-ant and easily packaged versions of a certain kind of identity which will be recognizable, exportable, and politically applicable has corresponded with the increasing dominance of form as a concern in his writing, and the prominence of difficulty in the writing's texture and allusive methods. Nevertheless, this is not academic game-playing on Muldoon's part, nor a narrow pedantry indulged in for its own sake, but a result of attempting to achieve something new, unexpected, and unprepared-for, in the poems themselves. For Muldoon, as for any real poet, this in fact boils down to the simple ambition (never simply achieved) of originality; the consequences of such originality, however, whether for literary criticism, for cultural politics, or for any other set of fixed agendas, are likely to be far from simple or comforting. A literary critic hoping to come to terms successfully with this poetry cannot afford to regard form as something simply described and accounted for, and will bring to the writing theoretical models of interpretation at his or her peril. Similarly, set notions of Muldoon's place on a cultural map of Northern Irish writing, and the meaning of his work in terms of defined identities and allegiances, are liable to be sabo-taged by the poetry's intricate (but deadly) ironies. Identity may be, for complex reasons, much valued in contemporary agendas for Northern Ireland, and poetry may be allowed an illustrative role in some of these agendas; but, for an artist like Muldoon,

[67] *Mules*, 11.

identity is just one of the available certainties (or determinisms) which originality has to understand and get beyond and which, in the inevitable embraces of poetic form, real poetry steels itself against.

7

'Silly like us': Anglo-Irish Accommodations

You were silly like us: your gift survived it all;
The parish of rich women, physical decay,
Yourself; mad Ireland hurt you into poetry.
Now Ireland has her madness and her weather still,
For poetry makes nothing happen: it survives
In the valley of its saying where executives
Would never want to tamper; it flows south
From ranches of isolation and the busy griefs,
Raw towns that we believe and die in; it survives,
A way of happening, a mouth.

(W. H. Auden, 'In Memory of W. B. Yeats', II)

In his late volume of memoirs *Recollections: Mainly of Writers And Artists*, the English poet and literary impresario Geoffrey Grigson offered his last thoughts on the 1930s generation of poets, and on W. H. Auden's pre-eminence amongst them, including his own reflections on the vicissitudes of critical success. In Auden's case, that success was not, evidently, all it might have been:

Thinking of Auden aroused only one disappointment, though I half expected it. I was driving home from France and knew Auden was one of the two favoured candidates for the year's Nobel Prize, and that the winner's name would be on the one o'clock news bulletin of English radio. I knew that the other candidate, the other likely winner of the one prize that seemed worth the bestowal, was Beckett, on account, I suppose, in chief, of *Waiting for Godot*. So we drew in beside a lane in Normandy under some pine trees, turned on the transistor, and waited. And it was Beckett, and I damned the gentlemen of the Swedish Academy for a brutish impercipience, and a sentimental, not to say provincial choice.[1]

*

[1] Geoffrey Grigson, *Recollections: Mainly of Writers and Artists (London: Chatto & Windus / The Hogarth Press,* 1984), 71.

The anecdote is a remarkable one, not least in the multiple ironies of its use of the word 'provincial': in what sense, it might be asked, was Beckett the more 'provincial' choice here? And if the Swedish preference for an Irish writer who worked in French is, indeed, 'provincial', how does this English memoirist, who has pulled in off a road in Normandy to listen to the 'English radio', understand the non-provincial claims of his favoured candidate? It is wisest, per-haps, to leave aside here the question of Beckett's and Auden's comparative merits as writers, beyond making the (fairly obvious) point that Beckett's claims are by no means self-evidently the weaker; more interesting is the question of how Auden can be set up to display, by contrast, the limitations of the 'provincial'. The 'brutish impercipience' of the Swedish Academy misses, Grigson implies, the universalism of a cosmopolitan Auden (with his addresses in New York, Ischia, Oxford, and Kirchstetten); but this universal worth is rooted in England itself ('His soil proved deep and extensive as the Fens'), so that 'Our English fortune is to share peculiarities with him'.[2] One peculiarity, Grigson's memoir seems to acknowledge, is the propensity to be undervalued in favour of the modish and the 'provincial'. But there is another—ultimate—horizon to the critical argument here, at which all such valuations and judgements fade away—as Grigson puts it: 'is it discreditable for a poet to find himself... outside and beyond poetry in the end?'[3]

How deeply is the poet W. H. Auden—beyond the context of Geoffrey Grigson's memoirs—really implicated in 'our English for-tune'? And what can a question like this have to do with the different fortunes of Northern Irish poetry in the contemporary literary world? One suggestion of the terms within which an answer would have to be framed comes just a few pages later in Grigson's book, when the author recalls (with admiration) Louis MacNeice, and claims simply that 'He is our Pasternak'. The possessive here needs to be distinguished from 'our English fortune', for it sets to one side questions of nationality, and speaks out of the apparently universal (and nationless) realm of art in praise of the unprovincial. As Grigson seems to grasp, it is in fact an *English* literary provinciality which has problems with MacNeice:

² Grigson, *Recollections*, 69.   ³ Ibid. 68.

Quite a bit could be learnt about English writers at present and recently by discovering their reactions to Louis MacNeice since his death in 1963— their reaction not *vis-à-vis* his poems directly, but in a reverse of reasonable generosity.

He is our Pasternak, less open to be sure, less concerned for us all, yet he is one of those poets who seem to excite the jealousy of contemporaries and slightly younger poets who were less gifted than he was. Here is a poet who propped up raffish bars near Broadcasting House, an elegant man and an elegant writer, and a scholar from an Oxford college and an English public school and English prep school, who looked all the same like the habitué of a zinc-topped bar among an Irish company painted by Jack Yeats, who yet was open to what Russia's Pasternak frequently spoke of in such terms as loyalty to the Earth of the World...

Talk of that specific kind often, I would say too often, embarrasses English poets (and novelists, and readers), leaving them at the same time jealous, and always wanting to go on in a restless way to something different, something new.[4]

Again, this is tonally an extremely complex passage, but it remains nevertheless illuminating. Grigson's sense of MacNeice's importance for literary history after 1963 takes stock of the reserves of grudge, jealousy, and ill will by which such history is often driven (and to which Grigson himself was no stranger); at the same time, an awareness of the strength of MacNeice's English affiliations is balanced by the acknowledgement that these were not enough— finally—to win the 'generosity' of the English themselves. In this passage, MacNeice's otherness is noticed very briefly, and almost immediately transcended in 'Russia's Pasternak' and 'loyalty to the Earth of the World'. Oddly, perhaps, that otherness is shown in how MacNeice looked (as though he was 'among an Irish company painted by Jack Yeats'), and this note is picked up a little later, when MacNeice is described as 'dark, handsome, tall, well-dressed; then, looked at more closely, almost squalid', and the elegance is tempered by a second glance which 'revealed that he had, as a rule, the dirtiest of finger nails'.[5]

MacNeice's degrees of inelegance are, on the face of things, what Grigson wants to forget in the interests of a more universal perspective; on the other hand (indeed, quite literally so) the hints of the 'squalid' and the dirty fingernails are precisely what the memoirist chooses to record. Where Auden has been allowed to

<hr>

[4] Ibid. 72.   [5] Ibid. 73, 74.

transcend the circumstances of his daily life and become a part of
'our English fortune', MacNeice's success appears still to face
greater odds. In point of fact (or, at least, in point of memoirs'
facts), Auden might not have been altogether impeccable himself in
terms of personal hygiene, though Grigson chooses not to bring this
to mind. To remember such things in public is not, perhaps, altogether in good taste, though this does not stop Paul Muldoon's
'Ben' [Britten] in '7, Middagh Street':

> And the Dean of St Pauls?
> 'Since you left us, the stink is less.'
> Then a question in the House.
>
> The Minister, in his reply, takes Wystan
> for the tennis-star H. W. Austin
>
> which, given his line in tennis shoes
> (though not the soup-stained ties
>
> and refusal ever to change his smalls)
> seems just. Perhaps the Dean of St Paul's
>
> himself did time
> with Uncle Wizz in an airless room
>
> (a collaboration on *John* Bunyan?)
> and has some grounds for his opinion.[6]

If it seems self-evidently true that the details of Auden's habits in
changing his underwear are irrelevant to the worth of his poetry, we
should pause to wonder how Geoffrey Grigson (whose voice was
not—or has not yet been—ventriloquized by Paul Muldoon) can
link the state of MacNeice's fingernails to his critical fortunes. As a
critic, Grigson has come to praise MacNeice, and not to bury him,
but it is the terms of this praise which are revealing, especially in the
contrast they present to the Auden encomium. For Grigson, Auden
and MacNeice are both 'ours', but in different ways, Auden by
sharing 'our' peculiarities, and knowing that there are things 'outside and beyond poetry in the end', and MacNeice by transcending
the marks of his origin and becoming an (international) artistic
resource. To simplify this, it is as though MacNeice can leave

⁶ *Meeting the British* (London: Faber & Faber, 1987), 46–7. For details of the
'question in the House', and the Minister of Labour's confusion of W. H. Auden with
H. W. ('Bunny') Austin, as well as the epigram on Auden by the Dean of St Paul's
('Since you have left us, here the stink is less'), see Humphrey Carpenter, *W. H.
Auden: A Biography* (London: Allen & Unwin, 1981), 291.

behind the Irish company and the dirty fingernails to become real poetry, while Auden can finally leave even the poetry behind in becoming fully 'ours'.

It has always been easy to complain about the English habit of considering everywhere other than England provincial; in terms of professional literary criticism, such complaints have become ever more sophisticated and deeply informed, but they still carry with them the undiscriminating desire to prove the point in as many instances as possible. In recent years, this impulse (a well-founded impulse, in many ways) has found numerous critical fronts on which to operate: as well as Irish literature, writing from women, or from positions of class disadvantage, from post-colonial cultures, or from Scotland or Wales has all been defended and promoted in terms of its rejection (or, almost always, its subversion) of monolithic 'English' cultural expectations. Robert Crawford's category of the 'Barbarian' manages to catch major writers from all these areas in its net, and calls for 'the constant assertion on the part of writers of their position in cultural politics' and 'a necessary sensitivity and alertness to the possibility of devolutionary readings which release texts and authors from easy, unconsidered entrapment in English literature.'[7] This sounds a useful warning, but it is not quite the barbaric assault on English cultural orthodoxy it supposes itself to be: the message Crawford picks up from a diverse range of poets (Les Murray, Tony Harrison, Douglas Dunn, Seamus Heaney, and others) is essentially an assertion of provincial identity (which English culture is, in any case, only too happy to grant). Thus, for example, 'If literature was important in the attempted formation of a British mentality, then it is also playing its part in the search for a post-British identity which has grown in twentieth-century Scotland.'[8] Crawford (like many others) will be happy to see literary devolution, but only if this leads to an 'identity': since English chauvinism always likes 'British' to mean 'English', this kind of devolution would remove the problem by settling for a 'post-British identity' of its own. The inequities resulting from one identity-discourse, then, have to be redressed by the formation and propagation of another, answering, discourse. However, what such approaches see as the failure of a British identity is the result

[7] Robert Crawford, *Devolving English Literature* (Oxford: Clarendon Press, 1992), 302.
[8] Ibid.

of forgetting that 'British' need not be complicit with the tendencies of identity, and their ultimately deterministic discourse, in the first place. In terms of literary criticism, such ideas are very blunt instruments indeed, for they insist on finding in writing the very identities they seek outside writing. There is always a certain complacency involved in talk of identity: it tends to be seen as a final destination (and implicitly it is one reached already by those who commend it); it is never a staging-post. Hence, an England at an intellectual and ideological standstill will have reasons for finding its own identity attractive, and irksome constructions like 'Britain' an inconvenience. A complacent Englishness is no more subverted by (say) complacent Scottishness than it is by the strident assertion of Irish identity; it is much more likely, in fact, to be reinforced by such pre-programmed systems of declaration.

But Irish writing, and Irish criticism, have been here before: in particular, the discourses of identity have been tried in (and tried on) Irish literature to the point of exhaustion, and their liabilities have had time to come fully into view. It is to risk understatement to say that English attempts to settle an identity on Ireland have a very long history, but events since 1969 have made even English observers aware that, in Ireland, identities tend not to stick, and that they become points of contention rather than consensus. In terms of literature, one might say that Ireland—and especially Northern Ireland—has profited from this state of affairs: it is evident that there are Irish literary careers in which England has played a centrally significant role. While Seamus Heaney is the most spectacular example of this, he is not by any means an isolated figure, and it could be shown that a Heaney-centred 'Northern Irish poetry' was thriving throughout the 1970s and 1980s (to go no further) on English soil. It may seem paradoxical that literary gestures such as Heaney's pamphlet-poem *An Open Letter* (1983), written in protest against his leading role in Andrew Motion and Blake Morrison's *The Penguin Book of Contemporary British Poetry* (1982) should have strengthened, rather than weakened the poet's (and Northern Ireland's) perceived relevance to British literary concerns. Yet Heaney's ability to decline the name 'British' is part of a process whereby the meaning of 'British' is broken down into the exclusivist discourse of identity: 'British' is taken as 'English', so a poet with Heaney's respect for the 'proper name' must 'draw the line' somewhere:

You'll understand I draw the line
At being robbed of what is mine,
My *patria*, my deep design
    To be at home
In my own place and dwell within
    Its proper name—[9]

This 'home' is completely unshadowed by uncertainty: after all, what *is* its 'proper name'? Is the propriety to depend on Heaney's own proprietorial claims, when there are others for whom these are (at the very least) 'improper'? But such reservations as Heaney allows into his poem come in the following stanza, where the 'Checkpoints, cairns, / Slated roofs, stone ditches' of the television news mourn for the whole country's 'lost, erotic / *Aisling* life'. In accounting for the extreme palatability of this 'deep design / To be at home', there is much to be learned from Robert Crawford's yoking together of Heaney and Douglas Dunn: 'Heaney the Irish republican and Dunn the Scot...are particularly wary of having their "barbarian" un-English identities submerged in an English-dominated "British" context.'[10] The scare-quotes around 'British' are eloquent, and respond attentively to the content of Heaney's poem, but again they are hardly contentious, confirming as they do that 'British' must be an identity-label, behind which the English deny everybody else the use of their 'home'. And who, in all reason, would wish to do such a thing?

If *An Open Letter* was a distinctly friendly slap on the wrist for the *Penguin Book* editors (whereas Crawford's later interpretation takes the opportunity to apply the tawse), it is important to remember that the editors' hands were, so to speak, being held out obediently for punishment. For Morrison and Motion, Heaney and other Northern Irish poets offered an object-lesson to English poets, in both the uses of identity and the capacities (and limits) of poetry in society:

The poets have all experienced a sense of 'living in important places' and have been under considerable pressure to 'respond'. They have been brought hard up against questions about the relationship between art and politics, between the private and the public, between conscious 'making' and intuitive 'inspiration'.[11]

[9] *An Open Letter* (Londonderry: Field Day, 1983), 10.
[10] *Devolving English Literature*, 290.
[11] Blake Morrison and Andrew Motion (eds.), *The Penguin Book of Contemporary British Poetry* (Harmondsworth: Penguin, 1982), 16.

These are weighty issues, of course, and they have been debated in Heaney's poetry; but the terms of the problem are older than recent Northern Irish poetry, and their relevance will also, for the editors, persist elsewhere:

So impressive is recent Northern Irish poetry... that it is not surprising to find discussions of English poetry so often having to take place in its shadow. This is not the first time this has happened. In 'How To Read' (1928) Ezra Pound claimed that 'the language is now in the keeping of the Irish'. But just as Auden and others rescued the reputation of English poetry in the 1930s, so in the 1970s and 80s a new generation of poets has started to do the same.[12]

The *Penguin Book*'s generosity towards Northern Irish writing is not, then, altogether disinterested; in one sense, the editors are waiting for history (as they perceive it) to repeat itself. Heaney's polite refusal of the crown in *An Open Letter* is anticipated by the terms of the anthologists' praise and, arguably, by their sense of what is coming next in *English* poetry. The citation of Ezra Pound disguises only slightly what is a very familiar paradigm in the reception of Irish writing, since Pound's reference is to Yeats and Joyce, and for Morrison and Motion it is therefore Yeats from whom 'Auden and others' 'rescue' English poetry in the 1930s. To preserve this paradigm, the complications of 'British' are better forgotten, and Heaney's insistence on the English identity of 'British' helps to simplify the agenda for the 'new poetic generation' in England for whom the *Penguin Book* hopes to clear the way.

Although the hopes of 1982 now look somewhat premature (not all the English horses backed by Morrison and Motion ran well through the 1980s, and Northern Irish writing continued to develop and proliferate), the process of Anglo-Irish literary accommodation at work in both the anthology and the reactions to it has maintained a steady course. Here, the acceptability of identity is central, and Heaney's continued critical success (owing primarily, of course, to his continued—though sporadic—excellence as a poet) has helped to entrench one particular version of the 'deep design / To be at home' as a touchstone of identity from which others can learn. In this sense, the poet has contributed to 'our English fortune' by the terms of his disavowal of the 'British' tag,

[12] Morrison and Motion, *The Penguin Book of Contemporary British Poetry* For the context of Pound's remark in 'How To Read', see *Literary Essays of Ezra Pound*, ed. T. S. Eliot (London: Faber & Faber, 1954), 34.

and has become the welcome face of the non-English in a literary culture busy defining a number of identities of its own. But the critical paradigm referred to above, in which Yeats passes the torch to Auden, is by no means compromised by Heaney's success. Where it is compromised, however, is in the critical arena, and over issues like the importance of Louis MacNeice. In this respect, the matters raised by Geoffrey Grigson have refused to go away: more than this, they have become increasingly problematic, since they call into question not just the neat paradigm of the poetic succession after Yeats, but the notions of identity, the separate spheres of influence and representativeness, from which that paradigm derives.

It is worth examining more closely the ways in which Auden's poetic fortunes have come to be paradigmatic in contemporary English literary culture. To do this, it is necessary to confront a poem which has good claims to be the most over-cited (though not the best understood) in Auden's *œuvre*, 'In Memory of W. B. Yeats' (1939).[13] The second section of that poem (quoted as an epigraph to this chapter) contains the phrase, 'For poetry makes nothing happen', which has come very close to the condition of cliché in the extent of its promiscuous over-employment amongst critics. To deal with this phrase outside the immediate context supplied by the poem is difficult; as a statement, it is ambiguous at least, and a stress put on any one word rather than another can send the phrase's meaning in a number of directions ('For *poetry* makes nothing happen'? 'For poetry *makes* nothing happen'? 'For poetry makes nothing *happen*'?) Nevertheless, such uncertainties tend to be put to one side in casual allusions to Auden's line, where the phrase functions as a handily compressed piece of common sense, a worldly-wise reflection on the necessary limitations of poetry in the real world: it points towards something 'outside and beyond poetry in the end', in Grigson's words. In fact, for Grigson this 'something' was, in Auden's case, a final belief in Christianity. But the value of the thing outside poetry, whose ultimate primacy even poetry acknowledges, need not necessarily be 'religious' at all, in any usual sense of the word. Rather, the burden of 'poetry makes nothing happen' is more often admonitory, and its function is close to that of a literary–critical safety-valve, reminding readers (and writers) of

---

[13] *The English Auden: Poems, Essays and Dramatic Writings 1927–1939*, ed. Edward Mendelson (London: Faber & Faber, 1977), 241–3.

poetry about limits best not ventured beyond. On this generalized level the phrase, like all such pieces of common sense, seems unexceptionable enough.

However, Auden's words have a specific context in his elegy for Yeats, and the uses of 'poetry makes nothing happen' carry with them traces, however subtle, of this original occasion. The whole second section of Auden's poem is a remarkable intervention in the question of Yeats's Irish meaning and its relevance for 'us', and its opening phrase, 'You were silly like us' is of great importance in establishing both the tone and the presumed authority of what is to come. In one respect, the phrase enacts an exemplary deflation of Yeats's pomposities and hieratic poses: to reduce these to 'silly' is to bring Yeats back, not to 'the foul rag and bone shop of the heart' but to the nursery, where such silliness can expect a firm, if bene-volent, reprimand. But 'silly like us' does something more than this, by effecting a link between Yeats's follies and the kinds of silliness in which 'we' engage: Yeats is, in fact, taken up as one of 'us' in Auden's casual line, and as someone whose poetry is to 'survive'. There are different kinds of survival going on in the poem: that of poetry, and that of the complex (elegiacally conditioned) survival of the poet in his work; but also, in this second section, there is an assumption that Yeats's 'gift' managed somehow to 'survive' Ire-land in his artistic life. It is customary, when discussing 'For poetry makes nothing happen', to direct the reader's attention to the lines which follow this apparent statement, and which modify it in significant ways; however, it is less usual to ask readers to think again about the lines that *precede* the phrase:

> mad Ireland hurt you into poetry.
> Now Ireland has her madness and her weather still,
> For poetry makes nothing happen...

Yeats's poetry, Auden says, has made not a jot of difference to Ireland's 'madness', any more than it has contrived to transform the Irish weather. It is worth pausing to consider the terms being used here, for Auden has drawn a line between 'silly' and 'mad-ness': Yeats's poetry is complicit with silliness, and with 'us', but it has to get the better of, and therefore to 'survive', 'madness' and Ireland (Auden does not write 'You were mad like us...'). Poetry's capabilities, then, do not extend to impossibilities, such as doing anything with Irish 'madness', but have their horizons with 'us' and our 'valley', 'ranches' and 'Raw towns'. In these lines of his elegy, Auden transforms Yeats into something other than, or more than, an Irish poet (in section III, he will be 'the Irish *vessel*'—my emphasis), while setting the terms for his 'survival' apart from the 'mad Ireland' which the living poet had to get beyond.

The question of 'survival' is a difficult one, and it is part of the power of Auden's poem to make that difficulty palpable even as it is transformed into an artistic resource. To survive is, on the one hand, to come through, to live through dangers; on the other hand, to survive may also be to live on after somebody else, and possibly inherit their estate. In this sense, it could be said that 'In Memory of W. B. Yeats' is a poem in which Auden survives Yeats, while at the same time being a meditation on Yeats's survival. It is 'poetry', of course, which seems to bridge the gap between the two kinds of survival at stake here; but this poetry, which is finally 'A way of happening, a mouth', has transcended more than just Ireland in the process of its survival. As Lawrence Lipking points out, it is (in critical terms) much more accurate to say that for Yeats 'Poetry makes everything happen', so that Auden's reformulation of what poetry can and cannot do is a decisive one. The need to employ Ireland in this reformulation is recognized in Lipking's reading, which notices the strong 'English' flavour to Auden's tone and manœuvre:

Auden's indifference to this argument [that 'Poetry makes everything happen'] may derive partly from his reaction to the propagandistic verse of the thirties, partly from the common impression, especially keen in England, that nothing ever happens in Ireland—nothing, at least, but 'weather,' endless rounds of the same old pugnacity and romanticism...[14]

Lipking identifies in Auden here a 'criticism of Yeats's provincialism', and notes that Yeats at the end of the second section 'now belongs less to his countrymen than to any lonely reader to whom his work gives "a mouth"'.[15] Nevertheless, it is far from clear that Yeats is left in the keeping of quite *any* reader here, for the Irish poet remains 'Silly like us'—not, as it were, mad like *them*—and his ultimate universality as 'a way of happening, a mouth' is made certain by his transcending (by way of Auden) the provincialities of

[14] Lawrence Lipking, *The Life of the Poet: Beginning and Ending Poetic Careers* (Chicago, Ill.: University of Chicago Press, 1981), 156.
[15] Ibid. 157.

'mad Ireland'. These are the conditions for 'survival'—for Yeats's survival as poetry, and for the poet Auden's survival of Yeats—which have been strong influences on Auden's own critical standing in England.

The fate of 'poetry makes nothing happen', as a phrase which, in its variously journalistic critical usages, seems often to spell out the conditions for 'survival', is keyed closely to the whole issue of Auden's centrality, his status as a norm against whom later careers in the post-1930s poetic world may be measured. As early as 1957, John Bayley was writing in praise of Auden's 'very English vision', and ranked him alongside John Betjeman as one of the 'two most considerable English poets writing today': 'no two have made so vigorous and fascinating—and in Auden's case so capacious—a myth out of the way in which people, for better or worse, are actually living.'[16] To make Auden's grasp of the actual clear, Bayley set him in contrast to Yeats, quoting some lines of 'Lapis Lazuli' and commenting:

Our individual lives, in the midst of the twentieth century, do not seem much related to this. They are complex, difficult, random, perhaps horrify-ing, certainly concerned with issues which appear to demand some other response than tragic gaiety. Yeats's 'acceptance' of life, in fact, often seems very much like a renunciation—where poetry is concerned—of what actually happens in life.[17]

Bayley's terms did not prove to be atypical, and were of use for other poets beside Auden: much of the reception of Philip Larkin's work, for example, was to follow a broadly similar course in its welcoming of the 'actual' in preference to 'renunciation', and with comparable closeness to and rejection of Yeats on display in the poet's artistic history. For Bayley and others, survival was a matter of succession, and of poetry becoming more and more something for and about 'us'; indeed, the strength of the critical paradigm involved here was shown by the ease with which a writer like Larkin could effectively supplant Auden within the same post-Yeatsian, Anglocentric framework. When Larkin's posthumously published letters caused public shock in 1992, and were attacked most vocally by Tom Paulin (who has never sounded more Irish to

---

[16] *The Romantic Survival: A Study in Poetic Evolution* (London: Chatto & Windus, 1957), 157, 185.
[17] Ibid. 128.

English ears than on that occasion), the safety-valve of 'poetry makes nothing happen' was put to the severest of tests; nevertheless, for many readers and critics, the deceased poet's political bile, his casual misogyny and unthinking racism, were things to be forgiven as 'silly', rather than signs of 'madness'. The poetry, even in an extreme case like this, could be assured that, in spite of it all, 'it survives'.

The lesson of Auden, then, is an adaptable one, but it begins in a struggle for accommodation and survival from which Yeats's Ireland and 'her madness' have to be excluded. Stan Smith has read Auden's elegy in terms of this struggle with the unacceptable opinions of the deceased poet, noting that 'Absolving Yeats of guilt in this elegy, Auden forgives the older poet as a surrogate, a scapegoat even, for his own crimes'. In identifying the battle for succession, Smith is alert to some of the costs of survival:

Auden will follow (succeed) Yeats by in his turn persuading us, like the poems he praises, to rejoice in and learn from his own verses. In doing so, he establishes his claim to supplant Yeats ('human unsuccess' establishing a poetic succession), writing Yeats's obituary in an act of homage which is also an oedipal celebration of triumph over the Father of Lies.[18]

Smith's identification of Auden's phrase 'human unsuccess' as the guarantee of poetic succession is acute, and it relates back to the tone of 'the way in which, for better or worse, people are actually living' (or, indeed, 'For poetry makes nothing happen') in its understanding of the centrality of disappointment and failure to the English post-Yeatsian paradigm. All the same, one notices Smith's (apparently unconsidered) use of 'us' in the passage, showing, perhaps, the critic's own failure to see quite what Auden is supplanting along with Yeats.

It is possible to formulate critical disagreement with what Auden says while remaining within the pull of this paradigm. Certainly, all kinds of subtlety and diversity of emphasis remain possible within a framework so shifting, adaptable, and (finally, at that point where poetry goes beyond poetry) so forgiving as this one. Frank Kermode, for example, is able to reformulate 'poetry makes nothing

[18] 'Persuasions to Rejoice: Auden's Oedipal Dialogues with W. B. Yeats', in Katherine Bucknell and Nicholas Jenkins (eds.), *W. H. Auden: 'The Language of Learning and the Language of Love'*, Auden Studies, 2 (Oxford: Clarendon Press, 1994), 163.

happen' to incorporate even the kinds of poetry with which that statement might seem to be most at odds, writing that 'Whether or not Auden was right to believe in the end that poetry can make nothing happen, it must be true that there can be poetry about the sort of thing that poetry cannot make happen, and about that failure.'[19] Even here, poetry's primary role in a process of 'survival' is quietly (but definitely) insisted upon, and the notion of an ultimate limitation to the power of literary art is crucial to the value being put on the art itself. Kermode, then, is remaining faithful to an orthodox reading of Auden, in which (as Michael O'Neill and Gareth Reeves put it) 'Auden implies the importance of poetry's survival even as he interrogates its capacity to alter history.'[20] The term 'survival' can turn up with reference to other poets, but tends to bring with it the expectations of the Auden paradigm. Symptomatically, this can happen in critical discussion of Seamus Heaney, the survival of whose poetry through the Troubles—and often its power to survive as poetry as a consequence of this—is a common matter for celebration amongst critics. Again, even dissent from this view is expressed in terms which scarcely threaten the paradigm of 'survival'. Here for example, in David Trotter's subtle questioning of Heaney's satisfactoriness as a 'public poet', the same key terms come into play:

All these analogies are adequate not so much to the Irish predicament as to the survival of Heaney's poetic gift, and to our expectations about the resilience of poetry. During the Troubles he has perhaps revised and protected an old aptitude, rather than forged a new one.[21]

The apparently neutral word 'poetry' here triggers 'survival', which in turn forces consideration of 'our expectations'. Trotter's critical scrutiny of Heaney (acute enough in itself) remains conditioned by Auden's far-reaching influence, putting Irish matters in relation to 'our' concerns, where what is 'ours' is also what is involved in poetry's 'resilience' and 'survival' beyond an Irish 'predicament'. It is worth remembering that the phrase of Heaney's which Trotter is considering here is 'symbols adequate to our pre-

[19] *History and Value: The Clarendon Lectures and the Northcliffe Lectures 1987* (Oxford: Clarendon Press, 1988), 70.
[20] *Auden, MacNeice, Spender: The Thirties Poetry* (Basingstoke: Macmillan, 1992), 160.
[21] *The Making of the Reader: Language and Subjectivity in Modern American, English and Irish Poetry* (Basingstoke: Macmillan, 1984), 188.

dicament';[22] this becomes 'the Irish predicament', while Heaney's 'our' is transferred to 'our expectations'. At a deep level, this is consonant with Auden's poetic appropriation of Yeats, even though Trotter's reading would appear to be suspicious of phrases like 'poetry makes nothing happen'.

Essentially, the post-Yeatsian paradigm which Auden's elegy may be seen to inaugurate is a means of combining the profit to be had from the 'provincial' and the advantages inherent in the non-'provincial': in the case of Heaney and the Troubles, the paradigm provides a way for English literature to gain all that the Troubles have to give (delivered, more often than not, by Heaney himself), while retaining (usually quietly, and without making a fuss) the air of universality that comes from distance and apparently diminished ambitions. The point needs to be made that this is a *mis*reading of a great deal of Heaney's poetry which, especially in a volume like *Seeing Things* (1991), is concerned with the propagation of metaphysical universalities of its own, and which has seldom since *North* (1975) offered itself as an experience in exemplary artistic suffering and survival. There is a sense in which Heaney's poetic development away from his earlier manner is uncongenial to English readers, but it may be Heaney's fate (amongst those readers at least) to be fixed for good on the terms of his greatest success, even when he has himself left them far behind. Such terms, as in all powerful critical paradigms, have a way of outlasting changes in the poetry they are employed to interpret.

Fundamentally, such issues concern the transmission of Yeats in post-war poetry, the full history of which still needs to be written; such a history would bring to light distinct divergences between English and American patterns of reaction and reception, and would chart the complexities of Ireland's uses for, and projections of, the poet in an Anglo-American context. It is doubtful whether Anglocentric notions of the 'provincial' could survive such scrutiny, just as it is likely that Auden's role in Yeats's English survival would appear more obviously problematic, owing not least to the significance of Louis MacNeice's role and example. [23]

---

[22] Seamus Heaney, *Preoccupations: Selected Prose 1968–1978* (London: Faber & Faber, 1980), 56.

[23] On Yeats's reception in Ireland, see Warwick Gould and and Edna Longley (eds.), *Yeats Annual*, xi; *'That Accusing Eye': Yeats and his Irish Readers* (Basingstoke: Macmillan, 1996).

In fact, Heaney's part in the presentation of Yeats is more challenging to orthodox English views of poetry's 'way of happening' than might initially be apparent. In the 1978 essay 'Yeats as an Example?', Heaney gave George Moore's satirical portrait of Yeats its full comic rein, and then invoked Auden and the key terms of the English post-Yeatsian paradigm, but with subtle changes in emphasis:

This is the Willie Yeats whom his contemporaries could not altogether take seriously because he was getting out of their reach, the Yeats whom Maud Gonne called 'Silly Willie' and whom W. H. Auden also called 'silly', in his 1939 elegy: 'You were silly like us, your gift survived it all.' But in setting the silliness in relation to the gift, Auden went to the heart of the matter—survival. What Moore presents us with is a picture of Yeats exercising that intransigence which I praised earlier, that protectiveness of his imaginative springs, so that the gift would survive.[24]

Heaney refrains from picking up on Auden's 'like us'; however, he makes it clear that 'survival' means something quite different from the transposition of the artist from his lifetime and country into his successors and a universalized centre, concentrating instead on the survival that comes of 'intransigence', of not moving from the 'imaginative springs'. Elsewhere in the essay, Yeats's 'peremptoriness' and 'apparent arrogance' are praised on the grounds that 'it is proper and even necessary for him to insist on his own language, his own vision, his own terms of reference', while this very insistence (Auden's 'silliness') 'is an act of integrity, or an act of cunning to protect the integrity'.[25] This echoes MacNeice, who had insisted in 1941 that 'Yeats, as a poet, is characterized by integrity',[26] and it returns Yeats to 'his own' ground, rather than evaluating him in terms of his mobility. Even the admonitory note of 'poetry makes nothing happen' seems to be adjusted in this treatment of Yeats, where, instead of the necessary limitations of art which are 'our' common fortune, Heaney draws attention to 'the humility of [Yeats's] artistic mastery before the mystery of life and death',[27] setting the stakes much higher, and refusing to apologize on Yeats's behalf.

[24] Gould and Longley, *Yeats Annual*, xi, 108.
[25] Ibid. 101.
[26] Louis MacNeice, *The Poetry of W. B. Yeats* (London: Oxford University Press, 1941; 2nd edn. London: Faber & Faber, 1967), 196.
[27] *Preoccupations*, 111.

There is a restrained quarrel with Auden throughout Heaney's essay which continues a more explicit disagreement in some of MacNeice's writing on Yeats. Like Heaney, MacNeice was not happy with the implications of calling Yeats 'silly', and in *The Poetry of W. B. Yeats* he made his objections (which were simple ones) very clear:

Many people, however, exaggerate Yeats's 'escapism'. He was neither so simple-minded nor so esoteric nor so dilettante a poet as he is often represented. I have met people whose attitude is: 'Yeats was a silly old thing but he was a *poet*.' This is a foolish attitude. No silly old thing can write fine poetry. A poet cannot live by style alone; nor even by intuitions alone. Yeats, contrary to some people's opinion, had a mind.[28]

This gains in resonance not just by being put in relation to Auden's pronouncements, but by comparison with other contemporary opinions, such as that of L. C. Knights in 1942:

Measured by potentiality, by aspiration, and by the achievement of a few poems, it is as an heroic failure that one is forced to consider Yeats's poetic career as a whole. The causes were complex. Something, no doubt, must be attributed to defects of 'character'...[29]

There is something in the timing of 'no doubt' here which catches precisely that tone of resigned but finally detached weariness which was to become essential in the formation of the 'poetry makes nothing happen' paradigm (compare Bayley's 'the way in which people, for better or worse, are actually living', with its similarly faked catch in the breath). In the post-war years, MacNeice continued to insist on the value of what Heaney calls Yeats's 'intransigence', praising him as 'an artist who remained single-minded in a world of trimmers and who, for all his posing, had integrity', and insisting that 'when in doubt about Yeats, we might well, I think, give him the benefit of it'.[30] This Yeats, whose 'drawbacks became steps forward',[31] does not fit the pattern drawn with such success

---

[28] *The Poetry of W. B. Yeats*, 31.
[29] 'W. B. Yeats: The Assertion of Values', *Southern Review*, 7 (Winter 1942), repr. in William H. Pritchard (ed.), *W. B. Yeats: A Critical Anthology* (Harmondsworth: Penguin Books, 1972), 186.
[30] Review of *Collected Poems of W. B. Yeats*, *Observer*, 27 Aug. 1950, repr. in *Selected Literary Criticism of Louis MacNeice*, ed. Alan Heuser (Oxford: Clarendon Press, 1987), 173, 172.
[31] MacNeice, review of *The Letters of W. B. Yeats*, ed. A. Wade, *New Statesman and Nation*, 2 Oct. 1954, repr. in *Selected Literary Criticism*, 194.

by Auden, and is much closer to the Yeats Heaney was to describe later, who is seen to insist on 'his own terms of reference'.

MacNeice's areas of disagreement with Auden have far-reaching implications, and Heaney's position a generation later is (like Northern Irish poetry in general) touched by these consequences. As he finished his book on Yeats, MacNeice turned to Auden's prose dry run for the elegy (the 1939 article 'The Public v. the late Mr W. B. Yeats'), and reflected on how Auden had been lured into a degree of distortion in his construction of a case for Yeats's defence:

Auden, however, as was natural in a poet who had abruptly abandoned the conception of art as handmaid of politics for the conception of art as autotelic, overstates his case; he says that the case for the prosecution rests on the fallacy that art never makes anything happen. The case for the prosecution does rest on a fallacy but it is not this. The fallacy lies in thinking that it is the *function* of art to make things happen and that the effect of art upon actions is something either direct or calculable.[32]

Here MacNeice sees into (or perhaps sees through) Auden's habit of separating out any difficulty into two opposing principles; the strength of the habit determines his treatment of Yeats, but with results that say more about Auden than they do about the Irish poet. Interestingly, it is this tendency in Auden which Heaney fastens upon in his essay 'Sounding Auden', where he reads Auden as divided between the 'Prospero' and 'Ariel', the 'rich' and the 'strange' of his philosophical and artistic allegiances. Heaney's praise is reserved, for the most part, for the younger Auden, who was prepared to do violence to poetic language, and thus 'brought native English poetry as near as it has ever been to the imaginative verge of the dreadful'.[33] Again, in his praise for the 'estranged and estranging words of his earliest poems',[34] Heaney is calling attention to a bifurcated Auden: the point of this bifurcation, moreover, is at the transition from England to the USA, where the line 'poetry makes nothing happen' (the wisdom of 'Prospero') has its origin. In 1941 MacNeice was also able to detect in Auden, and in that particular formula, a certain loss of contact with the kinds of reality (what Heaney calls 'the dreadful') known to Yeats:

[32] *The Poetry of W. B. Yeats*, 192.
[33] *The Government of the Tongue: The 1986 T. S. Eliot Memorial Lectures and Other Critical Writings* (London: Faber & Faber, 1988), 128.
[34] Ibid. 117.

It is an historical fact that art *can* make things happen and Auden in his reaction from a rigid Marxism seems in this article to have been straying towards the Ivory Tower. Yeats did not write primarily in order to influence men's actions but he knew that art can alter a man's outlook and so indirectly affect his actions. He also recognized that art can, sometimes intentionally, more often perhaps unintentionally, precipitate violence. He was not sentimentalizing when he wrote, thinking of *Cathleen ni Houlihan*:

> Did that play of mine send out
> Certain men the English shot?[35]

MacNeice will not settle here for Auden's over-simplified and misconceived alternatives; and the aspect of Yeats which provides MacNeice with his most powerful evidence is the very thing which Auden tried to push beyond—the fact of the poet's Irishness. In their different ways, and more than four decades apart, both MacNeice and Heaney question the adequacy of Auden's universalizing wisdom about Yeats, and raise doubts about the conditioning of the English poet's sometimes too ready perspective.

But 'Sounding Auden' is nothing if not well-mannered in its dealings with the poet, and MacNeice refrained from criticizing his friend's later poetry; today, apart from some lonely rumbles from what remains of the post-1930s political left in England, Auden's reputation is not exactly under attack, and floats successfully, buoyed up by both academic attention and popular taste. It is still rare to argue in print that the later Auden, and in particular that post-1950 Auden, was creatively exhausted, given to barren formalism, and addicted to an increasingly unrewarding indulgence in the camp, the donnish, and the 'silly'. If Auden is becoming secure in his position, embodying, like Larkin, Betjeman, and perhaps Hughes, 'our English fortune', that position depends on simple outlines for its sense of identity. Heaney's challenge to Auden remains implicit (and many English readers are much more interested in Heaney's exemplary sense of identity, his 'provincial' usefulness in confirming the 'universal' value of other poetry); the more formidable challenge posed by MacNeice, on the other hand, is beginning to come more clearly into view. Here, however, the apparently resigned air that usually goes with the post-Yeatsian paradigm in England—because under serious

---

[35] *The Poetry of W. B. Yeats*, 192.

attack—becomes more edgy and irritable, given to more vigorous and damaging application.

Like much Northern Irish poetry, and like much that is valuable in such poetry, Louis MacNeice's work continues to contravene the terms of Anglo-Irish accommodation. It is an important coincidence that there is common ground to be discovered here between literary opinion in the Republic of Ireland (and its out-stations in the world of Irish studies in the USA) and Anglocentric readings of the post-Yeatsian poetic world. For more than two decades after his death in 1963, MacNeice was kept at arm's length in many English readings of the 1930s poetic generation, valued as a bit-part player in that decade's larger literary drama, and the author of some vivid poetic reportage, tinged perhaps with a distinctive melancholy and sentiment. Beyond this, of course, lay the more complicated situation sketched in Geoffrey Grigson's memoir, and glimpsed from time to time in the accounts of some academic observers. In Ireland meanwhile, MacNeice had always been regarded by literary Dublin (which, in MacNeice's 1939 'Dublin' 'will not / Have me alive or dead') as tainted by his English education and employment;[36] after his death, he came under further suspicion on account of the admiration shown for him by young poets from Northern Ireland. Irish and English marginalizations of MacNeice were able (and are still able) to collude by providing their own dominant interpretations of post-Yeatsian poetry, each one effectively self-contained in its own version of identity. Where many English critics took from the Northern Irish Troubles the poetry of Seamus Heaney and little else (and even this little else, arguably, on terms deriving from their reading of Heaney), Irish commentators tended to play down poetry from 'the North' (again, however, taking it for granted that Heaney was the most important figure there), and treated MacNeice's place in this poetry with everything from suspicion to open scorn. It has been in the interests of both Irish and English readers of Northern Irish poetry after Yeats to keep MacNeice to one side.

From many Irish points of view, the MacNeice problem is a symptom of something larger, a distortion of Irish literary history in order to accommodate the tastes of Northern poets with a

---

[36] *The Collected Poems of Louis MacNeice*, ed. E. R. Dodds (London: Faber & Faber, 1966) 163.

mistaken claim to be parts of a distinctive literary 'renaissance'. Here, there are also dark suspicions of political manipulation; for are not presentations of poetry from Northern Ireland as somehow self-contained and coherent, as well as artistically successful, in fact subtle statements of Northern Ireland's *de facto* separateness from the Irish Republic, and therefore attempts to create an identity which traditional Irish nationalism must regard as perpetually mistaken? These issues were at stake in the battle of Irish poetry anthologies that ran through the late 1980s, and which provides an interesting parallel to the various disagreements that followed the 1982 *Penguin Book of Contemporary British Poetry*. The poet Thomas Kinsella, in his role as a mid-Atlantic embodiment of the Irish literary tradition, published his *The New Oxford Book Of Irish Verse* in 1986, including very little MacNeice, an equally small helping of Derek Mahon, and no Michael Longley at all, but with a few words in his introduction to explain his procedure:

The adequate presentation of contemporary careers would require another book. Similarly with any current 'movements'. Though it is clear already, with the most insistent of these, that it is in the context of a dual responsibility, toward the medium and toward the past, that Seamus Heaney's and Derek Mahon's poetry registers so firmly, rather than in any 'Northern Ireland Renaissance'.

The idea of such a renaissance has been strongly urged for some time (with the search for special antecedents usually settling on Louis Mac-Neice), and this idea by now has acquired an aspect of official acceptance and support. But it is largely a journalistic entity. The past, in Northern Ireland, is not.[37]

A 'responsibility... toward the past', for Kinsella, could only mean a responsibility towards the correct version of the past, and anything else put in place of this was part of mere 'contemporary careers' and thus complicit with the 'journalistic'. As with the campaign against historical 'revisionism', the reflexes played upon here are those of identity: *my* version of the past is consistent with who *we* are; *your* version of the past belongs nowhere, and is no more than the unmeaningful data of journalese. Literary history, like political or economic history, has people to answer to in the Irish Republic; the suggestion that MacNeice was, in his artistic

---

[37] *The New Oxford Book of Irish Verse* (Oxford: Oxford University Press, 1986), p. xxx.

posterity, a key element in the poetic success of a number of Northern Irish poets, was for Kinsella (and continues to be, for a number of critics) simply an unacceptable proposition. Thus, the appearance (also in 1986) of Paul Muldoon's *Faber Book of Contemporary Irish Poetry* was unlikely to please: besides its inclusion of generous amounts of poetry from 'the North', this volume began with a large selection from MacNeice, and had in place of an editor's introduction excerpts from MacNeice's 1937 radio discussion with (or against) the Irish poet F. R. Higgins. In 1990, a counterblast, of sorts, came in the form of *The Penguin Book of Contemporary Irish Poetry*, edited by Peter Fallon (founder and editor of the Gallery Press) and by Derek Mahon. Now, along with copious representation of poets from the Irish Republic (many of them publishing with Gallery), there came an introduction to set right the errors of both Muldoon and the whole 'journalistic' cabal. Usefully, the introduction begins by making clear what is at stake in such operations, stating that 'Among the contours of modern Irish poetry the work of Yeats is Everest', and adding that 'His poems and his other activities in the pursuit of a new national identity represent a monument which, more often than not, obscured the achievement of younger writers.'[38] The agendas of identity mean that the argument can turn in only one direction when it comes to consider MacNeice, and the editors begin their remarks on the poet by making it clear that 'From the beginning MacNeice was associated with the English tradition.'[39] The editors keep their distance when they mention that 'After his death he was adopted as what Michael Longley calls a "progenitor" by a number of new poets who emerged in Northern Ireland in the sixties', and their observations on MacNeice's poetry concentrate on his talent for reportage, his ability to take 'the measure of his time' in work like *Autumn Journal*, a 'long documentary [which] places a private life in the context of world events'.[40] Having agreed to the journalistic estimate of MacNeice (a version of the poet acceptable also in English studies of 'the Auden generation'), the editors tackle the whole phenomenon of recent poetry from Northern Ireland, and happily recycle Kinsella's 'journalistic' jibe:

[38] Derek Mahon and Peter Fallon (eds.), *The Penguin Book of Contemporary Irish Poetry* (Harmondsworth: Penguin, 1990), p. xvi.
[39] Ibid., p. xvii.
[40] Ibid.

ANGLO-IRISH ACCOMMODATIONS   211

The Northern experience has received a great deal of poetic coverage in the period with which we are concerned, to such an extent that it might almost seem abroad as if the only contemporary Irish poetry of particular interest had its origins there. The excellence and popularity of Seamus Heaney's work has much to do with this, but the Northern phenomenon remains, in Kinsella's phrase, 'largely a journalistic entity'. There was never, contrary to received opinion, a Northern 'School' in any real sense, merely a number of individual talents.[41]

The ease of connection here, from MacNeice to journalism to the 'Northern experience' and the 'individual talents' of Northern Irish poetry, is as remarkable as the shallowness of critical judgement which it reflects. The outlines of an *Irish* version of the post-Yeatsian paradigm are visible enough: a marginalization of Mac-Neice, a downplaying of shared aspects in poetry from Northern Ireland, and an insistence on the alien nature of 'the English tradition'. Behind it all lies the desire for a literature of 'national identity', in which Yeats himself is briskly but firmly accommodated.

The agendas of identity are not always quite so visible in English criticism, but the marginalization of MacNeice there, while it has become increasingly difficult through the 1980s and 1990s, remains a part of the way of dealing with post-Yeatsian poetry for a number of critics. Once again, the paradigm in play here is an extremely powerful one, which can adapt itself to admiration of the poet as well as dismissal of his work. In such cases, MacNeice has to become something *more than* Irish, and his poetry is read as transcending 'all the talk about contexts'[42] in achieving its 'universal' validity; indeed, among the smartest of the young English poets, for whom it is routine to wear their poetic allegiances on their sleeves, an admiration for (and emulation of) MacNeice along with Auden has become *de rigueur*. In some circles in the 1990s, then, MacNeice is very plainly back in fashion, his gift having survived it all; but he has returned as 'universal' rather than Irish, and in this sense Geoffrey Grigson's analysis of 1984 might well be seen as prophetic. Even so, the more traditional workings of the post-Yeatsian paradigm are still in evidence, and the publication of Jon Stallworthy's biography *Louis MacNeice* in 1995 allowed some older and still influential attitudes to be aired.

[41] Ibid., pp. xix–xx.
[42] Peter Forbes, review of Jon Stallworthy, *Louis MacNeice* (London: Faber & Faber, 1995), in *Poetry Review* 85/1 (Spring 1995), 15.

Ian Hamilton's assessment, for example, included moments of effortless superiority:

Being MacNeice, he may have feared that hard work—and how hard he worked: six hundred pages of close-packed *Collected Poems*, numerous now unreadable verse plays—could never compensate for an essential absence in his make-up, for a lack of that creative magic which poets like Dylan Thomas assumed that they were full of, head to toe.[43]

The casual condescension is familiar (very close, in fact, to that employed on MacNeice by A. Alvarez forty years earlier),[44] and the tone of voice is a slightly wry one, indicating quietly that the subject knew all the time how very dull he was. To reapply L. C. Knights on Yeats, 'Something, no doubt, must be attributed to defects of "character".' This instinctive mastery of tone is in evidence elsewhere in Hamilton's review, for which Grigson's anecdote offers the best kind of fuel, with its suggestive adjective in 'almost squalid':

'Squalid' seems a bit extreme. What is Grigson hinting at? He goes on to reveal that MacNeice 'had, as a rule, the dirtiest of fingernails'... Could this be *all* he meant by 'squalid'? Stallworthy does not say, or ask... I'd still like to know more about that 'squalid'.[45]

There is nothing in the 1995 biography to help Hamilton pursue this Grigsonian 'squalid'—a deficiency which the review turns into grounds for complaint. All the same, something ugly is going on here, and the undertones of Hamilton's repeated questions are troubling. In 1966, when he was editor of *The Review*, Hamilton printed a review of Seamus Heaney's first collection, *Death of a Naturalist* in which 'The Faber mantle falls flatteringly on Seamus Heaney... here is something like the real thing, mud-caked fingers in Russell Square, a Worzel Gummidge of metaphors.'[46] The 'mud-caked fingers', like the 'dirty fingernails' are the kinds of small detail which the trained English critical intelligence may be relied upon to detect.

[43] 'Smartened Up', *London Review of Books*, 17/5 (9 Mar. 1995), 3.

[44] See A. Alvarez, review of Louis MacNeice, *Autumn Sequel*, *New Statesman and Nation*, 11 Dec. 1954, p. 794, quoted and discussed in Peter McDonald, *Louis MacNeice: The Poet in his Contexts* (Oxford: Clarendon Press, 1991), 152–3.

[45] Ian Hamilton, 'Smartened Up', 4.

[46] Giles Sadler, review of Seamus Heaney, *Death of a Naturalist*, *The Review: A Magazine of Poetry and Criticism*, 16 (Oct. 1966), 43.

The significance of a figure like Paul Muldoon in the background to such arguments is considerable, for it is Muldoon who has, more than Heaney, made the complexities of the literary historical contours in Northern Ireland visible; Muldoon's success in contemporary British taste brings with it some element of the MacNeice poetry he admires, 'the tone of voice and the humour and the bleakness of it, and the fluency and the surreal element of it, and yet the fact that in the middle of all this great invention it never leaves the real world.'[47] Even so, again more than Heaney, it is Muldoon whose poetry threatens most seriously (and most subtly) the founding assumptions of the post-Yeatsian paradigms of critical reception in both Ireland and England. Writing since the late 1980s from America, Muldoon poses a problem for the mutually supporting provincialities of both an Irish identity-discourse and an English 'universality'-discourse of self-approval, not by explicit opposition but by the pervasiveness of his quizzical, ironizing perspective on the kinds of certainty both traditions hold dear. The elaborate circularities of '7, Middagh Street', for example, take in on their orbit around W. B. Yeats the 'poetry makes nothing happen' of Auden's elegy, but in such a way as to return the line to its original, undecidable status. In the first section of the poem, it is indeed 'Wystan' who condemns Yeats's 'crass, rhetorical / posturing', comically distorting and deflating the lines from 'Man and the Echo' which (the real) Louis MacNeice had quoted at the end of his study of Yeats. Muldoon allows 'Wystan' to speak with a kind of finality on the subject:

> For history's a twisted root
> With art its small, translucent fruit
>
> and never the other way round.
> The roots by which we were once bound
>
> are severed here, in any case,
> and we are all now dispossessed...[48]

This section of Muldoon's poem gives voice to a convincingly disillusioned Auden, who is speaking with the plangent resignation of 'our English fortune' as its horizons steadily contract. And yet, as '7, Middagh Street' circles back to its beginning, it is 'Louis' who

---

[47] Paul Muldoon, interview with Clair Wills, Nick Jenkins, and John Lanchester, *Oxford Poetry*, 3/1 (Winter 1986/7), 18.
[48] *Meeting the British*, 39.

comes back to Auden's dictum, insisting that 'poetry *can* make
things happen— / not only can, but *must*'.[49] What Muldoon does
here is to feed Auden's words into a complex matrix, in which their
weakness is sounded out by a double perspective: both 'Wystan'
and 'Louis' (like a pair of Yeatsian antinomies) say something
true—but the dramatic and ironic conditioning which Muldoon's
poetry and its circling form provide mean that such truths become
fatally (or, it may be, vitally) relative. Instead of concluding on his
notes of high seriousness (which were in fact constant artistic
liabilities for the real MacNeice), 'Louis' closes on a more problematic vignette:

> I left by the back door of Muldoon's
>
> (it might have been the Rotterdam)
> on a Monday morning, falling in with
> the thousands of shipyardmen who tramped
> towards the front gates of Harland and Wolff.
>
> The one-eyed foreman had strayed out of Homer;
> 'MacNeice? That's a Fenian name.'[50]

In the end (though, of course, '7, Middagh Street' does not exactly
end), 'Louis' is confronted with his own mistaken identity, and in
the process the certainty of 'Wystan''s 'The roots by which we once
were bound / are severed here' begins to look (to use Muldoon's
word) 'whimful' or (to use Auden's) 'silly'. If there is a lesson here,
it is again a double one: identity is not easily to be transcended, and
its nature is to be always mistaken.

Muldoon's critical success is important as well as encouraging;
but his work is not, finally, at home with the taste by which poets
like Heaney are enjoyed and poets like MacNeice are marginalized,
whether in Ireland or England. The issues at stake here are not, in
the end, those concerning the level of any one poet's critical standing; MacNeice's value in the context of the present discussion is
primarily that of an exceptionally revealing critical indicator. More
fundamentally, it is the terms of Anglo-Irish literary accommodation which come into view in such discussions, and these terms rely
increasingly heavily upon acceptance (implicit or explicit) of the
discourses of identity. It has been argued here that a reading of
'poetry makes nothing happen' is central to much contemporary

[49] Muldoon, *Meeting the British* 59.   [50] Ibid. 60.

English criticism, and that MacNeice, who kept his distance from the question (just as he held back from the post-mortems and fits of revision which characterize the 'Auden generation''s relation to their past) skews the tradition which Auden's dictum supports. In English terms, MacNeice's comparative silence here is proof (as it suits) either that he was failing to be wholly serious, or that he was failing to be in on the joke. There is some irony in the fact that Paul Muldoon's work often uses as a basic principle the generation of that particular unease which comes from suspecting that one is left out of the in-joke, is failing to see the point, or has been otherwise excluded: just one or two pieces of absent information, and all might become clear... The necessary incompleteness of 'what's knowable',[51] like the always illusory stability of identity, is central to Muldoon's writing, and makes him extremely difficult for ortho-dox critical frameworks to accommodate in Ireland as in Eng-land.[52] In Muldoon's poetry, a challenge to Irish and English orthodoxies continues to emerge, no less serious for its often playful tones, and criticism which attempts to acknowledge the importance of this soon finds itself unable to subscribe to identity-readings. It may be that the post-Yeatsian paradigms have only a limited shelf-life now, and that readings of Auden's great elegy may begin more commonly to answer back to its mas-sive reasonableness with their own quizzical obliqueness. The tone of such answers, their allegiances and hints of identity, are likely to be indeterminate, and themselves impossible to identify with any-

[51] Paul Muldoon, 'Our Lady of Ardboe', *Mules* (London: Faber & Faber, 1977), 26.
[52] For one English reaction against Muldoon, see John Carey, review of *Meeting the British*, *Sunday Times*, 21 June 1987: 'packed to the gunwales with higher education... The poems stand around smugly, knowing that academic commenta-tors will come running. His refusal to communicate is in itself a political decision—a cliquish nonchalance': quoted in Barbara Buchanan, 'Paul Muldoon: 'Who's to know what's knowable?", in Elmer Andrews (ed.), *Contemporary Irish Poetry: A Collec-tion of Critical Essays* (Basingstoke: Macmillan, 1992), 310. The critical and evalu-ative implications of Carey's hostility are provided in his *The Intellectuals and the Masses: Pride and Prejudice among the Literary Intelligentsia 1880–1939* (London: Faber & Faber, 1992), 214: 'In contemporary poetry, for example, obscurity is no longer the rule... The leading poets writing in English in the second half of the twentieth century, Larkin, Hughes and Heaney, have all written poems that—though not written with a juvenile readership in mind—can be readily appreciated by schoolchildren.' It is interesting that, even in the work of so unsympathetic a reader of Yeats as John Carey, the post-Yeatsian English critical paradigm becomes finally suitable for children.

thing like certainty: silly, perhaps, but not silly like 'us'. In this respect, Muldoon's work may be in the end a more decisive blow to common English orthodoxies than Heaney's; in Ireland itself, its consequences and fortunes are certain to be complex, and will be dependent in part on the capacity in Northern Ireland and the Irish Republic to think and imagine in terms that go beyond the categories dictated by identity. At the end of the process, it may well be that Northern Ireland, rather than providing a model of some exemplary provincialism, will come to be seen as the central, and critically defining, location for poetry in the archipelago over the closing decades of the century, having indeed 'survived it all'. But in literary criticism, as in politics, such optimistic agendas have to be tempered by the terms of their accommodation; the immediate task is always to make sure those terms are fully in view and in focus, having been decisively identified.

Select Bibliography

ANDREWS, ELMER (ed.), *Seamus Heaney: A Collection of Critical Essays* (Basingstoke: Macmillan, 1992).

——*Contemporary Irish Poetry: A Collection of Critical Essays* (Basingstoke: Macmillan, 1992).

BROWN, TERENCE, *Northern Voices: Poets from Ulster* (Dublin: Gill & Macmillan, 1975).

——*Ireland's Literature: Selected Essays* (Mullingar: Lilliput Press, 1988).

CARSON, CIARAN, *The Irish For No* (Dublin: Gallery Press, 1987).

——*Belfast Confetti* (Oldcastle: Gallery Press, 1989).

——*First Language* (Oldcastle: Gallery Press, 1993).

CORCORAN, NEIL, *Seamus Heaney* (London: Faber & Faber, 1986).

——*English Poetry since 1940* (London: Longman, 1993).

——(ed.), *The Chosen Ground: Essays on the Contemporary Poetry of Northern Ireland* (Bridgend: Seren Books, 1992).

CRAWFORD, ROBERT, *Devolving English Literature* (Oxford: Clarendon Press, 1992).

CURTIS, TONY (ed.), *The Art of Seamus Heaney* (Bridgend: Seren Books, 3rd edn. 1994).

DAWE, GERALD, *How's the Poetry Going?: Literary Politics and Ireland Today* (Belfast: Lagan Press, 1991).

——*A Real Life Elsewhere* (Belfast: Lagan Press, 1993).

——*False Faces: Poetry, Politics and Place* (Belfast: Lagan Press, 1994).

——and FOSTER, JOHN WILSON (eds.), *The Poet's Place: Ulster Literature and Society: Essays in Honour of John Hewitt, 1907–87* (Belfast: Institute of Irish Studies, 1991).

——and LONGLEY, EDNA (eds.), *Across a Roaring Hill: The Protestant Imagination in Modern Ireland* (Belfast: Blackstaff Press, 1985).

DEANE, SEAMUS, 'Remembering the Irish Future', *The Crane Bag*, 8/1 (1984), 81–92.

——*Celtic Revivals: Essays in Modern Irish Literature 1880–1980* (London: Faber & Faber, 1985).

——'Edmund Burke and the Ideology of Irish Liberalism', in Richard Kearney (ed.), *The Irish Mind: Exploring Intellectual Traditions* (Dublin: Wolfhound Press, 1985), 141–56.

——'Wherever Green is Read', in Máirín Ní Dhonnchadha and Theo Dorgan (eds.), *Revising the Rising* (Londonderry: Field Day, 1991).

DEANE, SEAMUS, 'Canon Fodder: Literary Mythologies in Ireland', in Jean Lundy and Aodan Mac Poilin (eds.), *Styles of Belonging: The Cultural Identities of Ulster* (Belfast: Lagan Press, 1992), 22–32.

——(gen. ed.), *The Field Day Anthology of Irish Writing*, 3 vols. (Londonderry: Field Day, 1991).

EAGLETON, TERRY, 'From the Irish', *Poetry Review*, 75/2 (August 1985), 64–5.

——*Nationalism: Irony and Commitment* (Londonderry: Field Day, 1988).

FOSTER, JOHN WILSON, 'Radical Regionalism', *The Irish Review*, 7 (Autumn 1989), 1–15.

——*Colonial Consequences* (Dublin: Lilliput Press, 1991).

GARRATT, ROBERT F., *Modern Irish Poetry: Tradition and Continuity from Yeats to Heaney* (Berkeley: University of California Press, 1986).

GRIGSON, GEOFFREY, *Recollections: Mainly of Writers and Artists* (London: Chatto & Windus/The Hogarth Press, 1984).

HAFFENDEN, JOHN, *Viewpoints: Poets in Conversation with John Haffenden* (London: Faber & Faber, 1981).

HANCOCK, TIM, 'Identity Problems in Paul Muldoon's "The More a Man Has the More a Man Wants"', *The Honest Ulsterman*, 97 (Spring 1994), 57–64.

HART, HENRY, *Seamus Heaney: Poet of Contrary Progressions* (Syracuse, NY: Syracuse University Press, 1992).

HEANEY, SEAMUS, *Wintering Out* (London: Faber & Faber, 1972).

——*North* (London: Faber & Faber, 1975).

——*Field Work* (London: Faber & Faber, 1979).

——*Preoccupations: Selected Prose 1968–1978* (London: Faber & Faber, 1980).

——*An Open Letter* (Londonderry: Field Day, 1983).

——*Station Island* (London: Faber & Faber, 1984).

——*The Haw Lantern* (London: Faber & Faber, 1987).

——*The Government of the Tongue: The 1986 T. S. Eliot Memorial Lectures and Other Critical Writings* (London: Faber & Faber, 1988).

——*New Selected Poems 1966–1987* (London: Faber & Faber, 1990).

——*Seeing Things* (London: Faber & Faber, 1991).

——*The Redress of Poetry: Oxford Lectures* (London: Faber & Faber, 1995).

——*The Spirit Level* (London: Faber & Faber, 1996).

HEWITT, JOHN, *Collected Poems 1932–1967* (London: MacGibbon & Kee, 1968).

——*Ancestral Voices: The Selected Prose of John Hewitt*, ed. Tom Clyde (Belfast: Blackstaff Press, 1987).

——*Collected Poems*, ed. Frank Ormsby (Belfast: Blackstaff Press, 1991).

HUGHES, EAMONN (ed.), *Culture and Politics in Northern Ireland* (Milton Keynes: Open University Press, 1991).

KENDALL, TIM, *Paul Muldoon* (Bridgend: Seren Books, 1996).

KINSELLA, THOMAS (ed.), *The New Oxford Book of Irish Verse* (Oxford: Oxford University Press, 1986).

LARRISSY, EDWARD, *Reading Twentieth-Century Poetry: The Language of Gender and Objects* (Oxford: Blackwell, 1990).

LLOYD, DAVID, *Anomalous States: Irish Writing and the Post-Colonial Moment* (Dublin: Lilliput Press, 1993).

LONGLEY, EDNA, *Poetry in the Wars* (Newcastle upon Tyne: Bloodaxe Books, 1986).

—— *The Living Stream: Literature and Revisionism in Ireland* (Newcastle upon Tyne: Bloodaxe Books, 1994).

—— 'Derek Mahon: Extreme Religion of Art', in Michael Kenneally (ed.), *Poetry in Contemporary Irish Literature* (Gerrards Cross: Colin Smythe, 1995), 280–303.

—— 'Irish Bards and American Audiences', *The Southern Review*, 31/3 (July 1995), 757–71.

—— (ed.), *Culture in Ireland—Division or Diversity?*, proceedings of the Cultures of Ireland Group conference, 27–8 September 1991 (Belfast: Institute of Irish Studies, 1991).

LONGLEY, MICHAEL, *Poems 1963–1983* (Edinburgh: Salamander Press, 1985).

—— Interview with Robert Johnstone, *The Honest Ulsterman*, 78 (Summer 1985), 13–31.

—— *Gorse Fires* (London: Secker & Warburg, 1991).

—— *Tuppenny Stung: Autobiographical Chapters* (Belfast: Lagan Press, 1994).

—— *The Ghost Orchid* (London: Jonathan Cape, 1995).

—— Interview with Dermot Healy, *The Southern Review*, 31/3 (July 1995), 557–61.

LYON, JOHN, 'Michael Longley's Lists', *English*, 45/183 (Autumn 1996), 228–46.

MCDONALD, PETER, 'Ireland's MacNeice: A *Caveat*', *The Irish Review*, 2 (1987), 64–9.

—— *Louis MacNeice: The Poet in his Contexts* (Oxford: Clarendon Press, 1991).

—— 'Difficulties with Form', *The Irish Review*, 16 (1994), 127–33.

—— 'Yeats, Form, and Northern Irish Poetry', in Warwick Gould and Edna Longley (eds.), *Yeats Annual*, xii: *'That Accusing Eye': Yeats and his Irish Readers* (Basingstoke: Macmillan, 1996), 210–38.

MACNEICE, LOUIS, *The Poetry of W. B. Yeats* (London: Oxford University Press, 1941; 2nd edn. London: Faber & Faber, 1967).

MacNeice, Louis, *The Strings are False: An Unfinished Autobiography* (London: Faber & Faber, 1965).

—— *The Collected Poems of Louis MacNeice* ed. E. R. Dodds (London: Faber & Faber, 1966).

—— *Selected Literary Criticism of Louis MacNeice*, ed. Alan Heuser (Oxford: Clarendon Press, 1987).

—— *Selected Poems*, ed. Michael Longley (London: Faber & Faber, 1988).

—— *Selected Prose of Louis MacNeice*, ed. Alan Heuser (Oxford: Clarendon Press, 1990).

Mahon, Derek, *Poems 1962–1978* (Oxford: Oxford University Press, 1979).

—— *Courtyards in Delft* (Dublin: Gallery Press, 1981).

—— *The Hunt by Night* (Oxford: Oxford University Press, 1982).

—— *Antarctica* (Dublin: Gallery Press, 1985).

—— *Selected Poems* (Harmondsworth: Penguin, 1993).

—— *The Hudson Letter* (Oldcastle: Gallery Press, 1995).

—— and Fallon, Peter (eds.), *The Penguin Book of Contemporary Irish Poetry* (Harmondsworth: Penguin, 1990).

Montague, John, *Selected Poems* (Oxford: Oxford University Press, 1982).

—— *Mount Eagle* (Oldcastle: Gallery Press, 1988).

Morrison, Blake, and Motion, Andrew (eds.), *The Penguin Book of Contemporary British Poetry* (Harmondsworth: Penguin, 1982).

Muldoon, Paul, *Mules* (London: Faber & Faber, 1977).

—— *Why Brownlee Left* (London: Faber & Faber, 1980).

—— *Quoof* (London: Faber & Faber, 1983).

—— Interview with Kevin Smith, *Gown Literary Supplement* (1984), [4–5, 12].

—— 'Toxophilus', *Times Literary Supplement*, 10 Feb. 1984, p. 137.

—— *The Wishbone* (Dublin: Gallery Press, 1984).

—— Interview with Clair Wills, Nick Jenkins, and John Lanchester, *Oxford Poetry*, 3/1 (Winter 1986/7), 14–20.

—— *Meeting the British* (London: Faber & Faber, 1987).

—— *Madoc: A Mystery* (London: Faber & Faber, 1990).

—— Interview with Kevin Smith, *Rhinoceros*, 4 (n.d. [1991]), 75–94.

—— *Shining Brow* (London: Faber & Faber, 1993).

—— Interview with Lynn Keller, *Contemporary Literature*, 35/1 (Spring 1994), 1–29.

—— *The Prince of the Quotidian* (Oldcastle: Gallery Press, 1994).

—— *The Annals of Chile* (London: Faber & Faber, 1994).

—— *New Selected Poems 1968–1994* (London: Faber & Faber, 1996).

O'BRIEN, DARCY, *W. R. Rodgers (1909–1969)* (Lewisburg, Pa.: Bucknell University Press, 1970).

O'DONOGHUE, BERNARD, *Seamus Heaney and the Language of Poetry* (Hemel Hempstead: Harvester Wheatsheaf, 1994).

PARKER, MICHAEL, *Seamus Heaney: The Making of the Poet* (Basingstoke: Macmillan, 1993).

PATTEN, EVE (ed.), *Returning To Ourselves: second volume of papers from the John Hewitt International Summer School* (Belfast: Lagan Press, 1995).

PAULIN, TOM, *The Strange Museum* (London: Faber & Faber, 1980).

—— *Liberty Tree* (London: Faber & Faber, 1983).

—— *Ireland and the English Crisis* (Newcastle upon Tyne: Bloodaxe Books, 1984).

—— *Fivemiletown* (London: Faber & Faber, 1987).

—— *The Hillsborough Script: A Dramatic Satire* (London: Faber & Faber, 1987).

—— *Minotaur: Poetry and the Nation State* (London: Faber & Faber, 1992).

—— *Walking a Line* (London: Faber & Faber, 1994).

—— (ed.), *The Faber Book of Political Verse* (London: Faber & Faber, 1986).

PEACOCK, ALAN, 'Michael Longley: Poet between Worlds', in Michael Kenneally (ed.), *Poetry in Contemporary Irish Literature* (Gerrards Cross: Colin Smythe, 1995), 263–79.

POLLAK, ANDY (ed.), *A Citizens' Inquiry: The Opsahl Report on Northern Ireland* (Dublin: Lilliput Press for Initiative '92, 1993).

RAMAZANI, JAHAN, *The Poetry of Mourning: The Modern Elegy from Hardy to Heaney* (Chicago, Ill.: University of Chicago Press, 1994).

RODGERS, W. R., 'Conversation Piece', *The Bell*, 4/5 (August 1942), 305–14.

—— *Collected Poems* (Oxford: Oxford University Press, 1971).

—— *Poems*, ed. Michael Longley (Oldcastle: Gallery Press, 1993).

STALLWORTHY, JON, *Louis MacNeice* (London: Faber & Faber, 1995).

TROTTER, DAVID, *The Making of the Reader: Language and Subjectivity in Modern American, English and Irish Poetry* (Basingstoke: Macmillan, 1984).

WILLS, CLAIR, *Improprieties: Politics and Sexuality in Northern Irish Poetry* (Oxford: Clarendon Press, 1993).

Index